ART AND PHILOSOPHY

ART AND PHILOSOPHY

A SYMPOSIUM

Edited by Sidney Hook

New York University Press 1966

LIBRARY OF CONGRESS CATALOG CARD NUMBER: 66–13841
MANUFACTURED IN THE UNITED STATES OF AMERICA

The contents of this volume comprise the proceedings of the seventh annual New York University Institute of Philosophy, held at Washington Square, New York, October 23–24, 1964. Previous volumes in the series, also edited by Sidney Hook, are:

Determinism and Freedom in the Age of Modern Science
Psychoanalysis, Scientific Method, and Philosophy
Dimensions of Mind
Religious Experience and Truth
Philosophy and History
Law and Philosophy

Contents

Preface

PHILOSOPHERS have concerned themselves with problems about the nature and function of art from the earliest times. What they have taught about these and related themes has had a continuing relevance to reflective interest in the subject. Plato on imitation, Aristotle and Hegel on tragedy, Longinus and Kant on the sublime still have a contemporary significance for us which their observations on cosmological and other scientific questions do not possess. Philosophical writings on art may not reveal the same depth and insight as philosophical writings on ethics, but they have had the same perennial interest.

The direct influence of philosophical thought about art on practicing artists has been small compared with the effects of the working tradition and actual training to which artists have been exposed but the indirect influence has been pervasive, varying in intensity from age to age. It is not without significance that church, state, and other social institutions have shown a lively interest not only in encouraging the arts but, unhappily, sometimes in coercively influencing their form as well as content.

The philosophy of art concerns itself with a multitude of problems ranging from the identification and definition of a work of art, analysis of the concepts of meaning, communication and truth in art, the criteria of judgment of excellence, the nature of the aesthetic experience, the place of art in human experience, and many others. Even without attempting to sort them out it is obvious that some of these problems are related to each other but all of them have become more difficult and challenging as a result of developments in modern art, music, and literature. Gertrude Stein was once asked: "What is your attitude toward art today?" "I like to look at it," was her whole reply. But most people, I believe, would say "I would like to understand it," whether they like to look at it or not. It is often assumed that liking grows with understanding but this is doubtful since sometimes understanding seems to increase aversion. It may be that mere liking is not as important as many assume. Even when we start from the aesthetic experience in order to get over the hurdle of determining what is an artistic object and what is not, the eye or ear or mind turn back more attentively to the aesthetic object itself, which has arrested our interest, for better understanding.

These considerations explain the topics selected for discussion out of the large number that might have also served for exploration by the Institute. The comments of the contributors have as far as possible been bunched together under the appropriate themes to which they relate. Since some participants made connected comments on all three main papers, their contributions have been printed in Part III, so that the reader will not come across references to any paper by a contributor before he has read the paper to which reference has been made. This explains the paucity of comments on the main papers in Parts I and II.

Once more I must regret that no feasible way has been found to capture and bottle the vitality, spontaneity, and fun of the Institute discussions so that they could be shared with the readers.

Sidney Hook

ART AND PHILOSOPHY

PART I

Grounds for Judgment of Artistic Excellence

A

On Perfection, Coherence, and Unity of Form and Content

MEYER SCHAPIRO
Columbia University

I

My aim in this paper is to examine the ascription of certain qualities to the work of art as a whole, the qualities of perfection, coherence, and unity of form and content, which are regarded as conditions of beauty. While rooted in an immediate intuition of the structure of the whole, the judgments of these qualities often change with continuing experience of the object. They are never fully confirmed, but are sometimes invalidated by a single new observation. As criteria of value they are not strict or indispensable; there are great works in which these qualities are lacking. Coherence, for example, will be found in many works that fail to move us, and a supreme work may contain incoherences. Order in art is like logic in science, a built-in demand, but not enough to give a work the distinction of greatness. There are dull and interesting orders, plain and beautiful ones, orders full of surprises and subtle relations, and orders that are pedestrian and banal.

II

The word perfection is often a rhetorical term expressing the beholder's feeling of rightness, his conviction that everything in the work is as it should be, that nothing can be changed without ruining the whole. Our perception of a work is not exhaustive, however. We see only some parts and aspects; a second look will disclose much that was not seen before. We must not confuse the whole in a large aspect, co-extensive with the boundaries of the work, with the whole as the totality of the work. Expert scrutiny will discern in the acknowledged masterpieces not only details that were defective when the artist produced them, but changes brought about by others who have repaired the work. Few old paintings are today in their original state. Even acute observers will often fail to notice these changes. A painting that has seemed complete and perfectly proportioned will, like Rembrandt's "Night Watch," turn out to have lost a considerable part. In Homer's *Iliad* numerous passages are later interpolations. Few visitors to the cathedral of Chartres can distinguish the original painted glass from the replacements made in the same windows in later and especially in modern times. The example of Chartres reminds us, too, that for the judgment of artistic greatness it is not necessary that a work be consistent in style or complete. Many architects, sculptors, and painters collaborated on this marvel. The varying capacities of these artists, their unlike styles, even their indifference to consistency with each other, have not kept generations of beholders from adoring this beautiful church as a supreme achievement. It is not a single work of art, but, like the Bible, a vast collection of works which we value as a single incomparable whole. If the Parthenon holds up artistically in its ruined state through the grandeur of its qualities in all that remains of the original, in Chartres we accept a whole in which very different conceptions of form have been juxtaposed. The two West towers, begun by two architects of the twelfth century, were completed at different times, one of them in the late Gothic period in a style that is opposed in principle to the rest of the façade. The great West portal, too, is not as it was originally designed; several sculptors of different temperament and capacity have worked together; and parts have been arbitrarily cut and displaced to adjust to a change in the construction.

Even where a single great artist has been responsible for a work one can detect inconsistencies brought about by a new conception introduced in the course of work. So in the Sistine ceiling, Michelangelo has changed the scale of the figures in mid-passage. One can recall other great works of literature, painting, and architecture that are incomplete or inconsistent in some respects. And one might entertain the thought that in the greatest works of all such incompleteness and inconsistency are evidences of the living process of the most serious and daring art which is rarely realized fully according to a fixed plan, but undergoes the contingencies of a prolonged effort. Perfection, completeness, strict consistency are more likely in small works than in large. The greatest artists—Homer, Shakespeare, Michelangelo, Tolstoy—present us with works that are full of problematic features. Samuel Johnson, in considering Shakespeare, drew up a list of weaknesses which, taken alone, would justify dismissing as inferior any other writer in whose poems they occurred. The power of Shakespeare, recognized by Johnson, is manifest in the ability to hold us and satisfy us in spite of these imperfections. Arnold, reviewing Tolstoy's *Anna Karenina,* remarked that it was not a well-constructed story and was defective as a work of art. But then he added—as others have done since in speaking of Tolstoy—his novel is not art, but life itself.

It is clear from continued experience and close study of works that the judgment of perfection in art, as in nature, is a hypothesis, not a certitude established by an immediate intuition. It implies that a valued quality of the work of art, which has been experienced at one time, will be experienced as such in the future; and in so far as the judgment of perfection covers the character of the parts and their relation to the particular whole, it assumes that the quality found in parts already perceived and cited as examples of that perfection will be found in all other parts and aspects to be scrutinized in the future. There is, of course, the negative evidence from the absence of observable inconsistencies and weaknesses. But we have learned often enough how limited is our perception of such complex wholes as works of art. In a circle a very tiny break or dent will arouse our attention. But in an object as complex as a novel, a building, a picture, a sonata, our impression of the whole is a resultant or summation in which some elements can be changed with little apparent difference to our sense of the whole; perception of such complexities is rapid and tolerant, isolating certain features and passing freely over others, and admitting much vagueness for the sake of the larger effects. We cannot hold in view more than a few parts or aspects, and we are directed by a past experience, an expectation and a habit of seeing, which is highly selective even in close scrutiny of an object intended for the fullest, most attentive perception. The capacity of an expert to discern in a familiar work unnoticed details and relationships that point to its retouching by others is therefore so astonishing. Here the sensibility of the expert, trained and set for such investigation, is like the power of the microscope to disclose in a work features beyond ordinary sensitive vision.

But even the experts are often blind or mistaken. To see the work as it is, to know it in its fullness, is a goal of collective criticism extending over generations. This task is sustained by new points of view that make possible the revelation of significant features overlooked by other observers. In all these successive judgments there is an appeal to the freshly seen structure and qualities of the work.

III

What I have said about the fallibility of judgments of coherence and completeness applies also to judgments of incoherence and incompleteness. These are often guided by norms of style which are presented as universal requirements of art and inhibit recognition of order in works that violate the canons of form in that style. The norms are constantly justified in practice by perceptions—supposedly simple unprejudiced apprehensions of a quality—which are in fact directed by these norms. This is familiar enough from the charge of formlessness brought against modern works and especially the Cubist paintings that were criticized later from another point of view as excessively concerned with form. It is clear that there are many kinds of order and our impression of order and orderliness is influenced by a model of the quality. For someone accustomed to classic design, symmetry and a legible balance are prerequisites of order. Distinctness of parts, clear grouping, definite axes are indispensable features of a well-ordered whole. This canon excludes the intricate, the unstable, the fused, the scattered, the broken, in composition; yet such qualities may belong to a whole in which we can discern regularities if we are disposed to them by another aesthetic. In the modern compositions with random elements and relations, as in the works of Mondrian and the early Kandinsky and more recent abstract painting, are many correspondences of form: the elements may all be rectilinear, of one color or restricted set of colors, and set on a pronounced common plane; however scattered they appear, these elements are a recognizable family of shapes with an obvious kinship; the density in neighboring fields is about the same or the differences are nicely balanced. In time one comes to distinguish among all the competing models of chaos those which have the firmness of finely coherent forms like the classic works of the past.

I may refer also to a striking medieval example of a long misjudged order, the Romanesque relief at Souillac, with the story of Theophilus, the Virgin, and the Devil. It had seemed to critical observers, sensitive to this style of art, an uncoherent work, in spite of its clarity as an image. Its defect was explained by its incompleteness, the result of a loss of parts when the large monumental relief was moved from its original place to the present position. Study of the jointing of the sculptured blocks of stone has shown that no part is missing; and a more attentive reading of the forms has disclosed a sustained relatedness in the forms, with many surprising accords of the supposedly disconnected and incomplete parts. It was the radical break with the expected traditional mode of hierarchic composition in this strange and powerful work that made observers feel it to be chaotic and incomplete.

IV

I shall turn now to the unity of form and content, a more subtle and elusive concept. As a ground of value, it is sometimes understood as a pronounced correspondence of qualities of the forms to qualities and connotations of a represented theme—a stimulating kind of generalized onomatopoeia. So in a painting of violent action, many crossed, colliding, and broken forms, even among the stable accessories, and in a scene of rest, mainly horizontal shapes and considerable voids. It is the poetic ideal of a marriage of sound and sense.

This concept of unity must be distinguished from the theoretical idea that since all forms are expressive and the content of a work is the meaning of the forms both as representations and expressive structures, therefore content and form are one. In a representation every shape and color is a constituting element of the content and not just a reinforcement. A picture would be a different image of its object and have another meaning if the forms were changed in the slightest degree. So two portraits of the same person, done with different forms, are different in content, though identical in subject. It is the specific representation together with all the ideas and feelings properly evoked by it that makes the content. And where there is no representation, as in architecture and music and abstract painting, the qualities of the forms, their expressive nature, in the context of the work's function, are the content or meaning of the work.

Conceived in this second way, the unity of form and content holds for all works, good and bad, and is no criterion of value. It is a sort of definition of art as well as of content, though it applies also to spoken language in which the physiognomic characteristics of speech are included with the intended message as part of the content. Unity in this indivisible oneness of form and content has another sense, it seems, than in the concepts of unity of form and unity of content, where distinguishable parts are judged to harmonize or to fit each other. What is expressed in this oneness of form and content need not, however, be unified in the sense of an inner accord; it is compatible with inconsistencies in the meanings themselves. To judge that a work possesses oneness of form and content it is not even necessary to contemplate it; the oneness follows from the definition of content in the work of art. The sense of the conjunction in "form and content" is not clear then; we do not know what it is that has been united with form as a distinguishable entity or quality in the work. It is different from saying that the content is the sum of the meanings—meanings given in the subject, the forms, and the functions of the work, with many different levels of connotation—a content unbounded rather than definite, and open to successive discovery rather than apprehended completely in a single moment of divination. The unity of form and content is then an accord of specifiable forms and meanings and may in certain works appear comprehensive enough to induce the conviction that everything in the work is stamped with this satisfying accord which is a ground of its beauty.

This judgment of an extensive unity is an interpretation, a hypothesis; there is no one perception or series of perceptions that make it complete and certain. Judgments of unity and perfection in art, as in nature, rest on a selecting vision, an unreflective and sometimes habitual choice of aspects, as in other engagements with complex fields. In attributing a unity of form and content to a work we are free to abstract the aspect of forms and meanings that might coincide. It is not *the* form and *the* content that appear to us as one, but an aspect or part of each that we bring together because of analogy or expressive correspondence. Content and form are plural concepts which comprise many regions and many orders within the same work. The vagueness of the form-and-content usage is due to the failure to specify in which region the connection or the unity lies. In any work form and meaning cover several layers and scales of structure, expression, and representation. Line, mass, space, color, dark-and-light constitute different orders in painting, as do words, actions, characters, and the large sequence of narrative in a play or story. Besides, within each of these aspects of the work are elements and characteristics that belong to the style of the time, others that are personal, and still others that are unique solutions for the particular work. To disengage these in their contribution to the content, even to interpret their expression, is beyond the power of an immediate apprehension of the whole.

In an extensive cycle of paintings—let us take Giotto's Paduan frescoes as an example—each scene has a unique form that builds its distinct image; but all hold together through common forms and colors, though the subjects are different. It would be difficult to match this large order of the whole—given at once to the eye and confirmed by scrutiny of the recurrent elements and connections—with a summating expression and meaning found also in Giotto's conception of the story of Christ. But even if found, it would remain true that we can respond to one without grasping the other fully. If there is a common spiritual attitude in all these scenes, which we regard as a quality of the content, there is a particular form in each scene with features that are not distinctive for the governing spiritual attitude.

How far the unity of form and content is an ideal hypothesis, even a program, is clear from the fact that we often appreciate forms without attending seriously to their represented meanings; for certain works we could not begin to consider that unity with content since so little of the original meanings is available to us. There are few works of older art that are legible now as they were to their makers. Some of the greatest are still problematic in meaning and continue to engage the ingenuity of iconographers. To assume that the forms would necessarily acquire another aspect if we knew what they represented or what their deeper content was originally is only a guess, although there are examples of works restructured after a new interpretation of their meaning. It is unlikely that Titian's "Sacred and Profane Love" would change in artistic character and value if one of the alternative interpretations of its uncertain subject were adopted as certain.

After long study the content of the Sistine ceiling is less

evident to us than the structure of the forms; to speak of a unity of form and content there is to pretend to a grasp that is still denied us. The uncertainty is not inherent in the untranslatability of artistic content into words, but in the difficulty of knowing fully enough the broad organizing ideas through which we can perceive the meanings as a unity embracing the subjects, the spheres of connotation, and numerous connections between otherwise isolated elements of representation.

For the painter each figure had a specific sense as well as many connotations, and his conception of the whole as a composition and many details of form were shaped by the need to make that sense visible. To ignore it and yet to speak of the unity of form and content is to strip the content of an essential core of meanings, and the work itself of a great part of its purpose. There is also the pictorial meaning of each figure as a form with a definite place and artistic function in the appearance of the whole. This can be grasped without our knowing what the figure represents or symbolizes, what is its role in the story. The fact that we are still deeply moved by the undeciphered whole makes us wonder at a theory that regards the experience of forms as necessarily fused with that of content. Here the forms have become for us the main content of the work in a literal sense; they speak to us powerfully and we feel that we have perceived through them the force of the artist's creative powers, his imagination and conception of man, his style as a living person.

If, before Rembrandt's famous picture of "Man with a Knife," a beholder is unable to say whether it's a portrait of a butcher or an assassin or of Saint Bartholomew who was martyred by a knife, he can still enjoy the painting as a beautiful harmony of light and shadow, color and brushwork, and appreciate the artist's power of making the figure visible as a complex human presence steeped in feeling and revery; and all this without linking in a specific way the qualities of the painting to the attributes of an intended subject. In a portrait we need not know the identity of the person in order to admire the realization of individuality by painterly means. Yet for the artist that identity was essential. Certain expressive forms were conceived as uniquely adequate to a particular sitter with traits of character and a significance that we divine only incompletely from the portrait.

Seen as form, different works have a different explicitness of structure. In a novel we often hardly attend to the form; in architecture, in music, in certain kinds of painting and especially in short poems, the form is more evident and is an unmistakable physiognomy of the work. Who, after reading a novel by Tolstoy, can recall the form as distinctly as he can retell the story or find summarizing words for the thought and feeling that pervade the action? Surely there is an order, a pattern of narration, peculiarities of syntax and phrasing, contrasts and repetitions of language, of character and of plot, that build the whole in its large and intimate meanings. But we do not fix upon these as we read; the style, the form of narration, seems a transparent medium through which we experience the action itself and the feelings of the characters. But this is true also of inferior writing for the reader who is completely bemused by a story. What is relevant for the problem of unity of form and content as a value is that we do not speak of Tolstoy's form—even when we recognize it—as we do of his content. One may find in the remarkable transparency of the medium in Tolstoy's writing the same purity and sincerity as in the substance of his narrative, a confirmation of the oneness of his art in at least certain aspects of form and content. Here again the unity would lie in a common quality rather than in an undecomposable resultant.

In practice form and content are separable for the artist who, in advance of the work, possesses a form in the habit of his style which is available to many contents, and a conception of a subject or theme rich in meaning and open to varied treatment. In the process of realization these separable components of his project are made to interact and in the finished work there arise unique qualities, both of form and meaning, as the offspring of this interaction, with many accords but also with qualities distinctive for each. The beautiful simple language of a writer in a complex story may be appreciated without being considered a property of the content.

The relation between forms and what they represent may be intimate or conventional, as in the beauty of a written or printed book as a work of calligraphic and typographic art. We admire the perfection of the script, the spacing of the page, the ornament, without ever referring to the meaning of the words. From the qualities of the page we cannot imagine the qualities of the text; and we know that this same artistic form can represent whatever text is committed to the calligrapher's art which is, in general, indifferent to the sense of the script. But if this is regarded as a low order of art because of the shallowness of its content, limited to the expressive import of the melody of script, we shall also find in the same books miniature paintings of greater complexity which we contemplate with delight while ignoring most of their meanings—they are inaccessible to any but scholars.

The concept of unity of form and content must contend with the fact that there are conventions of form which are independent of the subject and appear the same in a great variety of individual styles. In painting and sculpture, what is called the style of representation is a system of forms applied to varying themes. An example is the use of the black ground with red figures and the red ground with black figures in Greek vase painting, a highly characteristic and striking form. It would be hard to show that the choice of one or the other solution has much to do with the content of the painting, however broadly we interpret the latter. Themes of myth and everyday reality, the tragic and festive, the athletic and erotic, are represented alike with this contrast of figure and ground. Accepting the convention, artists of different style endow the basic form with qualities that might be connected with distinct features of a personal style and perhaps even with their individual conceptions of certain themes. But at least some characteristics of the form are distinguishable from the specific content and even from the content considered as a domain of subjects with a typical set of meanings. Perhaps the convention contributes a quality of feeling, an archaic strength consonant with the robust objectivity of the representations. But even if I accepted this interpretation, I would not dare to say in advance that all the conventions and motifs in that art could be seen as fused with the meanings of an image in a consistent expression—even if I felt the painting to be perfect. On the other hand, to connect such a form as the black and red of figure and ground with a world view implicit also in the choice and conception of a whole class of Greek subjects is to construct a special layer of meaning to which no explicit reference is found in the work. The Greek artist is not illustrating or presenting his world view as he illustrates the mythical tales; but he is expressing it somewhat as the structure of a language, it is supposed, embodies in certain features attitudes prevalent in a culture and found also in some revealing utterances in a more explicit way. Yet it must be said that while the assumed connection between form and world view is alluring to the imagination and as a hypothesis has become embedded in our perception of Greek objects until it has acquired for us the simplicity and self-evidence of a directly grasped meaning, the world view is not a clear expressive feature of the work of art like the feeling of a painted smile or the contrast of black and red, but a complex and still uncertain interpretation.

Both concepts of unity—the perfect correspondence of separable forms and meanings and the concept of their indistinguishability—rest on an ideal of perception which may be compared with a mystic's experience of the oneness of the world or of God, a feeling of the pervasiveness of a single spiritual note or of an absolute consistency in diverse things. I do not believe that this attitude, with its sincere conviction of value, is favorable to the fullest experience of a work of art. It characterizes a moment or aspect, not the work as disclosed through attentive contemplation, which may also terminate in ecstasy. To see the work as it is one must be able to shift one's attitude in passing from part to part, from one aspect to another, and to enrich the whole progressively in successive perceptions.

I have argued that we do not see all of a work when we see it as a whole. We strive to see it as completely as possible and in a unifying way, though seeing is selective and limited. Critical seeing, aware of the incompleteness of perception, is explorative and dwells on details as well as on the large aspects that we call the whole. It takes into account others' seeing; it is a collective and cooperative seeing and welcomes comparison of different perceptions and judgments. It also knows moments of sudden revelation and intense experience of unity and completeness which are shared in others' scrutiny.

B

Critical Comments

PAUL ZIFF
University of Wisconsin

PROFESSOR SCHAPIRO says that he is concerned with "the ascription of certain qualities to the work of art as a whole, the qualities of perfection, coherence, and unity of form and content, which are regarded as conditions of beauty."

I am afraid that I have but an imperfect understanding of what Professor Schapiro wishes to say, both here and elsewhere, in his paper. Arthur Murphy once spoke of a cultivated incapacity to understand and possibly I have overexercised that incapacity here, but what Professor Schapiro says is clearly obscure.

Is unity of form and content a quality of a work of art? Is perfection regarded as a condition of beauty? It makes some sort of sense, I suppose, to say of a painting 'It is not altogether beautiful for it lacks coherence'; but it would be more than curious and would it make sense to say 'It is not altogether beautiful for it lacks perfection'?

Professor Schapiro speaks of the judgment of perfection "in art, as in nature." It is not clear what he means to be referring to. If pointing to a painting by Kandinsky one says, 'That is a perfect circle,' has one made a judgment of perfection? Or what if one says 'The work has a perfect balance'?

He says that he is concerned with the ascription of the quality of perfection to the work of art as a whole. But does he mean to suggest that there is some important logical difference between speaking of a perfect circle, a perfect balance, and a perfect work?

He says "the judgment of perfection in art, as in nature, is a hypothesis, not a certitude established by an immediate intuition." Is the reference here to any judgment of perfection whatever?

If one says of a woman, fully clothed, standing before one, that she has a perfect figure, there need be nothing much amiss in characterizing that remark as a hypothesis awaiting further confirmation. But if one says this of a woman starkly displayed before one, hasn't the hypothesis been transformed, transmuted, to what Professor Schapiro calls "a certitude established by an immediate intuition"?

Professor Schapiro says that judgments of perfection in art are "never fully confirmed." He adds that such judgments are however "sometimes invalidated by a single new observation." Insofar as I understand these remarks I do not believe them, but then I don't really understand them. Talk about "confirmation," "invalidation," "observation" here arouses in me strong feelings of no enthusiasm: I doubt that such talk either has or can even be given any clear sense in connection with paintings.

Consider a particular painting, say Poussin's "The Rape of the Sabine Women" (the version in the New York Metropolitan Museum of Art), and consider the judgment "That is a perfect painting." I do not think that. Certainly it is a fine painting but, even so, imperfect: think of the stiffness of the figures, their posed look. If I look at the painting and the figures look a bit stiff to me, as they do, have I had an observation that suffices to "invalidate" the judgment of perfection? And if someone else looks at the painting and the figures don't look stiff to him, has he made an observation that serves to "confirm," or is it to "validate" the judgment?

Professor Schapiro says that judgments of perfection in art are never fully confirmed. Examples of perfect works of art are hard to come by; I have not been able to think of even one that seems plausible: in consequence it is rather difficult (for me anyway) to discuss his claim. But he also says that judgments of coherence as well as those of perfection are never fully confirmed and are sometimes invalidated by a single new observation. Does he mean that we never know that we are right in judging a work to be coherent but sometimes we know that we are wrong? Must we accept such a depressing conclusion?

Again consider Poussin's "The Rape of the Sabine Women": isn't it a coherent work? I certainly think so. I would and do judge it to be so. What sort of "single new observation" could serve to "invalidate" this judgment?

What if I have overlooked a certain part of the painting? Professor Schapiro says that "Our perception of a work is not exhaustive. . . . We see only some parts and aspects." It is of course true that we see only some parts of a painting, for any painting has submicroscopic parts, internal parts, parts that are invisible. But that of course is irrelevant here since seeing such parts is irrelevant to an appreciation of the work. Professor Schapiro adds that "a second look will disclose much that was not seen before." But will it? If he is to maintain, as he does, that we see only some parts and aspects of a work then he must argue that no matter how many looks one has had, another look will or would or could disclose something relevant not seen before. I should find that hard to believe, but then I don't mean to try. (How tiresome it would be always to be seeing something different, never to be seeing simply the same again!)

Perhaps what in part inclines Professor Schapiro to his Heracleitean view of viewing works of art are the examples he wades in. He thinks of Chartres Cathedral, the works of Homer, the Sistine ceiling. He stares at big works, large and pregnant, works that require years of exploration, consideration, study if one is merely to familiarize oneself with only some of their features. Possibly each time one hears Bach's *Passion According to Saint Matthew* one hears something new, but what about hearing Mozart's lovely little song "Come Sweet May"? Not every work is endlessly complex: there are some such that less than a lifetime will suffice for their appreciation.

Are there relevant parts of Poussin's painting that I have overlooked, such that were I to attend to them I should feel compelled to revise my judgment that the work is coherent? I see no reason to believe that. To judge the work coherent is after all not to stick one's neck out very far. I am not saying that the work is absolutely flawless. Possibly it is less coherent than some, certainly it is more coherent than many similar works.

But what if someone were to show me or teach me a new way of looking at the painting? Professor Schapiro speaks of new points of view that "make possible the revelation of significant features overlooked by other observers." Perhaps after learning to look at the work in this new way I might be inclined to say 'Yes, now the work seems less coherent than before; indeed, looked at in this way it really seems incoherent.' I might even be tempted to add 'I now see that the work really is incoherent,' but if I did, perhaps I would simply be confused.

New points of view are not always, if ever, unmixed blessings. If a new point of view provides the basis for the judgment that a work that has hitherto been deemed coherent must now be deemed incoherent, need one accept the new point of view as relevant? Why speak, as Professor Schapiro does, of the "revelation of significant features" rather than of, say, the arbitrary introduction of irrelevant considerations?

In Milton's *Lycidas* one finds the line "He must not float upon his watery bier": the pun was not intended, possibly it was not even possible in Milton's time. Is it nonetheless a significant feature of the work that has been revealed in time?

If you look at the Poussin in the way that you have learned to look at a Miró then possibly the Poussin will look incoherent. But then why look at it in that way?

This is not a simple matter. I would not suggest it. It is conceivable to me that there be a new way of looking at a work, such that when looked at in that new way the work would seem incoherent even though before it had not, and such that one would or anyway could sensibly maintain that

that new way was nonetheless a sensible way of viewing the work. To decide on the relevance of a new way of looking at a work it may be necessary to consider not only the work in question but other works in a similar style, the basis of the relevant stylistic classification, characteristics of the observers, and so forth.

Thus suppose we have hit on a new way of looking at, viewing, works of type *a*, which type presently comprises works *1* through *99*. Suppose that hitherto we have deemed work *64* to be a virtually flawless work, but now, viewed in this new way, we find it to be somewhat defective in certain respects. Then so far we have no reason to view *64* in this new way and we have no reason to adopt this new way of viewing works. But suppose that hitherto we had deemed works *1* through *63* to be largely defective but now, viewed in this new way, we find them to have become immensely rewarding works. Then certainly we would now have reason to view works *1* through *63* in this new way, but it would still be an open question whether this new way would be relevant in connection with works *64* through *99*. If we found that the new way was definitely not rewarding in connection with works *64* through *99*, then we might consider and tentatively adopt the hypothesis that works of type *a* are best considered to be of at least two distinct subtypes, that there are therefore important stylistic differences between works of type *a*. Whether type *a* can sensibly be seen as comprising works of at least two distinct subtypes, of two relatively distinct styles, will of course depend on certain characteristics of the works in question, those characteristics in virtue of which we could explain and account for the fact that the new way of viewing works is rewarding in connection with only some works of type *a*. Furthermore, even if we found that the new way of viewing works was rewarding and so of at least prima facie relevance in connection with works *65* through *99*, still it would not follow that it was relevant in connection with *64*. For possibly one could learn to look at works *1* through *63* and *65* through *99* in the new way and yet continue to look at *64* in some other more traditional way, a way in which *64* would continue to be deemed a virtually flawless work. Would this be possible? Perhaps. It is not possible to say in the abstract, for it would depend on specific characteristics of the observers, the way of looking, specific features of the works under consideration, and so forth.

Attention to complexities of the kind just indicated can, I believe, incline one to lend only a querulous ear to Professor Schapiro's occasional remarks about "inconsistency." He says "Even where a single great artist has been responsible for a work one can detect inconsistencies brought about by a new conception introduced in the course of work. So in the Sistine ceiling, Michelangelo has changed the scale of the figures in mid-passage." Why does Professor Schapiro here (perhaps or even no doubt rightly) speak of an "inconsistency" rather than of, say, a striking variety? Michelangelo has varied the scale of the figures. Why insist on inconsistency when it might be more satisfying to find variety? No doubt there are reasons but these reasons want spelling out. (Jeremy Bentham made the same sort of point a long time ago in a somewhat different connection: a man refuses to part with a dollar; whether you characterize this a prudential act rather than a manifestation of a miserly nature will depend on various other factors. There is a difference between a miser and a prudent man but to detect it is sometimes somewhat difficult.)

Professor Schapiro has spoken at some length about questions concerning the unity of form and content and I certainly think that what he says may be interesting. But it has made me realize that I have at best a very feeble grasp of the relevant meaning or meanings of the word 'form,' only a hazy conception of what one is referring to in speaking of the form or forms of a painting or building, and so forth.

For example, at one point Professor Schapiro considers what would happen if the forms in a painting were changed. He says "In a representation every shape and color is a constituting element of the content and not just a reinforcement. A picture would be a different image of its object and have another meaning if the forms were changed in the slightest degree." The suggestion here seems to be that a change of color would constitute a change in form. I can see how a change in color could occasion a change in form but I don't understand how it could rightly be said to constitute a change in form.

Professor Schapiro speaks of form in connection with music and in connection with paintings: is that more than a pun? 'This piece of music is in sonata form': what can one say about paintings in this way? Certainly nothing leaps to mind.

He says that in a novel "we often hardly attend to the form" but "in architecture the form is more evident and is an unmistakable physiognomy of the work." Does 'form' here mean shape? But then he would seem to be punning again. Novels don't have shapes in the way buildings have shapes. But of course there is such a thing as the novel form, a piece of prose may be in novel form. And what can a building be in? Steel or concrete or what have you? Why not speak of a building in, say, glass form?

In speaking of the form of a bit of prose Professor Schapiro evidently doesn't mean to be talking about what I have just referred to as the novel form. This is clear from the fact that he asks "Who, after reading a novel by Tolstoy, can recall the form as distinctly as he can retell the story. . . ?" If I am asked whether I recall the form of a certain novel I might hesitantly reply that I did, that it was in chapter form. Is it that that Professor Schapiro is suggesting that we have difficulty in recalling?

He says:

> Who, after reading a novel by Tolstoi, can recall the form as distinctly as he can retell the story or find summarizing words for the thought and feeling that pervade the action? Surely there is an order, a pattern of narration, peculiarities of syntax and phrasing, contrasts and repetitions of language, of character and plot, that build the whole in its large and intimate meanings. But we do not fix upon these as we read; the style, the form of narration, seems a transparent medium

> through which we experience the action itself and the feelings of the characters.

I am afraid I simply do not understand. Is the style of the writing supposed to be the form of the narration? The style does not seem to me to be a transparent medium for it does not seem to me to be a medium at all.

There is, I believe, a fairly easy distinction between what someone says and how he says it; so one can readily distinguish between what is said in a novel and how it is said. I suppose that what is said is what is likely to be in question when critics talk of "content." And perhaps there is supposed to be some sort of connection between how what is said is said and "form" or "the form." But it is not easy to make sense out of talk about the unity of form and content when 'form' and 'content' are so understood. Professor Schapiro suggests that the unity of form and content would then be a matter of each having a common quality. Thus he says "One may find in the remarkable transparency of the medium in Tolstoi's writing the same purity and sincerity as in the substance of his narrative, a confirmation of the oneness of his art in at least certain aspects of form and content." How can how what is said is said have the qualities of purity and sincerity?

C

Originality as a Ground for Judgment of Excellence

H. W. JANSON
New York University

WHAT I HAVE to say is not really a comment on Professor Schapiro's paper. If I were to follow my instructions literally and confine my remarks to "Perfection, Coherence, and Unity of Form and Content," I could do so in a single word: Amen. That these concepts are of little use as criteria of value Dr. Schapiro has, I think, made abundantly clear. I venture to guess that he would arrive at the same conclusion regarding similar terms, such as "balance" or "proportion." He does not commit himself, however, on what he regards as valid criteria of value. Surely he must have some; along with the rest of us, he constantly makes value judgments about works of art, judgments that are understood and widely shared by his colleagues. I hope that Dr. Schapiro will consent to tell something of the criteria governing his judgments. Meanwhile, I should like to venture a tentative sally in the same direction.

Let me begin by affirming that the problem itself is a valid one. Since it is quite impossible to act as an art critic or art historian without judging artistic value, we ought to be able to formulate the criteria of such judgments. I propose, however, to limit myself to the visual arts; not only because I know more about them than I do about music, literature, and the dance, but also because I am not sure that there can be criteria of value which hold true for *all* the arts. The roof concept of "art" as that which unites music, literature, painting, architecture, etc., only dates from the late eighteenth century, as Paul Kristeller proved in a well-known article in the

Journal of the History of Ideas some years ago; perhaps the concept has done more harm than good. Be that as it may, as an art historian I am embarrassed by the need to generalize. If I stay within the area I know best, I may be able to avoid at least the more obvious empirical objections to my theorizing.

In his paper, Dr. Schapiro has emphasized that our perception of works of art is always selective, limited, explorative, and conditioned by previous experience, our own as well as others'. Such complexity of response suggests that we may be chasing a will-o'-the-wisp if we assume a single "aesthetic value" as the common focus of all this activity. Perhaps there is instead a multiplicity of aesthetic values, possibly unrelated, or related in ways still unknown. What are some of these values? Let us look, not at a hypothetical situation, but an everyday one: the art historian confronted with an object he has never seen before, an object presented to him as a work of art. What questions will he ask of this object? How will he evaluate it? That depends on the circumstances of the confrontation, which may cast our art historian in more than one role, as it were. Suppose, then, that he is an acknowledged expert on Rembrandt, and a Dutch seventeenth century drawing is brought to him that has been attributed to Rembrandt: his role, in that event, is narrow and specific—he is the connoisseur who must decide whether the attribution is correct. Having spent the better part of his career scrutinizing the work of Rembrandt, our art historian has developed a special sensitivity, an "eye" as we say, comparable to the "nose" of the wine expert who need only sniff the cork in order to diagnose the vintage and place of origin of a given bottle. Such authenticating, on the basis of long experience, need not involve a value judgment at all; a drawing *not* by Rembrandt is not necessarily less good than a drawing by Rembrandt. To the outsider, the process of scrutiny here—involving, probably, comparison with other, "safe" drawings by Rembrandt and by various followers and disciples—may look very much like the process by which the handwriting expert authenticates a signature. Yet the two procedures are not as analogous as they may appear. While I am not prepared to assert that the handwriting expert's work involves no value judgments whatever, that of our Rembrandt expert involves a whole succession of them, though none of them need be articulated. He must decide, first of all, "Is this a work of art?" It could, after all, be a facsimile reproduction, or it may be a hand-drawn copy of an authentic Rembrandt made by a student for practice; or a forgery. Of these possibilities, only the first can be dealt with on technical grounds alone; all it takes to spot a facsimile reproduction is a powerful magnifying glass and an intimate knowledge of printing techniques. Once our expert has satisfied himself that what he has before him is not a facsimile, he can no longer proceed without value judgments. From here on, he must be guided by what the connoisseur calls "a sense of quality," an elusive yet palpable thing which more often than not will lead him and his fellow experts to the same conclusion. This conclusion is, of course, not always verifiable, but it has in the past been verifiable often enough to confound the scoffing layman. It has happened, for instance, that an expert diagnosed a drawing as a copy after an unknown work by a certain artist, and a few years later the hypothetical original turned up. The "sense of quality," then, is real enough; but how does it involve value judgments? It rests, I think, on a whole series of unspoken assumptions about the nature of works of art and the values they embody. What is on the expert's mind when he asks, "Is this a copy? A forgery? A drawing by a Rembrandt imitator? A work of the master's own hand?" is not the difference in monetary value between these classifications; that's merely the outward reflection of the underlying aesthetic values he believes in. The expert asks these questions, rather, because the answer will determine the rank of our particular drawing in a hierarchy of artistic qualities: a forgery ranks lowest—so long as we see it "merely" as a forgery, it is assumed to have no aesthetic value at all. (Paradoxically, however, this condition is a temporary one; the "life expectancy" of a forgery—that is, its capacity to deceive—rarely exceeds one generation. A forgery older than that no longer looks like a forgery to us and thereby achieves a limited aesthetic value in its own right.) Next in rank are copies: here the assumption is that no copy can capture the essence of the original, hence the more faithful the copy, the lower its aesthetic value. "Creative" copies, in contrast, such as Rembrandt's drawings after Indian miniatures or Dürer's copies after Mantegna, are accorded equal rank with other drawings by these masters, since they were not intended as substitutes or reproductions. Instead, we think of them as "interpretations"; Rembrandt's response to an Indian miniature, we believe, is in essence no different from his response to a view of nature, both having in common that unique quality which makes it so important to differentiate between an authentic Rembrandt drawing and one that merely approximates his style.

'Twas not ever thus. The Romans, for instance, saw little difference between original and copy. If we share Plato's view that a statue is no more than the imperfect material embodiment of the shapes that existed in the mind of its creator, it is indeed difficult to understand the modern cult of the original. Academic doctrine perpetuated this blurring of the distinction between original and copy far into the nineteenth century, as the collections of dusty plaster casts in the basements of art schools used to attest (they have all been smashed by now, I suspect). Yet our present-day faith in the uniqueness of the original work of art as a physical object also has deep roots in the past. It began with the cult of genius in the Renaissance, exemplified by the worshipful awe in which Leonardo, Michelangelo, and Raphael were held by their contemporaries and the bestowal upon them of the epithet "divine." It was only in the sixteenth century that people began to speak of painters and sculptors as "creators"—until then they had simply been "makers." And with this began the cult of the *non finito*, the imputing of aesthetic value to unfinished works, fragments, sketches, etc.; drawings, for instance, hitherto discarded when their usefulness as intermediate stages in the working process was at an end, were now eagerly collected, and have been ever since. One is tempted to think of the cult of the fragmentary work of art as the secularized counterpart of the medieval cult of holy relics. The merest scrap of paper touched by Michelangelo conveyed "the breath of genius," and thus achieved a potency equivalent to that of a splinter from the True Cross.

It will be clear from the above that the *summum bonum* of our Rembrandt expert scrutinizing that drawing is *originality*. His efforts are bent on finding out whether or not the drawing before him is "an original Rembrandt" and not something that derives from Rembrandt (e.g., a copy, a product of the Rembrandt school, a forgery). An original is assumed to have a uniqueness, or individuality, that places it at the top of the aesthetic hierarchy. And Rembrandt is valued as a great master because his work has a greater measure of uniqueness, or individuality, than that of his Dutch fellow artists. We might say with George Orwell, "All works of art are unique, but some are more unique than others."

Originality as a measure of artistic value has its pitfalls—to which I shall come presently—but it does seem a bit more manageable than perfection, coherence, unity of form and content, balance, and similar criteria. While we cannot measure it or fully know it, we have methods of estimating it. And in order to do this, we must compare the work of art in question with other works of art in every possible way, rather than contemplate it in isolation as we do when we try to judge its perfection, coherence, balance, etc. Originality, after all, is by definition relative. We can grasp it only by matching the work in question against those done before, in an effort to determine how far, and in what respects, it departs from them. We can grant, presumably, that to duplicate what already exists is easier than to make something that is novel in some sense. It is also less interesting. But to achieve something that is significantly new entails an effort of the imagination, a willingness to take risks and to overcome the resistance of established practices and convictions, that few of us can manage. Hence we marvel at this minority of creative individuals, and attribute their accomplishments not to their own endeavors but to some outside influence, such as divine favor or "genius." (Originally, genius meant a spirit that seizes a person and makes him act as if in a frenzy, or "beside himself." Even today we can speak of an artist as being "in the grip of his genius," or as a "mad genius.")

We still have to define—if we can—how originality in art differs from originality in science. From what we know of the actual process of creation, it seems to me, we may conclude that the difference lies not in the process—creation in both art and science demands the peculiar psychological impulse summed up in the term "inspiration"—but in the goal. Science is perfectible, progressive; its tasks are thus defined by the state of its development in a given field at a particular time. Its inner dynamic is such that, broadly speaking, we can say that once a discovery becomes possible it also becomes inevitable. Scientific discoveries have indeed been made independently and simultaneously by workers who had nothing in common except an up-to-date knowledge of their discipline. It is probably for this reason that creative scientists rarely achieve enduring fame: their discoveries soon become outmoded, overtaken by more recent discoveries. Artistic achievements, of course, do not become obsolete. Which is not to say that there is no inner dynamic in the history of art. But an attempt to formulate any sort of "principles of growth" here would take far more time than I have at my disposal. Perhaps eventually we shall learn to interpret the history of art, along with the history of everything else, as a special case within a general theory of evolution.

Let us return once more to the concept of originality as a measure of aesthetic value. It implies, I think, that no meaningful statement is possible about the aesthetic value of a given work of art except by comparison—overt or not—with other works. I believe this is true. All of us, experts and laymen alike, approach works of art with certain expectations based on other works of art that we happen to be familiar with. The "Man who knows nothing about art" does not exist; to be a member of any human community means, among other things, to know something—however little—about art. Acceptance of originality as a measure of aesthetic value also implies that no judgment based on it can ever be final, since we can never, in a given instance, hope to carry out all possible comparisons. Our Rembrandt expert (whom we left some time ago scrutinizing a supposed Rembrandt drawing) is in rather a good position in this respect, because of the extraordinary wealth of related material available to him. But let us suppose we confront him instead with a piece of wood carving from Central Africa. How will he be able to evaluate *that*? Presumably his general training as an art historian will enable him to place it in the proper context ("Primitive sculpture, Central Africa"), but how is he to know how good a piece it is? A hundred years ago, the problem would not have troubled him; he would have admitted, grudgingly, that the object was a work of art of some sort, but he would have responded to it as an anthropological exhibit rather than as an object of possible aesthetic value. Today, thanks to what has happened in Western art since 1900, he does respond to the beauty of primitive sculpture, and hence is concerned with the rank of the wood carving in question. By immersing himself in the specialized scholarly literature and assembling related objects from the same tribe, our art historian will be able to gain some idea of the merits of the piece in question, yet he is likely to feel far less certain of his conclusions than in the case of the Rembrandt drawing. For one thing, the related material is apt to be much less plentiful; and he will find that primitive art is extraordinarily conservative, so that the "margin of originality" may be very narrow indeed. There is, in addition, a more basic difficulty here. In Western art, we assume that the most original artists were also the most influential, so that we often can measure the degree of originality of a work of art by tracing its impact upon the art of its time. We are therefore encouraged to believe that we can measure the quality of a Rembrandt drawing by seventeenth-century standards. But how are we to acquire the aesthetic standards of the tribe that produced our wood carving? Are we not bound to see that object with Western eyes, measuring it against its relatives as we would measure a work of Western modern art against *its* relatives? Every student of primitive art will readily admit how uncertain aesthetic judgments are in his area. Even so, I do not believe that these difficulties invalidate the "originality theory of aesthetic value." Over the past fifty years, we have certainly learned a great deal about primitive art; we find that we now can to some extent differentiate the mediocre from the outstanding, and we have achieved this with basically the same tools we have developed for dealing critically with works of art in the Western tradition.

1

'Perfection' as a Term in Aesthetics

MAX BLACK
Cornell University

I WONDER, to start with, whether I have adequately grasped Meyer Schapiro's general position. (I am the more eager to understand him because I have profited so much in the past from his perceptive and illuminating remarks about particular paintings.) His emphasis throughout, if I am not mistaken, is upon the richness, the complexity, the profundity of great art. A work of art—or at any rate a work of "the most serious and daring art"—is essentially reticent, slow to reveal its significance and value. Great works of art cannot be grasped in single acts of observation, however sustained and perceptive: "To see the work as it is, to know it in its fullness, is a goal of collective criticism extending over generations." Aesthetic appreciation is more like the achievement of scientific understanding than one might initially have supposed: an aesthetic judgment, at its best, has to be a "hypothesis," that is "beyond the power of an immediate apprehension" to confirm. So precarious and tentative, indeed, is the aesthetic hypothesis that it may be "sometimes invalidated by a single new observation." (But surely the "single new observation" will itself, on this view, embody a new hypothesis, itself liable to be "upset" by collective criticism?) Seeing the work of art in its fullness is like scientific theorizing—tentative, exploratory, qualified by a knowledge of its own fallibility, undogmatic. What then is the ultimate test of the work's value? Perhaps its capacity "to hold us and to satisfy us," not today or tomorrow, but *in the long run*? (I suggest this, because it seems to follow that *any* test or criterion of value is at best an expedient, to be used for what it is worth as a clue, but no more, to the ultimate long-run satisfaction that is the hallmark of successful and authentic appreciation.)

Have I seriously misrepresented Schapiro's position? I hope not. At any rate, the program I have sketched engages my sympathy as a corrective against facile reliance upon immediate judgment. Of course, one begins to wonder whether this moderate pragmatism may not have weaknesses of its own. It seems plausible enough when applied to Schapiro's examples of a Gothic cathedral or a novel by Tolstoy, but less appropriate to smaller and more tightly constructed works. Perhaps even the most erudite and resourceful criticism might find little to say in the presence of a Brancusi egg? (Though I would be astonished if Schapiro did not come up with some surprisingly apposite remark even on that subject.) After all, even sceptical and undogmatic scientists don't indefinitely agonize about the boiling point of water. One wonders also about the character of that terminal "satisfaction" that seals and crowns the protracted process of progressive correction of defective preliminary insights.

Putting these questions aside for discussion on another occasion, let us concede the undeniable merits of Schapiro's general position. What is puzzling, and remains so after further reflection, is the strategy he has adopted in this paper. I would have expected a *general* argument against the relevance of ready-made "criteria of value"; instead, we get a vehement attack upon the usefulness of appeal to "perfection, coherence, and unity of form and content," as if such appeals were sufficiently frequent and influential to demand attack. I am too much in the dark about the presumed targets of Schapiro's criticism to know whether he is flogging dead horses; in any case, he seems to me to be conceding too much in the manner of his rebuttal.

To start with what is perhaps a trifling point of logic: it seems odd to couple together "perfection, coherence, and unity of form and content" as if a single *fundamentum divisionis* could be in question. Doesn't that phrase sound about as ill-formed as "Beef, custom, and incorporated butcher"? And is it really justified to speak, as Schapiro repeatedly does, of perfection as a *quality* and as a *criterion of value*? A criterion is, I suppose, an applicable test or standard; but how are we to teach somebody to look for perfection in a painting *in order* to discover whether it is good? To call something perfect is already to imply, with strong emphasis, that it is supremely good. So it looks as if by the time we are ready to award the accolade of perfection, the work of aesthetic appraisal has already been accomplished. 'Perfect' is appropriate in a *terminating*, a final judgment (however misguided and in need of correction in the light of further experience). To use perfection as a "criterion" of value looks about as plausible as using guilt as a criterion of crime. To be sure, Schapiro argues that perfection is not a "strict or indispensable" criterion, but he overlooks the extreme oddity of treating perfection as a criterion at all. Can it be that he is here operating with some special notion of perfection?

I have tried to discover how Schapiro actually *uses* the word 'perfection' and its cognates in the paper. Sometimes it has the force for him of 'unfinished,' 'incomplete'; sometimes the force of 'containing no weak or defective part,' 'unflawed,' 'unblemished.' So perhaps what he wants to say is that in the case of "serious and daring art" failure to complete a design, or local weakness in its execution, is compatible with high achievement? Well, *that* must be conceded, of course. Yet the very assumptions behind this conclusion suggest, surely, that the unfinished symphony might have been *better* if brought to completion; and the language of 'weakness' and 'defect' suggests that to eliminate flaws or blemishes is to *improve* the work as a whole? Altogether, Schapiro's remarks about perfection remain puzzling, even to a sympathetic reader, and after several readings.

One puzzling feature about Schapiro's language is connected with a fairly obvious feature of the use of 'perfect' and 'perfectly' in ordinary contexts. Something can be sweet, or red, or round, *simpliciter;* but nothing can be *just* perfect, without being a perfect *something.* If I say such-and-such is perfect, I am either merely praising it or else inviting the relevant question, 'Perfect *what?*' To say something is perfect, and nothing more, is about as awkward as saying something is *utterly!* (Indeed, this is more than a rhetorical analogy: in ordinary use, 'perfect' has approximately the force of 'utterly, surpassingly, good of its kind,' so that something is 'imperfect' to the degree that it falls short of reaching a predetermined or desirable standard or goal. Where there is no limit on a scale of comparative achievement, it makes no sense to speak of perfection or imperfection.) If Schapiro persists in using 'perfection' as a term of aesthetics, he will be committed to specifying the respect in which, the standard with reference to which, a painting is properly to be called perfect. It looks to me as if there can be no such standard. Of course, we may judge sometimes that a painting has 'perfectly' realized the intention or design manifested in the work itself, so that nothing could have been done to have improved the execution, given *that* intention. But an artist may have "brought off" something that he would have been better advised not to have attempted. If that is Schapiro's point, I must agree with him. But I would respectfully ask him to consider whether 'perfect' might not be left on the shelf with the other grandiose terms that do more to obfuscate than to illuminate aesthetics.

2

Perfection as an Aesthetic Predicate

CHAUNCEY DOWNES
New York University

IN HIS PAPER Professor Meyer Schapiro spoke of perfection as a *quality* possessed by certain works of art. Professor Max Black questioned whether perfection was in fact a quality; he suggested that perfection was rather a higher order predicate that served to indicate the presence of all the requisite features of the object in question. As, for example, we can speak of a perfect circle because we have certain criteria for what it is to be a circle. I shall follow the matter somewhat further along the lines suggested by Professor Black.

I find Professor Black's point quite convincing; it certainly seems that in any nonaesthetic use of 'perfect' we do have a standard of some sort in mind. If this is the case, and I shall now assume so throughout, we must try to see if the use of 'perfect' in aesthetic contexts does involve the use of standards or criteria, and, if so, where these are to be found.

There is a host of standards often appealed to in aesthetic contexts, or contexts that are at least marginally aesthetic. These include standards of technique, conventional standards as enunciated by critics, and so on. Such standards as these have one feature in common: they are all external to the work itself. Now it may be that such external standards have their use. But Professor Schapiro, in claiming that perfection was a quality *of the work* was, I think, trying to get away from this idea of perfection as something imposed on the work of art from the outside. There is an obvious way in which Professor Schapiro's aim might be reconciled with Professor Black's comment, viz., find a way in which the notion of a standard may be retained but in such a manner that no appeal need be made to anything outside the work itself.

I think it possible to work out this notion somewhat along the following lines. Let us say that the use of 'perfect' as a ground for a judgment of aesthetic merit is appropriate when the work itself implies, indicates, points to, an aim or objective of its own, and then fulfills, satisfies, or carries out all the requirements of *that* aim or objective. In phenomenological language, the work evokes intentions which the work itself fulfills. Now there are numerous difficulties and even obscurities in this formulation. Let me first offer some considerations in favor of an account along these general lines. I will then return to my formulation in the hope of refining and clarifying it. Some of these considerations are:

(1) There is a familiar state of indecisiveness before an unfamiliar work of art. When asked for an opinion we sometimes have to respond that we just don't know—the work confuses us. We may note a certain rhythm in a painting starting from one corner, but this rhythm is broken up and finally fades as it moves across the picture. We may not yet see the point of this. Insofar as we do not see the point, are confused, don't know what the work is up to, we are unable to evaluate the work.

(2) But even when we grasp the intent or point of the work we still do not have all that we need in order to judge the work. We may say 'Yes, I see what is going on, but I am not sure that it succeeds.'

(3) And, of course, understanding what the work is up to does not entail a favorable evaluation. We may well say 'I understand perfectly well what is going on, and I think it is atrocious.' Such expressions as this make quite clear what may be called the difference between promise and performance. (Of course, we must speak only of the promise made by the work itself; of this more below.)

(4) A consideration of a quite different kind is to be found in the familiar experience of the development or

growth that occurs when we reexperience the work on numerous occasions. It is perhaps possible to account for this by mere accumulation. But I think we can recognize that such an account fails to do justice to the peculiar tension that we experience before good works of art. That there exists such a tension, that it may sometimes be almost spellbinding I think we can agree. But we must also note that in works we are inclined to call perfect this tension is not at all an irritation or a strain. Rather it is satisfying and at the same time stimulating. Hence the poles between which the lines of tension run are not opposed but rather complementary. And this is, of course, precisely the case with the relation between a meaning intention and a meaning fulfillment. Our excitement about the work is generated as we alternately grasp intentions and grope for the fulfillments on the one hand, and note features and aspects while seeking their roles, functions, and appropriate intentions on the other.

I suggest then that the predicate perfect is properly applied when (i) there are no intentions without fulfillments, (ii) every feature of the work is indeed a fulfillment of some intention of the work and is not merely there, and (iii) there is a sufficient degree of complexity of intentions and fulfillments to create in the viewer that tension which both stimulates and satisfies. (It would seem that (i) and (ii) would also be relevant to an analysis of the *coherence* of a work of art.)

Now there are surely problems connected with the idea of a work that itself implies or indicates intentions. First of all, I think we can avoid both pathetic and intentional fallacies; i.e., we need not attribute states of consciousness to works of art, nor need we concern ourselves with what was going on in the mind of the artist. Let us then confine ourselves to the features of the work itself. Now when one begins to speak of features of the work of art that lead the viewer to expect other features of the work it is natural to consider *conventions*. If the use of 'perfect' as an aesthetic predicate is to be explained in terms of the satisfying of a convention then it would seem that

Professor Schapiro's attempt to consider perfection a quality of the work itself must fail. For a convention is something external to the work. Hence a perfect work would be so in relation to something external to it, and the perfection would not belong to the work itself.

I cannot here undertake any detailed analysis of conventions in art, but I will try to make clear the direction I think such an analysis ought to take. Briefly, I suggest that the objective features of the work of art itself and the intentions and fulfillments of the work itself are fundamental; conventions are derived from and dependent upon successful works of art, and not the other way around. Hence while a work of art may be called perfect in the light of some convention or other, this is a derived and ultimately unimportant (and perhaps even sterile and degenerate) use of 'perfect.' A detailed defense of this claim would require much more space than is available. However, Professor Schapiro has, in his paper, given a variety of illustrations of ways in which a work may be 'imperfect' from the point of view of some convention or other, and yet be perfect.

So much for some of the mistakes we must avoid. The question now is, in what proper sense can a work of art be said to imply or indicate intentions and to furnish fulfillments? Intentions and fulfillments involve consciousness, and since we have set aside pathetic and intentional fallacies we must examine the way in which the features of the work relate to the consciousness of the viewer. I think a rather general, formal answer may be given: the work of art possesses features which have the capacity to evoke in a viewer certain orientations, sets, attitudes, expectations, etc. These are objective features of the work itself which may be experienced, in principle, by anyone. Of course these features may be quite subtle; it may take years of training and experience before the viewer is able to see them; they may require a certain background in the non-artistic culture of which the work is a part, etc., etc. But when apprehended these features will in fact create in the viewer states of consciousness of the kind noted above. These states are perhaps partly cognitive, but I think they are better described as having to do with feelings, emotions, affects. However, it is necessary to my argument that these states be intentional. Now I would certainly not deny that states such as these sometimes occur in nonintentional forms. For example, we may have only a generalized anxiety with no specific object; we may be simply hungry. But it is also true that we are sometimes anxious *about* and hungry *for*. And, of course, insofar as we deal with attitudes, expectations, etc. we have clearly an intentional or referential element. The intentionality of emotions is a tricky business, but I think it is at least clear that there exists a range of emotions, although perhaps not all, that have this directional feature. Insofar as the forms of consciousness are cognitive they are clearly intentional.

Indeed, terms like orientation, attitude, and expectation may seem to beg the question in that they are clearly referential. Well, it is of course the relation of intentionality to perfection that I am discussing. But suppose we try some term that seems clearly nonintentional, say, 'calm.' It would surely be unusual, although perhaps not impossible, to say that one was calm *about* or calm *toward;* any uses of such an expression of which I can think do not seem to be really intentional. (It might be interesting to pursue the analysis of, say, 'He received the news calmly.' Is his calmness logically independent of what the news was?) Nevertheless, even in cases such as 'calm' I think we can see the relevance of intentionality. For we surely do not mean that the picture makes us feel calm; we can get that result from a tranquilizer. Rather we mean that the picture *is* calm, and we would point to 'calm-making' features—horizontal lines, muted colors, etc. But so far, I would argue, these features of the picture would not move us to call it *perfect.* If we were to go on and argue that the picture is perfect, I think we would in fact try to show how the various aspects of the picture cooperate to yield calmness; how what is suggested here is carried out there; an orientation set up by the use of a color is complementary to that satisfaction received from an element of the composition, and, of course, vice versa. There is no feature of a work that is intrinsically an intention or a fulfillment; each feature may function as either, or, ideally, both.

I have chosen a hard case, viz., 'calm,' because it enables me to formulate the most obvious objection to my general contention about intentionality. The objection runs as follows: why not simply say that the picture is calm because it has many calm-making features; further, that if someone is impelled to say that the picture is perfect, all he means is that it contains all the calm-making features he can think of or that convention requires. In summary my reply is (i) conventions are derived, etc. as indicated above, and (ii) that mere accumulation does not seem to me to yield that simultaneously stimulating and satisfying tension that is required for the appropriate use of 'perfect.' This contention can be defended only vis-à-vis a particular work of art. But, in general, it still seems to me that legitimate use of 'perfect' requires a closure, a fittingness (as Professor Black pointed out), that no more heaping up can ever attain. And it is precisely such a closure and fittingness that is characteristic of the relation between a meaning intention and a meaning fulfillment.

3

The Abiding Values of Art

RICHARD KUHNS
Columbia University

A CONCERN common to all three main papers in this symposium is the search for the abiding in art: given the erosion of time, eccentricity of interpretation, relativity of affect, what is there in works of art which stays as a permanent value, something to which we may return again and again with the assurance that *here* we have that which makes art worthwhile?

Professor Schapiro selects three traditional attributes of art to which he assigns the virtue of being "regarded as conditions for beauty." If perfection, coherence, unity of form and content are the conditions for beauty, their ascription to works of art ought to be of great concern to us, for the degree to which we use them appropriately will determine the degree to which we will apprehend the value of art as such. Of the three writers who seek to define the abiding in art, Professor Schapiro has come closest to specifying and analyzing artistic properties; his suggestions deserve careful consideration.

In looking over Professor Schapiro's discussion of these concepts one is struck by his assumptions. He seems to assume, for example, that art is something mysterious, difficult, never apprehended in its totality, but always known in its "aspects" and "partialities." This is something Professor Ziff questioned, as do those who share his attitude: how can anything man-made be that complex, they say. Yet Professor Schapiro gives persuasive testimony to show us by example how long and difficult is the way to understanding. I am convinced by this, as well as by my own experience, that a great deal of art one works at and knows incompletely, one returns to with profit. Of course, we want to know why this is the case.

Professor Schapiro assumes further, and tries to illustrate with brief comments, that the most abiding aspect of art, that to which we are apt to be most drawn and of which we can have the best understanding, is "the structure of the forms." Content, he asserts, is less definite and sure, for we "often appreciate forms without attending seriously to their represented meanings; for certain works we could not begin to consider that unity with content since so little of the original meanings is available to us." At the same time he points out that the identity of form and content can be of great importance to the artist: "The expressive forms [in the case of a portrait] were conceived as uniquely adequate to a particular sitter with traits of character and a significance that we divine only incompletely from the portrait." It is difficult for us to know "fully enough the broad organizing ideas through which we can perceive the meanings as a unity embracing the subjects, the spheres of connotation between otherwise isolated elements of representation."

Separation of form and content exists initially for the artist who "in advance of the work, possesses a form in the habit of his style which is available to many contents, and a conception of a subject or theme rich in meaning and open to varied treatment." Although artistic realization joins these components in unique ways, an incompleteness of understanding seems to be our fate where, at least for certain works like the Sistine ceiling, "to speak of a unity of form and content here is to pretend to a grasp that is still denied us."

The weight of this conclusion falls on the side of a formalistic approach to art which, we know from his other writings, is not representative of Professor Schapiro's own position. But this kind of formalism has attracted many art critics who want to defend art values as empirically grounded, discoverable, articulable. I assume, then, that despite his disagreement with such a position elsewhere, Professor Schapiro wants to propose and defend a formalism that, most radically stated, comes to this: (1) Most art is known only partially; (2) the abiding aspects of art are its forms; (3) though identity of form and content was of crucial importance to the artist, we are in most cases unable to perceive it and must rest content with the forms alone, ignorant, except within limits, of the content in its original significance; and even if we recovered the original significance we would find *artistic* character and value little changed by this knowledge.

At first consideration, if only on the ground of human fallibility, point one would seem to be unassailable, but what we can infer from it is not clear to me. For instance, we cannot infer from it that we will be rewarded by returning to a work, nor that we can define a "coefficient of satiation" for art experiences generally. The difficulty turns on the word "partial," a term which has a special relevance to our experience of art. "Partial" does not mean simply fragmentary or incomplete; it has to do, rather, with an essential property of art, a property, I believe, not related solely to the form of art, nor a property to be, as it were, perceptually neutralized through the acquisition of the total content of the work. Even with an absolute grasp of content (assuming we know what that might consist in) there is a reason why our apprehension of a work or works would be partial, for our experience of art is necessarily cumulative without being exhaustive.

While Professor Schapiro assumes that "partial" is a function of the separation of form and content, he insists that the identity of form and content is crucial to the artist. It follows that in his view partiality is the consequence of a loss, of an incongruity we find in the object but not intended by the artist, and certainly not perceived by him, discounting his own dissatisfaction with his work. Other traditions, however, would find this hard to understand. The Chinese painter, for example, has psychological and spiritual aims which depend upon the content of his work. He would think it odd that we, in our appreciation of our own painting, can separate the "aesthetic" from the presented content. Color, line, shape are chosen for their appositeness to content and themselves are part of content. Are we then the inheritors of an art in which this integrity did not exist, or do we in fact decompose the art we receive in destructive ways? The position I have formulated seems to defend artistic values through the acceptance of such a decomposition. What is to be gained from this? The reason why it is often claimed that the formal elements are the bearers of *artistic* values is that the content appears to be relative to an outlook, point of view, set of beliefs, while the forms are abiding in their structural integrity and fixedness. In this connection it is worth recalling that Professor Schapiro is suspicious of a Weltanschauung in art interpretation: "The world of art is not a clear expressive feature of the work of art like the feeling of a painted smile or the contrast of black and red, but a complex and still uncertain interpretation." Admission of a world view threatens *artistic* values because it translates the artistic forms into something else. The Hegelian type of interpretation seeks the abiding values of art in an ultimate spiritual meaning, while the formalistic approach seeks permanence in something perceptual. But art is both ideational and perceptual; its values are to be established in defending wholeness and integrity rather than defending either an extravagant or a safe partiality.

The two directions in which the abiding values of art are sought are unsatisfactory because the experience of partiality remains, in either effort at interpretation, a fact about our experience of art. We find unity only in simple cases: advertising, comic strips, industrial design, which may be one reason for their attractiveness for Pop art and the novels of writers like Michel Butor. Here we are not so much puzzled by content as soon bored by it; there is a unity of banality which is artistically intentional because it solves difficult artistic problems. But this solution, while it helps the troubled critic, is like banishing the problem of war through a return to bows and arrows.

The values of art which make it worthwhile in an abiding way are values found in works of considerable complexity and richness, and even then those values are insufficiently confirmed when confined to a single object. It is when the individual work is known alongside others that the partiality to which Professor Schapiro draws our attention becomes evident. One aspect of our experience with art, no matter how well we know the art structures, is an awareness of incompleteness. The experience itself testifies to the fact that art values are not to be found in a permanence of structure available in its dimensions to all, but rather that they are found in the experience we have of a growing, changing object to be explored, never exhaustively disclosed in all its aspects.

In the process of exploring the domain of art, as individual works are set beside others in a larger acquaintance, the abiding values we discover are found in orders of relationships, ideas, arguments possibly different from those which counted most for the artist. He, unlike those who follow, cannot see his work as past, nor as leading to whatever it is that follows. What he values may well be different from what his later admirers will value. However, I think it a mistake to see this change as a loss or a partial grasp in a pejorative sense; rather, it may be a fuller, and I would think ultimately more valuable, realization of the art.

There is, I am suggesting, a wholly artistic value, essential to art, perhaps *the* defining characteristic of art, since perfection, coherence, and unity are meaningfully predicated on other human achievements. This value is recognized in the complicated interplay of direct confrontations with cultural assumptions, artistic methods, critical knowledge. The consequence for us is the sense we have of a reality revealed, but only partially. The partiality of which we are aware is due not to a decomposition within the work (a separation of form from content), but rather to the incompleteness of single encounters which, in revealing more, yet offer differing aspects of the work itself. What is revealed is not a reality ontologically prior to the work, or something more real than the work, but what the work is in itself as a work of art. Yet what it is in itself requires for discovery a willful act: the individual object is made to reveal itself through our impelling its participation in larger orders of artistic reality to which we usually give the name "style."

The fact of style itself—one of the most important conditions of art to which little attention was paid in these discussions—forces a selection of artistic methods and subject matter which makes us aware of a partiality. Everything is left out except what the style admits; yet everything omitted is relevant to the experience by a kind of artistic negation. Style, in working by means of rejections and exclusions, offers the possibility of completeness in contiguous endeavors: contiguous temporally in that clusters of works share techniques, purposes, visions; contiguous synaesthetically in that various genres in the different artistic media are complementary. No one style, no one medium, is exhaustive of the values of art. Acquiescence in the partiality defended by extreme formalism is apt to prevent our continued exploration of those values which are most art-full in that they go beyond the formal conditions of an individual object. Partiality is not the consequence of loss, but the recognition that there is something more to be gained.

Turning now to the second and third propositions: aware as we are of the overburdening freight of critical interpretations, we fear a work may be submerged, or forced to speak in tongues it does not understand. This danger is not avoided by limiting the obligations of criticism to the articulation of perfection, coherence, unity, for this leaves the ultimate values of art out of consideration. I see the prime responsibility of criticism as the making of a decision which is itself interpretive. What values are to be found in a given work as it participates with other works in a common artistic endeavor? Criticism is comparative always, its search for the abiding but directives for exploring a growing, changing reality. The recoveries of criticism are necessarily new artistic values.

Artistic values, I have argued, include more than coherence, perfection, unity; in selecting them as the conditions of beauty in art we are in danger of locating artistic value in properties we think of as analogous to the elegance of a formal proof. Artistic beauty is not that sort of property, though that sort is relevant to and is found in some art. The emphasis on artistic beauty as formal organization depending upon those conditions misleads us by suggesting beauty is, as well, the prime value of art. Not only is it not the prime value of art, but also those characteristics named as the ground of beauty are the ground for other values as well. Just as these grounds are contributing conditions for art values generally speaking, so beauty is a function of and a contributor to other values which we recognize as our awareness extends to its fullest grasp. When this occurs, as it can in the work of Michelangelo and Tolstoy, the two examples given, it occurs not because in one case there is perfection of form and in the other richness of content, but because in each perfection, coherence, and unity are structural characteristics of a reality to which we gain access. That reality exhibits values of vast variety and range. The steadfastness we seek is here, in the art object as part of a realm which in creative fertility does not copy or rival, but outstrips nature itself. The philosophy of art has hardly begun to explore this realm.

4

Are There Universal Criteria of Judgments of Excellence in Art?

SIDNEY HOOK
New York University

WHEN WE SAY something is an excellent work of art we mean to praise it and to call attention to an objective achievement by the artist with respect to the whole or part of his creation. When we call a work a masterpiece we imply that it is excellent but there are many works we find excellent that we would hesitate to declare masterpieces. None of the participants in the symposium on the grounds of judgment of excellence in art has been able to make clear how he himself was using the term "excellent" or "masterpiece." But a satisfactory analysis should be adequate at least to our own judgments. The criteria which Meyer Schapiro mentions—even where the term "perfect" is interpreted as a specific quality in context as in expressions like "a perfect fit" or "a perfect circle"—are obviously neither necessary nor sufficient conditions of excellence. Just as soon as anyone offers a criterion or rule for a judgment of excellence, someone else will show that in fact we make judgments of excellence, which are widely shared by competent critics, independently of the criterion, or that some work of art to which the criterion or rule clearly applied was not uniformly judged excellent by competent critics.

This is obviously also the case for the criterion Professor Janson mentions and which he gently chides Meyer Schapiro for neglecting. Originality is a quality that often plays a powerful role in determining our judgment of excellence. But unless it is arbitrarily asserted that when we say something is a great work we already mean that it is original, it seems to be true that we sometimes find great loveliness and delight in works of art, ranging from a new suspension bridge or a repeated rendition of a symphony or a performance of a play, that are not noteworthily original.

Whether originality is a necessary condition, it certainly is not a sufficient condition of excellence in any of the arts. *Some other element of significance must be present before the originality becomes a relevant aesthetic quality.* Otherwise some excellence would be attached to any new combination or permutation of elements in any composition. But there is an irreducible difference between an original Rembrandt and an original Hook. We make the same point when we distinguish between the original or creative, on the one hand, and what is merely novel, on the other. I can very well imagine works of art that are highly original in some respect and yet would never be judged great or even interesting. Puzzled by the appearance of a landscape, I may discover that it has been painted by an artist who looked at the world through his legs. Or someday I may read a novel whose first page describes the last moments on earth of some character and whose last page contains an account of his first moments on earth. By themselves these features of a work of art would hardly warrant a judgment of excellence although the perspective in the painting and the order of events in the novel would be declared original.

It seems to me quite true that sometimes when we declare or imply that a work of art is "unoriginal," we insofar intend to deny it aesthetic excellence. The critic who characterized *Herzog* as a minor Jewish version of *Ulysses* was uttering a judgment of disparagement. Professor Janson is right in asserting that statements about the originality of a work of art are comparative. This is analytically true. "Original" is a relational term. But I am not convinced that "no meaningful statement is possible about the aesthetic value of a given work of art except by comparison—overt or not—with other works." A work of art may move me to make a judgment of excellence with respect to a certain experienced quality without my making any comparison "overt or not" with other works. My judgment may have a history and be influenced by previous funded experiences but it is not necessarily comparative. At any rate, I do not believe that any significant correlation can be established between the rank order of originality and the rank order of aesthetic excellence. There is a difference between saying "This work shows greater artistry than that," where there is no doubt that both rate as significant works of art, and saying of two daubs "This is even cruder and uglier than that," where we are uncertain whether we would regard either one as legitimate works of art.

All this suggests that when a critic characterizes a work of art as a "masterpiece" or pronounces it "excellent," the term does not have the same meaning for him on each occasion of its use. It may function like the word "good." The history of aesthetic taste seems to me to reinforce this suggestion. A study of the judgments of excellence made by Professors Schapiro and Janson in the course of their workaday evaluations will show the same thing. We are often surprised by our own reaction—even by our reflective reactions—to works of art. It may be that, except in a special sense I shall propose later on, the entire quest to discover grounds for judgment of aesthetic excellence is ill-conceived. I used to believe that one sure sign that I was in the presence of a great work of art was that it commanded my attention again and again, that I could return to it and find a never failing source of freshness and delight. A great work of art does not pall on one. Just as one never tires of seeing a beautiful face so one never tires of rereading some of Shakespeare's passages or of hearing some works of Bach over and over again. Nonetheless I am beginning to wonder whether this is invariably true of works I regard as excellent. While seeing the movie *The Pawnbroker*, I judged it to be a remarkable film, and in retrospect I still believe it to be one of the most excellent productions of the cinematographic art. Nonetheless wild horses could not drag me back to see it again. The experience was too lacerating. It may be a great picture but I don't like it. It is unsafe to ground a judgment of excellence merely on one's likes or dislikes.

It therefore seems to me that when a critic makes a judgment of excellence with respect to any work of art, or any rendition or performance, aside from indicating something about his personal liking, the objective ground of the judgment must lie in some technical achievement recognized or recognizable by controlled observation or analysis of the art object. Such a judgment invites our approving attention to skills and to the complex effects of these skills in the work of art, their difficulty, their uniqueness, their interrelatedness with other objective features discoverable in the work. It is pointless, even senseless, to make aesthetic comparisons of rank order between different genres of art. Among the excellences of a poem may be its musical overtones and of a symphony its dramatic contrasts, but it would be malapropos to compare the excellence of a poem with that of a piece of music or the excellence of a symphony with that of a play except for certain formal purposes irrelevant to aesthetic judgment. I have always had an uncomfortable feeling in listening to, or reading, much art criticism, especially criticism of modern music or nonobjective art or certain kinds of writing, that my leg was being pulled, that the critic was really talking about himself and his reactions, rather than about the work itself. One can learn a great deal from the reactions of the critic about many different things, but in the end if his words are to be aesthetically relevant they must be related to the art object. When I look for something to control the critic's judgment, I must find it in what is before me or in an experience directly attributable to what is before me. Words can make anything suggest anything but we must have some way of ruling out the arbitrary suggestion. A critic who is talking about the excellences of a work of art must, when I dispute his judgment, be able to make me see in a painting what I did not see before, lead me to hear a piece of music with a greater degree of perceptiveness and discrimination, or relate incident, characters, and expressions in a novel which at first reading appeared inconsequential or disconnected. These are the experiences which are relevant to the control on the objectivity of his judgment, not my reactions *to* the experiences. The critic who is saying something significant about a work of art is teaching us something about the techniques of that art as practiced by the artist who himself may be completely unaware of how he gets his effects and even of what effects he gets. This seems to me to be particularly true of music.

Judgments of excellence of a work of art will reflect the developments and stages in the evolution and history of different techniques. And it is to be expected that because of the open character of techniques, which is comparable to the open texture of discourse, no one criterion of excellence will do justice to the variety of art-forms and the multiplicity of achievements a developing technique makes possible.

Where the rules of performance are given for any activity, it is easy to determine excellence or degrees of excellence. For example if I say that "X has pitched a perfect game," everyone knows that he pitched a no-hitter. But in the light of the rules of baseball I can refine the judgment. My judgments of excellence will differ depending upon the number of batters who were struck out. A no-hitter may result not from the excellence of the pitching but from the superb character of the fielding which converts almost sure homers into fantastic fly-outs. It is conceivable that a no-hitter can be pitched with 27 balls, but a perfectly pitched game is a no-hitter which results from 81 pitched balls—every batter struck out. (The assumption, of course, is that the players are normal—not drunk or corrupt.) Here the fixity of the rules makes it easy to determine the validity of judgments of excellence. But the analogy with judgment of artistic excellence breaks down because there are no fixed rules which an art must follow. Even when an existing tradition suggests compliance with rules, the artist's intent may require the abandonment of the old rules and the adoption of new and strange techniques. That is why the illustration of an excellently pitched game is not a good paradigm for an excellent work of art. The norms are too quantitative and the quality or style of the pitching is ignored. Games are not works of art. But the relevant point here is that the judgment of excellence is based on the objective technical achievement. The criteria of excellence in art are not rules or fixed "eternal" standards imposed from without upon the creative effort of artists. The history of criticism is largely a history of lost reputations because of the fetishism of past standards of excellence—the flaming rebel often becomes the conservative philistine. But because some theories of objective judgment of excellence are false, it does not follow that all criticism is a matter of gush and go, of riotous impressionist rhetoric.

The processes of creation are sure to produce not only variations on established forms of artistic excellence but radical novelties. Our age has a bias for the startling, the unexampled, and the shocking. The canons of the academic, the formal, the classical may be redefined to embrace violations but it is always after the fact. The challenge to understanding will always remain. This imposes the critical necessity of being able to distinguish at any definite time between new musical patterns and an arbitrary succession of sounds, between new configurations of color and design and a meaningless jumble of pigment and lines. The meaning must be embodied in the work so that intelligent and informed viewers or auditors may find it. And that is all that can be reasonably expected from criticism. It is true that some works of art or great technical facility in some respect seem to lack excellence, but when they do, it is because of a technical defect in *other* respects. Defects are remedied by better techniques not by abandoning all the disciplines of one's craft.

Where differences in judgments of artistic excellence cannot be resolved by reference to the embodied technical achievement in the broadest sense, then the differences reflect personal predilections that are not negotiable by aesthetic considerations but which *may* be reasonably resolved by other considerations. But "may" implies "may not." Sometimes the theme of a work of art or of the artist's intention is so foreign to our interests, sometimes so hateful to us that we are indifferent to the skill or brilliance of his technical achievement in carrying it out. There is no confusion here provided we can distinguish between what we judge to lack excellence because of shoddy or confused work and what we judge to lack excellence because we do not approve of the theme or the fashion in which it has been executed. Distinction, of course, is not separation but surely one can appreciate and enjoy Wagner's music even if one detests the non-musical values of his work. Sometimes this is not possible. But whether it is possible or not seems to me to be a psychological question not strictly germane to the quality of the work of art. Can an anti-Negro joke be funny to one who is morally outraged by racialism? It seems to me that it can, although I doubt whether I would *call* it an excellent joke and would prefer that such jokes not be cracked in a society in which racial antagonisms and tensions are found.

Despite what some critics have claimed, there are limits which our moral sensibilities impose on our capacity to appreciate or enjoy "the true" and "the beautiful." Knowledge is an intrinsic value but the most ardent devotee of knowledge for its own sake will draw the line about the value of experiments designed to further knowledge of how to increase the sufferings of human beings under torture. The wholesome recognition that all values are limited by other values sometimes leads to a converse error. Sometimes we mistakenly deny the truth or artistic achievement in what we cannot really enjoy. There are to be sure normative judgments also involved in the judgments of truth and of artistic excellence. But they are not normative moral judgments. In cases of conflict, and we sometimes must choose between the true, the good, and the beautiful, the primacy of moral judgment in the life of man must be acknowledged without denying autonomy of meaning to the true and the artistically excellent.

5

Merit as Means

NELSON GOODMAN
Brandeis University

IF I ASK YOU to rank according to excellence the Brahms Double Concerto, the Battle of Britain, springtime, *Hamlet* and charity, you may well protest that the question is either ambiguous or meaningless. The ranking will vary with the sort of excellence in question; and if I demand a single overall evaluation, I am either asking you to add elements as alien as apples and asteroids or talking in terms of units so denatured as to lack all significance.

Trouble of the same sort arises, I think, when the items compared are far less heterogeneous—even, for example, when all are works of painting or sculpture. If we are confronted with a Donatello marble, a Goya 'black' painting, a medieval illumination, and a Shang bronze, the question which is best, is ridiculous and may be vicious. Works vary in power, subtlety, vibrancy of color, justness of proportion, etc.; but to ask whether a supremely subtle work is better than a supremely powerful one is like asking whether a very tall man is bigger than a very stout one.

What I object to is not merely the oversimplification but the overvaluation of value. Not only is excellence at best multidimensional rather than linear, but also concentration upon questions of excellence diverts attention from more important concerns. It distorts and even inverts the whole task of the philosophy of art, and obscures its relationship to the general theory of knowledge. To understand works of art we must be able to tell power from bluster, subtlety from sophistry, vibrancy from raucousness; and a primary task of aesthetics is to discriminate and interrelate the aspects under which works of art are to be perceived and comprehended. Rather than judgments of specific aesthetic characteristics being mere means toward an ultimate appraisal, judgments of value are often mere means toward discernment of specific characteristics. If a connoisseur tells me that one of two Cycladic figures that seem to me almost indistinguishable is much finer than the other, this inspires me to look for and may help me to find the significant differences between the two. Estimates of excellence are among the minor aids to understanding.

In short, I suspect that the emphasis on excellence in art has been partly to blame for the lack of excellence in aesthetics. Judging the excellence of works of art or the goodness of people is not the best way of understanding them. And a criterion of artistic merit is no more the major aim of aesthetics than a criterion of virtue is the major aim of psychology.

PART II

Interpretation of Meaning in Art Criticism

A

The Limits of Critical Interpretation

MONROE C. BEARDSLEY
Swarthmore College

WHAT INTERPRETATION encompasses, in the context of the present discussion, will be plainer as we go on, but no doubt some initial effort should be made to fix this overworked term. I am talking about interpreting works of art (not scores or scripts) —one of the main things a critic or teacher does with them. Definition: to interpret is verbally to unfold or disclose meaning (either sense or reference).

The scheme I am operating with can be outlined this way:

I. Description
1. The painting includes a mauve elliptical area.
2. The sections of the music are balanced.
3. The sculpture has a quality of barely contained frenzy.

II. Interpretation
1. The painting represents a Conestoga wagon.
2. The metaphor connotes helpless and merciless desire.
3. The object in the literary work symbolizes the separateness of human beings.
4. The object in the painting symbolizes the depersonalization of modern man.
5. The (nonrepresentational) visual design denotes madness.
6. The music refers to the (composer's?) fear of death.

Parts of the discussion below will have to be adjusted if we differ about the exact line between I and II or about the location of some of the examples. Charles Stevenson, in his famous paper,[1] would have placed statements I, 2 and I, 3 under interpretation, because he would hold that they, like the examples under II, are subject to a certain irremediable sort of dispute. W. E. Kennick, in his recent book,[2] would have placed II, 1 under description; that is because he equates description roughly with statements about what is "obvious" in the work. In my earlier treatment of these problems,[3] I would have put II, 2 under description as analyzing the texture of the poem, considered as a composition of meanings—and I was pleased by my distinction between interpretation, elucidation, and explication. I haven't altogether abandoned my earlier classifications. But the six types of statement exemplified above have all, quite frequently, been called "interpretations," and I am willing to consider them as such on this occasion. Moreover, their similarities and differences, and even more the order in which they are listed, will prove to be instructive later.

The problem before us has to do with the nature and validity of critical interpretation-statements. And certain points that are to be stressed can most sharply be brought out, I think, if we begin with what might seem to be something of a digression. I would like to contrast, in a broad fashion, two general ways of viewing art—two attempts, we might say, at monolithic theories. It will appear that they bear more than a casual resemblance to theories that have actually been held and defended, though representing them somewhat crudely. What will help us most is to look carefully for the seams in these theories, to note the points at which a certain strain and artifice is required to keep them in one piece.

I

The first theory is one that takes art—*all* art—as inherently referential. According to this theory, it is the very nature of a work of art to point beyond itself to something else; the work is always, in a broad sense, a sign or symbol of something; it copies, or imitates, or represents, or expresses. Of course we must distinguish among all these different concepts. But those who hold this theory are after a concept more abstract than any of them. And perhaps I will be excused if I make the term "significance" do. According to the Significance Theory then, all works of art have a meaning, in this exceedingly broad sense, and therefore all works require to be interpreted—or at least are capable of being interpreted (though what the work means may often be too obvious to mention).

The Significance Theory, in its various forms, has been supported by many studies of particular works and particular arts—studies that have, incidentally, contributed much to our knowledge of them. But I want to sketch a generalized argument for this theory in order to see how persuasive it can be made.

Consider first literature—surely the most favorable case. Whatever else a poem may be, it is at the very least a series of sentences in a natural language. And what is a sentence (even a one-word sentence) if it is not *about* something? The sounds a poem makes may seem to please us in themselves, but their full force comes only with the support they give the sense; and a senseless poem is a contradiction in terms.

It may be possible to take issue with this, though I think not for long. The strings of more or less random words, or nonsense-syllables, or even mere letters, set down by Dada writers, should not trouble us. I do not think we have to be counted as enemies of art if we refuse to call these productions poems, or as dull in spirit if we fail to find much of aesthetic interest in them. But suppose the Dada poet defends his nonsense-syllables. What might he say? "My poem is not intangible in the ordinary sense, for it is not an ordinary poem. It has not been grasped by the critics, because they were looking for familiar elements of poetry and are bogged down in the traditional stereotypes. By breaking away from the limitations of English syntax and word-construction, I demonstrate the freedom of the creative artist, who has the boldness and imagination to be different. So if I had been a little more conventional, I could have called my poem 'Freedom,' instead of 'No. 97.'"

It turns out that the poem *is* about something, after all, namely freedom—however obscure it seems to those who lack the skeleton key. Though ostensibly about nothing, it speaks (on a deeper level) of the poet's freedom to talk about nothing if he wants to.[4] I don't say that the defense is a good one—my point is that if he *makes* a defense at all (which he may be too proud to do), then it looks as if his defense would have to consist in showing that the poem does indeed signify something, as the Significance Theory declares.

After that, we shall not be surprised to find that the theory can be made to cover many other unlikely cases as well. Probably the next easiest is the painting or sculpture that is plainly and thoroughly representational. Let's say there is a statue on the campus, its pedestal reading "Elihu Yale (1649–1721)." Certainly in a fairly clear sense this statue calls attention to Elihu Yale—it aims to preserve in the minds of living men the memory of this person, whom it represents and (I suppose) resembles. But now what if the name and dates were effaced—by time or by undergraduates—so that we had no verbal clue to the identity of its prototype? Would it then no longer refer to anyone? There is still the resemblance, to be sure. If it was not carved or moulded from the life, it was probably copied from a contemporary portrait—and if we could dig up the portrait for comparison, we would have our clue. The statue doesn't have to be *named* Elihu Yale to represent him.

Let us make things harder, and suppose that the face, too, has been so worn away that it no longer much resembles either the man himself or any existing portrait of him. *Now* shall we say that it has lost its reference? Well, still there is its bulk and location. We would recognize it as a statue of a man. And to make him larger than life, and place him on a pedestal in the middle of the campus, where he serves no apparent utilitarian purpose (where, indeed, people have to walk around him to get where they are going)—doesn't all this implicitly claim that he is *somebody,* at least—a worthy man, even if we don't know on what account he is worthy, or what he is worthy of? So even if the statue no longer refers to Elihu Yale, it may refer to *worthiness* in general, and to any other qualities we find depicted on that countenance, such as dignity, scholarly pride, strength of character.

Let us carry the matter further. Let us do as perhaps some archaeologist may in fact one day do: cart the partially ruined sculpture off to a museum—making way for someone more memorable, such as the late president of the University or its most eminent fund-raiser. Standing (or sitting) there in the art museum, shorn of name, individual features, and campus context—is the statue still a bearer of meaning? Yes, the Referentialist will say, for it still represents a man, and a man of a certain sort—a strong or weak man, a rough or kindly man, a reflective or impulsive man. Now suppose the statue is slowly melted down. As long as its recognizable resemblance to the human form remains, however abstract it may be, it still speaks to our human condition and about our human nature. Toward the final stages of melting, we may be able to say of it nothing more than that it is (1) vaguely humanoid, (2) droopy or humble or dejected. Still it depicts sorrowing humanity. And when, finally, we can no longer even say that—when we can say no more than that it is brown, bronze, and rounded—then we no longer have a piece of sculpture, no longer a work of art. We have a lump. We are back to the material.

In this way the Significance-Theorist makes out his case for the view that even nonrepresentational paintings and sculpture are, in a broad sense, meaningful—they don't just sit there; they have relevance to the deep concerns of man, his needs and aspirations; there is more in them than meets the eye. And once we have made out this case for purely formal art, there is no great difficulty in extending it to music. There is, of course, no difficulty at all about music that comes with words, or about music in which we can hear birds twittering. But take the most austerely formal music you can find, the most remote (at first glance) from all apparent interest in birds. Still, the Significance-Theorist would say, it has a reference. Consider a familiar example: the first six notes of "The Star-Spangled Banner," in B flat—as usually written, to make what accommodation it can to the limits of the ordinary human voice. Forget the words, and the voice of Lucy Monroe. Consider the notes only as a sequence of events in time. Something is happening—how shall we describe it? The melody dives down abruptly from fifth to tonic, by way of the third, and then with great determination and decisiveness climbs through the third and fifth to the octave. The downward plunge, as we see it in retrospect, while we are on the way up, was like a catching of breath, a stepping back to leap better, and this preparation makes the rise to the octave all the more emphatic. It is not aggressive, since the phrase ends at the octave, at home; it is an assertion of right, a resolution not to be dispossessed—like free men standing guard before their loved homes, or a flag waving amidst the smoke. There is nothing perfunctory, or hesitant, or languid about this little bit of musical action—it is at the opposite extreme, for example, from the opening bars of Wagner's *Tristan*. It has a quality of self-assurance, strength of will, defiance.

Stop right there, says the Significance-Theorist, and you have it. For quite apart from its patriotic lyrics and official status as National Anthem (and even if it lost these, the way Elihu Yale was imagined to lose his name and lineaments), the melody would still breathe these human qualities of will and strength. And it is capable of reminding the listener who really hears (or better, the hearer who really listens) that such qualities exist: it displays them, and shows them off admiringly, you might say. Thus music, too, without external aid, may have external reference. We need not give examples from architecture, the dance, and so on—we can see how the Significance Theory would deal with them. The strength of the argument lies in the continuity of cases. It seems that no one can deny that literary works are significant, but then by easy and apparently inescapable extensions of the method of analysis, representational works of fine art, then nonrepresentational works, and finally music, turn out to exhibit something of the same sort of significance—though of course more subtle and perhaps more difficult to put your finger on and describe as you go down the list. The heart of the arguments is this challenge: if you admit that there is signification at one end (in *Paradise Lost,* which surely refers to the creation of the world and man), and deny that there is signification at the other (say, in Bach's two-part inventions), where and with what excuses do you draw the line?

II

The second general theory of art relies upon the same argument from continuity. But it begins at the other end and works in the opposite direction.

Let us consider again a simple strain of melody. We can agree that the first six-note phrase of "The Star-Spangled Banner" has the qualities of vigor and forcefulness. But why must we go on to say that it *refers* to vigor and forcefulness as qualities existing in man and in man's behavior? It is perfectly all right to say:

1. The music *is* vigorous and forceful.

It is also all right to say:

2. The music's vigor and forcefulness *resemble* the vigor and forcefulness of human beings and human actions.

It is in fact this resemblance—vague and fleeting as it sometimes is—that justifies us in transferring these terms from human beings, where they literally apply, to music, where they apply only metaphorically. This little snatch of melody certainly acts as if it knows where it is going and is determined to get there; there is no nonsense about it, and no subtlety, either. Its motion is something like that of a man making a decisive gesture, or uttering a few short words of definite commitment to a cause, or rising to show where he stands on an issue. One could say a lot more about this, but that's enough to convey the general idea—if you don't find it too fanciful. The music *is* vigorous; its vigor is *similar* to human vigor. But that is still not the same as saying what the Significance Theory says:

3. The music *refers to* (means, signifies, expresses, represents, indicates, communicates) vigor.

From our second point of view, then, the music is not a sign of anything at all, but simply an object, or event, in its own right with its own shape and qualities. Its parts are purely musical happenings: upward and downward movements, speedings and slowings, swellings and fadings. They fit together and make something of a whole precisely because, far from pointing beyond the music to something else, like the dots and dashes of a Morse transmitter, they actually point to what is coming next in the musical process itself. When we hear the first sudden descent of "The Star-Spangled Banner," we do not ask what sort of human trait it is starting to imitate, but rather we find ourselves expecting (indeed, demanding) that it will turn in its course to rise again—though we are somewhat surprised to have it rise so far and so fast. This following of the music's course with intentness, with absorption, and with interest just in what is going on there, rather than anything else, is exactly *the* musical experience. Music essentially is a moving pattern of rhythmic and/or tonal happenings that permits this absorbed attention; and good music is music that rewards it. We might call this the Immanence Theory of Music.

As with music, so with nonrepresentational visual designs, including the freest products of the abstract expressionists, insofar as they can truly be called designs at all. Here the relationships holding the work together and making the wholeness of it, are a web of contrasts and similarities, tensions and oppositions, tendencies toward motion or rest, repulsions and attractions of kindred or jarring shapes, colors, and lines. Think of the painting—or the abstract sculpture—in this way and see it as it really is, says the Immanence-Theorist. And if you note also, as you should, that the design has vigor and force, as some designs undoubtedly do, then remember that these belong to the design, which is quite content merely to hang together and show off its qualities, and has no desire to direct our attention elsewhere; in fact, it wants all our attention on itself.

Now imagine we are able to reverse the process by which we gradually melted down the statue of Elihu Yale into a more and more abstract design until it became a formless (though, of course, not a shapeless) lump of metal. First we see the lump stretch itself into a more complicated form with certain vague qualities: of humility, contrition, or perhaps of power and drive. It doesn't *suggest* these qualities; it *has* them. A little later as this form becomes more and more articulated, it begins to resemble a human being, and later a man—not any man in particular, yet, but some man, any man. At that point, we say, it becomes representational. And as it individualizes itself more and more, it comes at some point to resemble Elihu Yale in particular (or his portrait, anyway) so closely as to allow us to say that it is a statue of him—not of *a* man, but of *this* man.

How could an Immanence-Theorist deny that at this point we have reference to the world? Elihu Yale was a historical person who existed before his statue did. But perhaps there is a way around this. Of course, we cannot dispute the fact that there is a resemblance between the statue and the man, and this resemblance justifies us, if we wish, in carving his name on the pedestal and setting him up on the campus in memoriam. The statue can be *used* to refer, by being named and exhibited, especially in a suitable location. But let us consider the statue as a statue—in the fine arts museum. Then what have we got before us? We have shapes and forms, well or ill put together. Some of the shapes are round, some oval or angular; some of them happen to be eye-shapes, finger-shapes, leg-shapes, and that's a perfectly fair way to describe them. But we have here two different modes of expression:

1. This part of the statue is an eye-shape.
2. This part of the statue represents an eye.

The Significance-Theorist moves without hesitation from 1 to 2—just as he moved from "resembling" to "referring" in music.

But this is a distinction that the Immanence-Theorist is inclined to draw with firmness. What is the justification, he asks, for jumping from one to the other? Of course there is such a thing as representation—the photograph with "Khrushchev" printed under it. Certainly, with its caption, the photograph represents Khrushchev. Statues, too, may have labels, but the labels are not part of them as statues: and the statue itself, the work of art, is not a representation of anything, but simply (or complexly) a form. So the Immanence-Theorist would maintain.

Does this seem too paradoxical? Then what difficulties will this philosopher face when he moves one step further along, and arrives at literature? The nonsense poem, made up of odd syllables, gives him no trouble, of course. He merely calls attention to a distinction that ought not to evoke a protest from any of us, though it could easily be overlooked by a mad Dada poet. It is surely one thing to *act* freely, and another thing to *refer* to freedom. If a person pretends to fall downstairs, as in a charade, you can say that his act (for he is acting) signfies *falling downstairs;* but if he really falls downstairs, then he is not referring to it, he's doing it. So even if the nonsense "poem" is the product of freedom, that doesn't make it a poem *about* freedom.

But after all there *are* poems about freedom (though not as many as one might expect). Byron's sonnet to Chillon is one: and surely, therefore, in literature we have works of art that are inherently and inescapably significant.

But at this point we are called upon to examine more closely this concept of signifying. We may say that the name "Khrushchev" signifies Khrushchev. But what about the name "Oliver Twist"? There is evidently one important sense, after all, in which novels and poems don't signify anything, but rather create and manipulate their own entities, which are purely imaginary. Some of these entities have names, some of them, like the lads who are hanged or killed in war in A. E. Housman's poems, are nameless. Of course you may say that lads have often enough been killed, and that's what Housman's poems are about. But the specific lads he talks about are not the real ones.

The night my father got me,
His mind was not on me. . . .

Who is the "me" in this poem? Not Housman, of course, for the speaker is hanged, whereas Housman died of heart disease. The speaker is not an actual, news-story criminal at all. And even when a poem or a novel happens to contain the names of genuine historical characters, like Mary Queen of Scots, there is only a pretense of history, not history itself—as we acknowledge in granting the writer the license to change dates and events if he can make his work more interesting that way.

Even if we concede, however, that a poem may contain only fictional characters and events, there remains a question about the abstractions it also deals with: freedom, faith, mutability, the chanciness of life—in short, its subjects and themes. The chanciness of life is surely a feature of the world, and a poem that speaks of it speaks therefore, the Significance-Theorist would say, about the world. But what is this "speaking of," in the case of poetry? A man who says the sky will be sunny tomorrow is speaking of something, namely tomorrow's sky; and he is saying something about it. But the ideas that turn up in poems, the Immanence-Theorist holds, are not handled this way. They do not purport to be predictions of future events, or laws of nature or of man. The poet uses them in a different fashion. He is interested in them, all right, vitally and passionately. But he is interested in their qualities—their grandeur or pettiness as ideas, their sweep and magnificence, their subtlety or ridiculousness, their connection or lack of connection with other ideas entertained by someone at the same time. He uses ideas the way he uses visual and auditory images, sounds and smells—the way a novelist uses his characters—that is, to build a complex pattern or design that will be somewhat of a whole, but yet be full of action and tension. He is like a child playing store who happens to get hold of real money to play with, or a sculptor who steals automobile parts from a stockroom in order to make an abstract sculpture of them.

This is the way some critics think of literature: when the

poet speaks of freedom, he is only trying to give the *feel* of it —to show what it would be like to love freedom of a certain kind with a certain quality of love—and his poem has really nothing to do with the Bill of Rights. Freedom, some would say, is more important than poetry—hence the comparative shortage of freedom poems, because the lovers of freedom would rather work for it than play with the idea (freedom *songs,* of course, are in a different category, for they are themselves weapons in the struggle for the real thing). In any case, the point, says the Immanence-Theorist, is that poetry and Bills of Rights are different things, with different uses. And to enjoy poetry *as poetry* you have to abstract from practical affairs and be prepared to contemplate patterns of concepts and of emotions, of images and of experiences, for their own sake, as patterns. For that is what a poem is—and that is all it is.

The Immanence-Theorist, then, sees works of art as variegated wholes, as more or less coherent and complete complexes of elements and qualities, which present themselves to us for absorbed contemplation. Their apparent references are pseudo-references; they are, so to speak, transformed into qualities. Just as the statue uses only the shapes of people, not people themselves, so the literary work uses only the possibilities of human action and experience, the surface and contour and texture and emotional impact of ideas, but not their living substance—that is, their capacity to compel belief, to work practical results. How else could we enjoy the horrors of tragedy? How else could we even laugh at comedy, which is composed, in the last analysis, of the same unhappy elements —deceit, misunderstanding, failure of purpose, helplessness under chance and fate, the painfulness of guilt and shame?

III

What is the fundamental character of the dispute between the Significance Theory and the Immanence Theory? That is one of my main questions, but it will be approached by stages.

First, it is to be noted that the Significance Theory accepts all the examples in Group II above as making good sense. Either the painting—probably entitled "O Pioneers!" or "The Last Stand on the Prairie"—does represent (in this case, I use the term "depict" [5]) a Conestoga wagon, or it does not. And, at the other end of the list, either the music refers to the fear of death or it does not. Of course, it may be hard to tell, and there may be borderline cases, where the graphic depiction or the musical reference is so gentle or subtle as to escape the detection of all but the most sensitive and sharp-eyed critical interpreter. But there is at least one kind of meaning in every work of art, and it can in principle always be disclosed.

The Immanence Theory, on the other hand, must make some distinctions. Statements like II, 1 have a clear status. It is either true or false to say that a painting with a general term as caption (the newspaper ad that says "Turkeys 69¢ a pound") depicts a turkey; it is either true or false to say that a painting with a singular term as caption (the newspaper photograph with "Khrushchev") portrays Khrushchev. But it is always false to say that a painting without a caption depicts or portrays anything. The Immanence Theory must undoubtedly accept statements like II, 2—that is, explications of metaphors—as true or false; however, it treats these not as interpretations but as descriptions. And I think that examples II, 3 to II, 6 would be regarded as neither true nor false by the Immanence Theory. Though the key terms, "symbolize," "denote," and "refer," have legitimate uses in other contexts, they would be said not to make sense as applied here.

In short, the Significance Theory declares all works of art to be interpretable (in principle), and the Immanence Theory considers no work of art, taken by itself, as being interpretable (unless the explication of metaphor—and, it might be added, the elucidation or analysis of implied character and motive in novels—be considered interpretation). Evidently, to adjudicate this dispute we must take a closer look at interpretation.

As I have defined it for present purposes, interpretation is essentially connected with meaning, in a broad sense. One who advances an interpretation tacitly claims correctness for it, and thus allows the logical possibility that it may be incorrect. He purports to be giving information about the work he is interpreting, and one who accepts a new interpretation typically feels that he thereby learns something (perhaps even something valuable and interesting) about the work that he did not know before. When an interpretation is challenged, the interpreter has the responsibility of backing it up by appeal to the work in question; it is understood to be checkable in some way. There must be, in other words, criteria of interpretation.

All this follows from the connection of interpretation with meaning. As far as linguistic meaning is concerned, its dependence on linguistic rules is now widely agreed upon. I don't say the thesis goes unchallenged, but it seems clear that, in the customary phrase, the use of language is a rule-governed or rule-guided activity, and linguistic meaning is best understood in terms, not merely of regular, but of regularized, use. Much thought, of course, has been given to the indicia of regularized behavior—though more is needed. How do we know when someone recognizes a rule, acknowledges an obligation to obey it, takes responsibility for certain conditions that are required in order for his linguistic performance to be correct? [6] We inquire whether he can state the rule as a rule. And, if not, we see whether he follows a fairly constant procedure, admits the possibility that he might be going wrong, gives evidence of a sense of requiredness, feels regret and tends to correct himself when he deviates, is able to settle disputes in an orderly fashion, and so on. In the light of such an inquiry, we may be able to say that infant speakers of a language are following syntactical rules even when they cannot formulate them, just as in playing a simple game they may follow rules that remain largely unspoken—except when violent disagreements occur.

If the concept of meaning is generalized by the art critic from certain linguistic contexts to more specialized linguistic contexts (poems and novels) and to the nonlinguistic contexts (paintings and music), the regularization of use must accompany it. Otherwise, the corresponding activity of interpretation will lack criteria of correctness. Now, it is well known that activities may vary considerably in the degree to which they are regularized. There are at least two dimensions of this variation—degrees, let us say, of rule-government and of rule-guidance. A person's actions are rule-governed to the extent to which his acceptance of certain rules leads him to follow them. His actions are rule-guided to the extent to which he subscribes to rules. It is this second feature that concerns us most here. Between a neighborhood game of hide-and-go-seek, whose participants often think of things to do that nobody has prohibited but some object to, and, say, baseball, where practically anything that could conceivably happen is provided for in the rule book or in the ground rules, there are many possibilities. One of the points I want to argue is that this range of variation is also to be found in interpretation of the arts. As we go down the list of examples in Group II, from 1 to 6, the rules of use (so to speak), and consequently the criteria of interpretation, become less and less stringent. Therefore what the critic is doing deserves less to be called interpretation at all, since the act of interpreting becomes itself less rule-guided. I believe that a recognition of this point will clarify some puzzling features of art criticism, and will dispose of some unnecessary conflicts. To make it stick would require a much fuller argument than I shall give, but perhaps brief remarks about a few of the examples in Group II will show the plausibility of the general line of argument.

Starting at the top, it seems to me that statements about what paintings represent (in the sense of depicting) are probably the most thoroughly regularized of all interpretations. Not that there are no paradoxes and difficulties about depiction.[7] But both in the practice of fine arts critics and in analytical studies by aestheticians, it is very clear for the most part when a painting depicts a Conestoga wagon, and when it doesn't. And (usually) if a dispute occurs, it can be settled by methods agreeable to all. The main problem about depiction arises in the following way. Let us say that objects of a certain kind, whether existing ones or imaginary ones possessing a defined general name, have visual aspects (the term comes from Paul Ziff)—that is, all the different ways they might appear at various angles, in various directions, under various atmospheric and lighting conditions. When a painting presents one of the visual aspects belonging to the set of visual aspects associated with a Conestoga wagon, then the painting may be taken to depict a Conestoga wagon. But it may happen that there is some other kind of object, X, the set of whose visual aspects overlaps with that of Conestoga wagons, and that the visual aspect presented in the painting belongs both to those associated with Conestoga wagons and those associated with X's. In that case (and it is the usual case) there is apparent ambiguity of depiction; and if that is all that can be said, the ambiguity is real and no decision is possible. However, as Ziff has cogently argued, a decision can be made if, on a frequency basis, the probability that the particular visual aspect is associated with a Conestoga wagon is greater than that it is associated with an X. In that case, we will say that the painting depicts a Conestoga wagon, rather than an X.

This analysis of depiction could be refined further, but surely it is a very good description of the grounds on which we actually decide what pictures are pictures of. Consequently, it makes explicit the operative criteria for interpretation-statements of this sort; it shows that within fairly narrow limits there are generally accepted rules for determining what is depicted. Moreover, these rules refer to quite objective features of the world. They do not depend on verbal captions (except in the case where the painting portrays a nonexistent individual person). Nor do they depend upon intention. Concerning one of his most famous cartoons, James Thurber explained to Harold Ross:

> that I had tried to draw a wife at the head of the stairs—at the head of a flight of stairs waiting for her husband. Having no skill in draftsmanship, I lost perspective and the stairs turned instantly into a bookcase or what looked like a bookcase, if

> you made transverse lines—so I made it into a bookcase—and there was this naked lady on top of a bookcase.[8]

It is an important rule about the general use of the term "represent," in the sense of "depict," that a drawing can represent something accidentally. The sole test is a relationship between the visual design and its object. There are other tricky points that a full analysis would have to clear up—for example, when a visual design depicts another depicting object: [9] say a photograph of a waxwork effigy of Mahatma Ghandi. But perhaps they can be taken care of by the principle of frequency—the only way one could unambiguously depict a waxwork effigy would be by giving it a stiff and glassy quality that would not be as likely to appear in a visual aspect of human beings.

The problems about representation in the visual arts may serve to point up one way in which some of the conflicts between the Significance Theory and the Immanence Theory might be resolved. We can say a painting depicts a house, or that it portrays the White House; it can't do the latter without doing the former, but it can depict *a* house without portraying any particular house. These two notions can be compared to familiar ones: the depiction is the *sense* of the picture (Mill's connotation), whereas portrayal is *reference* (denotation). Or it might be more correct to say something different: A picture depicts in virtue of its characteristics and those of the world (including worlds already imagined or described previously). So depiction *is* like a sense. But portrayal is a *use* of the picture. If it *has* a sense, then it can be used to portray. And a good support for this view can be found in the woodcuts in *The Nuremberg Chronicle,* where the same cut (that is, many tokens of the same type-woodcut) is used over and over to portray (inaccurately) a number of different cities, by being given a different label, though it always depicts (by definition) the same city. So perhaps the Significance-Theorist is right when he says that paintings can depict, and perhaps the Immanence-Theorist is right when he says that they do not in themselves portray anything.

I believe that explications of metaphors in poetry (such as the example in Group II, 2) are only slightly less well provided with criteria than statements about depiction. A study of the actual practice of literary explicators—their manner of explicating, and of defending and attacking proposed explications—reveals a fairly definite commitment to some general rules. The essential point is that the emergent meanings of the metaphorical construction are treated as functions of the standard meanings of the constituent words. The nature of this function is still subject to dispute among those philosophers who have tried to formulate it. And it is not conceived so exactly that no metaphors defy explication, and no unresolvable disagreements arise, and there are no residual ambiguities. Nevertheless, I believe this activity is largely rule-guided, and since it has been discussed in some detail elsewhere, I set it aside here.[10]

My example II, 4 should really be a series of examples, for when we get this far down on the list the regularization of interpretation begins to relax considerably. In this category, we are dealing with representational paintings (and sculptures), and with critical statements to the effect that some depicted object symbolizes some abstract quality or condition. (There are other complications about symbolism, of course, but we will have to ignore them here.) At the upper end of II, 4, we would still have fairly circumscribed interpretations —examples of traditional iconography. The symbolic reference of the emblems of the saints is thoroughly regulated—there are official rule books. Toward the lower end of the series we come to what might be called *free symbolism*—for example, the interpretive writing currently pouring forth about Pop art. The hundredfold repeated tomato soup can, the blown-up comic strip frame, the life-size wooden caricatures of people, with real dirty sneakers on—these things are said to have enormous symbolic weight, carrying the burden of abstractions like the conformism of modern life, the loss of individuality, the growth of *Angst*.

> The ten photographed images of forgotten men (pasted in a row on the ten white spools, one photo to a spool, arranged in two rows, on two platforms, of five each) express the Existential situation with poignant, noble, bittersweet clarity (*Art News,* April 1962, p. 23).

We need not deny that in such art, and in such criticism, there is a species of exhaustible fun. But the nature of that fun becomes understandable, I think, when we take such statements at their face value and look for criteria of interpretation, or rules of symbolic reference. For, in the first place, there is one sort of rule that continues to operate—as it has for a long time in pictorial art. Roughly, it is that any object prominently displayed in depiction, given special emphasis, is worthy of particular attention and has symbolic significance. To multiply the tomato soup cans, or to magnify the comic strip, is to claim and insist that there is meaning here, beyond what would ordinarily be noticed by the grocer or weary businessman. It is only the general acceptance of this rule, as part of the game of fine arts viewing, that gives momentary interest or excitement to the work. But, in the second place, there are no distinct rules to guide us in deciding *what* the symbol means. We know the soup is symbolic, but we can't know what it symbolizes—that is the irony, the mystery, and the amusement. Of course, we can think of what it *might* or *could* symbolize: anything we can associate with tomato cans, if we have the strength and patience, may be brought in. But there is hardly any restraint on the harassed reviewer for *Art News* when the time comes for him to retire to his desk and compose his lyric little paragraph. I do not say that there is no restraint at all, for the interpreter takes off from an intelligible and often familiar object, and there hovers about his symbol-reading the shadow of a methodology that suggests some sort of line. Tomato soup cans cannot possibly symbolize, I suppose, the pioneer spirit—any more than Conestoga wagons can symbolize the affluent society.

Yet the rules are so lax and the license has such latitude

that this sort of symbol-reading can not be said to be very regularized. It reminds me of the struggles of poor Ishmael in *Moby Dick* (Ch. 3) to make out the subject, and then the significance, of that grimy painting in the Spouter-Inn.

> But what most puzzled and confounded you was a long, limber, portentous, black mass of something hovering in the center of the picture over three blue, dim, perpendicular lines floating in a nameless yeast. A boggy, soggy, squitchy picture truly, enough to drive a nervous man distracted. Yet was there a sort of indefinite, half-attained, unimaginable sublimity about it that fairly froze you to it, till you involuntarily took an oath with yourself to find out what that marvellous painting meant.

For the most part, there is no way of disqualifying anyone's guess, and therefore there can be little achievement in maintaining one. The participants—neither the painters, the critics, nor the dealers—have hardly any rules, so what they are doing hardly deserves to be called the interpretation of meaning. The talk goes on, but it is a mug's game.

Somewhat more respectable than this free symbol-reading in painting, because more ancient and generally more self-restrained, is the interpretation of "meaning" in music. It is my view about music—and here I am speaking of music without words—that we have not even the first sort of rule that exists for allegedly symbolic depictions: we have no warrant for taking a musical composition to refer to anything at all outside itself. If we did, we would perhaps not be much worse off than with Pop art. That is, if music has to refer to something, we could certainly find *less* appropriate things to say,[11] for example, than that "the agony with which Mahler viewed the subject of death is undoubtedly expressed in" the Andante of his last symphony (this from Winthrop Sargeant), or that grief for their daughters "colors," or is "reflected" in, certain works of Smetana (Op. 15) and Dvořák (String Quartet in E Major), as we are told in the Penguin volume on *Chamber Music* (1957).

Here, it seems to me, if not in the case of symbolic meanings ascribed to Pop art (and to nonrepresentational designs; see II, 5), we must call a halt. Certainly anyone who wishes can ask himself whether the music reminds him of something, and can put down what comes to mind as his "interpretation." But the term is badly misused, for it involves a claim to criteria distinguishing correct from incorrect ones. Since there are no rules for musical significance, there is no such thing as interpreting music.

IV

It has long been realized that there is a curious division in discourse about music. The majority of competent critics and musicologists write as though it would hardly occur to them to take music as referring to something external to it—though some of them, like Sir Donald Tovey, may use rather elaborate, or even whimsical, metaphorical phrases to describe what they hear the music doing. But those who do find musical references write as though there were a fairly clear-cut rule, as though they knew what they are up to and are only doing their duty. True, they may contradict each other, but this does not seem to discourage them. Should we say that *they*, at least, do have rules, and do engage in interpretation, even if the others don't?

Let us see where this thought might lead. What if there were a rule for meaning in music? What would it have to be like to justify the sort of interpretation we find some critics giving? Since in discussing music we are at the bottom of my list of examples in Group II, this question can be broadened out by a kind of a fortiori reasoning. If music has interpretable meaning, there shouldn't be any difficulty about those examples higher on the list. What we are asking for, then, is a defense of the entire Significance Theory. On what general principle could it be argued that there is in fact a rule for interpreting all art?

The relevant point of view might be summarized this way: Works of art are made by human beings; they are characteristically fashioned with care. To make any object deliberately is implicitly to claim that it *has* a purpose and a value. But, generally speaking, works of art are, by intention, incapable of fulfilling any practical need, or at least designedly poor at it. They seem bent to the will of the maker rather than to the demands of the environment. The maker has put something of his own, indeed of himself, into the object. Thus for him to publish or exhibit or perform it, can only be to call attention to his own experience, his thoughts or feelings, and indirectly to the world around him (and us), for this is the world his thoughts and feelings are *about*. In short, a man-made object must be a sign if it is nothing else. Now every work of art resembles something in the world to some extent, and what it resembles it can be taken to refer to. Therefore every work of art is an intentional object—it makes a reference to the world and to the human condition. It cannot help being so, for it has to be something (it claims to be something) and it is prevented from being anything but a seeming, a show, a likeness. To draw a picture of a house under conditions when we can neither live in the picture nor use it for finding our way, for building or buying—this can only be to suggest something about houses, or some houses, and the way one can feel about them. And to compose a passage of sorrowful music can only be to allude to grief.

The Significance-Theorist will need two general rules. The first might be called the Rule of Indication (for music and visual designs): Whenever an object satisfies the following conditions: (1) it has been made deliberately by a human being, (2) it serves no practical end, and (3) it resembles, in form or regional quality, something already found in the world or in human experience, then we may take it that the object indicates what it resembles. By this rule, paintings can be said to depict, abstract designs and musical compositions to have not only a quality but a meaning. The second rule might be called the Rule of (free) Symbolism: Whenever an object that plays a role in human life is depicted in a painting, or introduced into the world of a literary work, then we may take it that the object symbolizes any general qualities that can be connected with it via the activities in which it usually plays a part.

But the permissive phrase "we *may* take it that" makes these rules too weak. Consider the second one. We may, if we wish, take absolutely anything as in some way symbolic. The cheerful suburbanite can cook on his barbecue pit and toss his salads without a qualm after a hard day's work. But his college-age son who comes home fresh from a course in sociology sees the barbecue pit as the symbol of an other-directed culture, the hearth of the home moved outdoors in full view of everyone. He notes the conspicuous waste of steaks that fall into the fire, sending up their aromatic smoke as a visual and olfactory signal to the neighbors. And to him the tossed salad marks the family's status in the higher echelons of middlebrow culture. Many of the 1200-car salesmen who were lured into becoming agents for the ill-fated Edsel some years ago thought they were selling a car—but to its more dedicated promoters it was mainly a symbol of the younger executive's "upward mobility."

In such cases as these it is evident that making a symbol consists in getting people to take something as a symbol—that is, to approach it with that peculiarly detached, searching, and diffuse attention that enables us, with a little imagination, to transform any object into a symbol by dwelling on its relation to forms of human life. And so the phrase required for these rules is not permissive but injunctive: "we are to take it," or "it is to be taken." Thus Rule 1: Works of art, as nonutilitarian human artifacts, are to be taken as indicating what they most resemble in form or regional quality. Rule 2: Utilitarian objects prominently depicted or described in works of art are to be taken as symbolizing the dominant qualities of the activities in which they usually function.

The basic character of the Significance Theory and the Immanence Theory can now be made plain. For these two rules, which in effect define the Significance Theory, have a peculiar status. There is no doubt that some critics (allowing this term to encompass all who talk much about works of art) more or less tacitly subscribe to these rules, and follow them as best they can much of the time. And there is no doubt that other critics do not follow them at all, and would repudiate them if explicitly invited to adopt them. We cannot say that critical activity in general is guided by these rules. And we therefore cannot escape the question whether or not it ought to be. In short, if taken as general theories about art, the Significance Theory and the Immanence Theory are, at bottom, not descriptions of what in fact prevails, but recommendations about how works of art are best approached. And more fundamentally still, they are pedagogical proposals about how people should be induced to approach works of art. Should we teach children to look for meaning in music or not? Some of the older psychological research on responses to music led the investigators to the conclusion that there are different types of listeners, but the evidence never (as far as I can see) showed any more than that people can be taught to expect different things from music and to make something different of it.

The Significance-Theorist, then, is recommending that we follow his rules; and the Immanence-Theorist is advising us not to follow those rules. A modified Immanence-Theorist, of course, might acept Rule 1 as far as representation in painting is concerned (II, 1), and Rule 2 as far as symbolism in literature is concerned (II, 3), but reject them for free symbolism in painting and for music and nonrepresentational painting. The crux of the issue is really whether the rules are to be extended to II, 4, 5, and 6. How, then, is a dispute over art education to be resolved? Evidently by going back to the question of aesthetic value. If both parties can agree on what aesthetic value consists in, and on the elements of art and of aesthetic experience that contribute to it, then it will become a factual question whether or not, in the long run, aesthetic value is maximized by following the two meaning-rules. If it turns out that besides the aesthetic value of art there are other extremely important values, the question might be whether these other values can be realized best with or without the rules. The kind of thing I have in mind here can be illustrated by an example from Bernard Bosanquet, expounding his "festal or social view of art":

> Suppose a tribe or a nation has won a great victory; "they are feeling big, and they want to make something big," as I have heard an expert say. That, I take it, is the rough account of the beginning of the aesthetic attitude. And according to their capacity and their stage of culture they may make a pile of their enemies' skulls, or they may build the Parthenon.[12]

Whether or not this is the beginning of the aesthetic attitude, it is certainly an instance of what might be called the *commemorative impulse,* of which Dewey has so much to say in his *Art as Experience.* Satisfying our need for a symbolic intensification and a lasting reminder of social achievement is one of the values that art can provide, even when it is not great art (the campus statue of a departed university worthy may be no great shakes as sculpture, after all). In order to recognize the commemorative character, and appreciate the commemorative value, of that pile of skulls, we would have to approach it under the guidance of the Rule of Symbolism.

If there are both aesthetic and nonaesthetic values in art, then there is the possibility of a conflict of interest—and this conflict may be reflected in some areas of disagreement between the Significance Theory and the Immanence Theory of art. In that case, the issues between these two theories will require even more delicate adjudication. Should we, for example, approach music in churches under the Rule of Indication, but lay that rule aside when we enter the concert hall?

These normative problems underlie the problem I have been discussing—though not quite in the way argued by Charles Stevenson, who was the first to explore carefully the interrelations of interpretive and normative issues (in "Interpretation and Evaluation"). My conclusion differs from his in that I do not regard each interpretation-statement as normative (it does not have to be formulated with an "is to be" or "is properly interpreted as"), but only the underlying theories of interpretation. But one of the main implications of Stevenson's work still holds good, I believe—that until we are reasonably confident that we know what aesthetic value is, the nature of interpretation will continue to puzzle us.

NOTES

1. "Interpretation and Evaluation in Aesthetics," in Max Black, ed., *Philosophical Analysis* (Ithaca: Cornell University, 1950), pp. 342–48, 358.

2. Ed., *Art and Philosophy* (New York: St. Martin's Press, 1964), p. 498.

3. *Aesthetics: Problems in the Philosophy of Criticism* (New York: Harcourt, Brace and Co., 1958), pp. 130, 242, 402–403.

4. G. S. Fraser has come pretty close to this in his argument on behalf of the "coherence within incoherence" of Pound's *Cantos* in *Ezra Pound* (Edinburgh and London: Oliver and Boyd, 1960), p. 77: "what the *Cantos* in the end are 'about' is the isolated artist, and his struggle through an *idea* of tradition and community, towards sanity."

5. See *Aesthetics*, pp. 269–78, where "depiction" and "portrayal" are distinguished.

6. Cf. William Alston, *Philosophy of Language* (Englewood Cliffs, N. J.: Prentice-Hall, 1964), pp. 41–44.

7. See, for example, Paul Ziff, "On What a Painting Represents," *Journal of Philosophy*, 57 (1960), 647–54.

8. Interview with Henry Brandon, *New Republic* (May 26, 1958), p. 12.

9. It was David Lewis, as a student at Swarthmore College, who showed me this difficulty.

10. See *Aesthetics*, Ch. 3; "The Metaphorical Twist," *Philosophy and Phenomenological Research*, 22 (March 1962), 293–307; Alston, *op. cit.*, pp. 96–106.

11. Remarks like these do not have the complete freedom from rule-guidance that we find, for example, in Titchener's image of "but" as the back of a speaker's head or Kandinsky's association of

green with bourgeois smugness, because in it the "concentricity" of blue is locked in a static and nullifying mixture with the "eccentricity" of yellow.

12. *Three Lectures on Aesthetics* (London: Macmillan, 1915), p. 75.

B

Significance and Artistic Meaning

ALBERT HOFSTADTER
Columbia University

THE FORM-CONTENT CONTROVERSY in aesthetics is not easily dispatched. Here it raises its head again in Professor Beardsley's charmingly written essay—a fresh essay on a familiar theme. His Significance Theory is plainly Content Aesthetics under a new name. And his Immanence Theory—for which "the statue itself, the work of art, is not a representation of anything, but simply (or complexly) a form" and which "sees works of art as variegated wholes, as more or less coherent and complete complexes of elements and qualities, which present themselves to us for absorbed contemplation"—what could this possibly be but Form Aesthetics, indeed in the version of an extreme Formalism?

The force and novelty of Beardsley's essay lie in his attempt to shift the contrast from the plane of nonnormative description to that of normative prescription. Content Aesthetics and Form Aesthetics then become opposing types of prescription regarding our approach to works of art. Content Aesthetics, in the guise of the Significance Theory, proposes the application of Beardsley's two rules of Indication and Symbolism, thus grounding the possibility of interpretation of works. Form Aesthetics, represented by the Immanence Theory, rejects all interpretation by rejecting the two rules. (A mitigated or eclectic aesthetics also is conceivable, in which different rules may be adopted or rejected for the different arts or kinds of art.)

Decision between the two now becomes a matter of determining their respective contributions to the realization of value, namely, aesthetic value in the first place and, perhaps, nonaesthetic value as well, if it is involved in art. Such decision faces its own problems, and they are great enough if not insuperable; but, it would seem, we know at least where we stand with the controversy. Our decision, for instance, whether sculpture—including, say, the Praxitelean "Hermes" and the "St. Theresa" of Bernini—is to be viewed as having or not having content, must rest on determining first how effective such a decision and its approach to art would be in leading to the realization of aesthetic, and perhaps also nonaesthetic, value.

Now I must say at the outset that I cannot share this ingenious thesis of Beardsley's. Works of art of all sorts, whether representational or nonrepresentational, seem to me, in my own encounter with them, to be full of meaning. Indeed, they seem to me to be the most intensely meaningful forms with which I am acquainted. Waiting to decide whether I am to treat them as having meaning until I can tell whether it would be valuable to make that decision consequently appears to me to be an exceedingly odd enterprise. It is in my view a *fact* that art is meaningful, not a matter subject to prescription and the pragmatics of choice.

The meaning that occurs in art is meaning in its most concrete and immediate form. Art is the domain in which man articulates his being. The form of art is the articulation of this meaning. Its content is the meaning articulated. Form and content are not separable and isolable, except in badly articulated (i.e. inarticulate) art. The presence of this meaning is not prevented by so-called abstraction and nonobjectivity, such as occur in pure music and nonrepresentational visual art. Art, as such, is preeminently meaningful, and one importance of form (in a sense of form that relates to its contrast and union with content) is that content is artistic when and only when it is articulated in form. The general principle is: All art is essentially meaningful, and in art it is meaningful form that counts.

The chief drawback in Beardsley's approach is the concept of meaning, namely "significance," which he assigns to the Significance Theory and which, apparently, he believes to be adequate for dealing with the claims of the theory of content in art. In his own terms, "significance" is supposed to signify a concept more abstract than any of the particular semantic concepts such as being a sign of, being a symbol of, copying, imitating, representing, expressing. The Significance Theory is represented by Beardsley as seeking a concept of meaning of which all these particular concepts would be varieties. This is clearly implied by his description of the significance concept as the most abstract and inclusive meaning concept. It is also implied by his statement of the Significance Theory in its non-normative form. On this theory, "all works of art have a meaning, in this exceedingly broad sense, and therefore all works of art . . . at least are capable of being interpreted." In other words, "there is at least one kind of meaning in every work of art, and it can in principle always be disclosed." Indeed, the intended concept of significance is to be so broad—since it is meant to cover every variety of meaning—that not only art works but all symbolic forms, including the scientific, religious, mythical, and other cultural forms, would have to fall under it. At least, Beardsley draws no explicit line delimiting the extension of the concept.

I doubt very much that such a concept exists—namely, a single abstract sense of "meaning" that would apply identically to all so-called kinds of meaning. But this doubt may be left aside. Beardsley in fact employs a more or less definite concept under the heading of "significance" which, I think, is demonstrably not as universal as he thinks, but which is quite abstract and, because of its limitation and simple abstraction, incompetent to deal with artistic meaning in its specificity as such.

Beardsley's concept of significance is indistinguishable from the abstract generic concept of reference. Notice the semantic terms he uses in his series of interpretation statements II, 1–6: "represents," "connotes," "symbolizes," "denotes," and "refers to." In each case there is something, the signifier, and something else, the signified, and the former in some way refers or points to the latter, whether by denoting, connoting, symbolizing, imitating, or otherwise referring. And, in fact, when Beardsley advances his first and most general statement of the theory, he describes it exactly in these terms. The Significance Theory, he says, "is one that takes art . . . as inherently referential. According to this theory, it is the very nature of a work of art to point beyond itself to something else. . . ."

This abstract concept of significance, which means nothing less and nothing more than "being referential," "pointing beyond itself to something else," is chosen by Beardsley to represent the ground of possibility of the interpretability of works of art. That choice is a fateful one. For anyone who proposes to deal with artistic meaning by means of a concept that applies indifferently to the meanings of a noun, a verb, a road sign, a map, a photograph, a statement in theoretical physics, a ritual act, a storm cloud, a wedding ring, a halo, and the label on a broom, and that consists in nothing but the abstract idea of referring or pointing to, has maneuvered himself into a position in which all he will be able to see in artistic meaning is just what is common to it and nonartistic meaning. But this means that he will have left the art out of the meaning.

As to the fatality of the choice of the abstract concept of significance, we may observe it at work leading Beardsley to impute plainly inappropriate meanings to art works—naturally, in the name of the Significance-Theorist, but nevertheless *in* his name and on the basis of the meaning concept that Beardsley supplies to him. I shall take note here of two sorts of illustrations that I hope will lead us to a perception of the nature of the inadequacy of the significance concept. I select the two from the first and the last types in Beardsley's list of interpretation statements, represented by II, 1, "The painting represents a Conestoga wagon," and II, 6, "The music refers to the (composer's?) fear of death." The utility of taking the two extreme types is that we can see in them the same defect exemplified in contrary contexts.

In representational paintings objects such as Conestoga wagons are in fact represented. In order to interpret such paintings one has to be able to establish the truth of statements like "That is a representation of a Conestoga wagon." And it will be true or false, depending on the facts, to say, "The painting represents a Conestoga wagon."

Nevertheless, in a strict sense of interpretation, this statement is not, as Beardsley thinks, interpretative of the painting as a painting. It is only an auxiliary statement that an interpreter makes use of in developing his interpretation of the painting. In order to interpret the painting as a painting one has to do more than point to a certain objective representation, such as that of a Conestoga wagon, in the painting. To understand the painting as a painting, we have to grasp it in its subjective aspect as well, and eventually in its total related subjective-objective structure. For a painting—so far as it is a work of art—does not merely represent an object or even an objective world. It also articulates a concrete spiritual attitude—containing elements of feeling, cognition, and conation—of a subject toward the objective content that is represented. The painter develops in his objective reference those features and aspects of actual or imagined reality that are important in building up the articulation of the subjective-objective whole of content that constitutes the meaning of the painting.

This is well known to artists, critics, art historians—and aestheticians. Everyone is familiar with the reminiscence of Ludwig Richter, repeated by Wölfflin as the very first paragraph of the Introduction to his *Principles of Art History:*

> Once, when he was in Tivoli as a young man, he and three friends set out to paint part of the landscape, all four firmly resolved not to deviate from nature by a hair's-breadth; and

> although the subject was the same, and each quite creditably reproduced what his eyes had seen, the result was four totally different pictures, as different from each other as the personalities of the four painters. Whence the narrator drew the conclusion that there is no such thing as objective vision, and that form and color are always apprehended differently according to temperament.

And the mention of temperament immediately brings to mind Zola's famous definition: a work of art is a corner of creation seen through a temperament. Far too narrow to hold of all art, this definition already testifies however, in the view of the outstanding theoretician and practitioner of naturalism, which is itself the outstanding style of art devoted to the representation of factual reality, that representation becomes artistic only when it is brought into the context of the mind's concern with what is represented.

Tragedy expresses our serious concern with the pitiful and terrible situation of man in reality. It would make no sense to think of tragedy as merely representing man's situation without recognizing the attitude of profound concern expressed about this object in the work. Oedipus is presented as undergoing a terrible and pitiable disillusion about his status in reality, one which he eventually accepts. What happens to him *is* terrible and pitiable, and his acceptance *is* great and noble; and the play can only be understood in its projection, at once and in essential unity, of the objective predicament of Oedipus and a correlative subjective concern regarding his predicament. We are given a point of view, an attitude, an understanding, a differentiation of importance and triviality, in essential correlation with an objective picture of a man in a world. To understand *Oedipus the King* we must be able to understand a symbolic form that articulates the meaning of the terrible, pitiable, great, and noble in human existence. This is possible only if we are able to understand the concern, as well as that which the concern is about, that gets articulated in the work.

But, to return to Richter's anecdote, it is not only unintentionally that representational paintings differ in articulation. There is, as Riegl maintained, such a thing as intention or volition, a *Kunstwollen* or specifically artistic conation, in art, which works itself out in the form as well as in the represented subject matter of the painting. The forms and the subjects of representation are not treated in the same way in classical and in mannerist painting, in the painting of Raphael and of El Greco, because such differences are necessary in order to articulate a total content that includes feeling, understanding, and conation as well as that toward which they are meaningfully directed.

Thus a Rembrandt painting of a Bathsheba is not a merely objective depiction of a naked woman but the articulation of a profound concern, of the nature of deep and understanding love, penetrating insight, and tender compassion, regarding human beings and the mysterious truth of their existence. The naked woman is used by Rembrandt to get this concern *visually* articulated. The visual articulation is the form of the content. To understand a Bathsheba by Rembrandt is eventually to grasp such an integral concern (bringing together the elements of emotion, cognition, and volition into a real unity) in and through its articulation in the symbolic mode of vision.

A statement like "This painting represents Bathsheba at her toilet" does not even begin to touch upon the essential artistic content or the equally essential visual form of the painting. Hence it is not competent as an instance of the interpretation of art. It is usable at most as a datum for the construction of an interpretation. But for an interpretation we need statements of the sort that I have indicated above, namely, statements in declarative language that try to name and describe the integral concern, the integral structure of subjectivity-objectivity, as it is articulated in the painting as a painting, that is, as an artistic visual form.

The defect in Beardsley's concept of significance is that it is too simple and abstract in its construal of artistic meaning. It thinks of meaning simply as reference, as pointing toward something. This could, perhaps, hold in part of the phase of objective representation in a work, but it cannot hold for the phase in which subjectivity is articulated. A work of art does not refer or point to its subjective content. It does not do this because subjectivity, as content, is not itself an object to be pointed or referred to. Our consciousness of subjectivity is nonreflective, nonthetic. Even if we were to use the phenomenological notion of intentionality here, we should have to say that conscious intending of the subjective is essentially different from conscious intending of the objective, and that the difference is that between the reflective and thetic on the one hand and the nonreflective and nonthetic on the other. To articulate the content of subjectivity in a symbolic form, in addition to the presentation of objective matter, we must make use of nonreferring devices—accent, emphasis, rhythm, tempo, and the like. By their proper organization it becomes possible for the beholder's understanding to fit the posture belonging to the articulated subjectivity and thus to become aware of it nonthetically, hence nonreferentially.

In the case of objectively representational art, then, the defect of the significance concept lies in its overlooking the difference and interconnection of subjective and objective components of the artistic content. The same defect manifests itself in the case of nonobjective, nonrepresentational art. Consider the musical illustration. The only way in which Beardsley's concept of significance can make music meaningful is to make it in some way resemble something and to use this resemblance as the basis of a relation of reference. Thus, because the first phrase of "The Star-Spangled Banner" is supposed to resemble vigorous human beings and actions, it can therefore become a sign of human vigor in being and action.

Here, the music is made a copy of something external to it, being able to imitate it through likeness, just as the painting of the wagon is (more correctly, includes) a copy of a wagon, imitating it through a certain likeness. This simple and abstract concept of reference through resemblance, however, is insufficient to take account of or to describe adequately either the subjective or the objective components of musical meaning. It therefore affords only an external approach to music and obstructs the way to a full understanding of its nature. This is a large subject and obviously I cannot undertake to present here a whole theory of musical meaning. I will, however, point to a special kind of highly emotional music, such as that of nineteenth-century romanticism, along with which there flourished the idea of music as expression of emotion.

Some music, like the opening of the slow movement of Tchaikovsky's *Fifth Symphony*, the famous theme of his Romeo and Juliet Overture, or the opening of Wagner's prelude to *Tristan*, is highly emotional. It has an essentially and predominantly lyrical nature. It is much like a cry of woe and anguish or a moan of yearning or grief, with the difference that it is more expressive of woe, grief, anguish, or yearning than most, if not all, such cries or moans. What is true about the expressiveness of a cry or a moan ought to be suggestive in regard to such emotively expressive art. Let us therefore look at a cry or a moan.

What do we hear when we hear a moan of grief? Surely not a sound on the one hand and grief on the other hand, and the sound like the grief, and the sound pointing to the grief in virtue of its apparent likeness! Also, surely not a sound that itself literally *has* grief or is *in* grief as a sound! Thus, neither does grief belong to the moan as a quality of it, nor is it an object referred to by way of the moan's resemblance to it. A moan of grief is neither itself grieving nor a copy of grief. The two categories by which Beardsley tries to construe the musical symbolism of life or emotion, namely, having a quality and resembling what is meant, simply do not apply here. A moan of grief does not in any way *signify* grief, in Beardsley's sense of signification, as pointing beyond itself to grief as something else.

Nevertheless it is a moan *of* grief, and we understand it as such in hearing it. It is full of the meaningful content of grief. It articulates grief in a way that is not yet described when we use quality, resemblance, and reference as our conceptual tools for analyzing meaning. What, then, is the sense of "of" when we say that the moan is a moan *of* grief?

I take the liberty of citing something that I have said elsewhere on this matter:

> Each cry of pain has, as such, the concrete character that belongs to an utterance by one who can both experience pain and utter a cry "of" it. Take as example a moan of grief. The one who moans is moaning *over* the loss or destruction of something cherished. Unless the moan makes use of names and other forms to specify the loss, what is lost remains indefinite. But we do not mistake it. There is a grievous loss over which the moaner moans. And, in response to this loss, the moaner grieves. We hear his moan *as* the moan of one who is grieving over a loss. All this we *hear*. Our hearing is intelligent, an understanding hearing. We do not have to make a special inference, just as in looking down the corridor we see the corridor and do not have to infer it. . . .
>
> In hearing the moan as the moan of one who is grieving over a loss, we hear one who is grieving over a loss; and in hearing him, we hear his grieving over his loss. That is, the one who grieves, the loss, and the grieving are all grasped in the act of grasping the moan *as* such a moan. We could not hear the moan as the moan of one who grieves over a loss unless the loss, the grief, and the one who grieves were elements in our interpretive hearing of the moan as such. . . .
>
> Here, at this primitive level, we experience the mysterious and wonderful phenomenon of speech: *the hearing of a piece of human existence in the very process of hearing a human utterance*. In hearing the utterance as what it is, we hear the human existence of which it is the utterance. The cry may be sincere or lying; the piece of human existence heard in hearing it may be real or fictional. But the question of its fictionality or reality has not yet arisen, for the hearing, merely as such, constitutes the act that is first required before this question can be raised, namely, the auditory act of linguistic imagination. . . .[1]

A moan of grief, then, is a sound that articulates such a particular piece of human being, which includes phases of objectivity and subjectivity in their essential union. The objective factor is relatively undeveloped, left in predominant indefiniteness and obscurity. The subjective factor is developed in quality and intensity, but along with the absence of development of the objective correlative it lacks a corresponding inward articulation. A poem of grief—"She Dwelt among the Untrodden Ways," say, or Milton's sonnet on his deceased wife—distinguishes and relates and organizes both objective and subjective factors, and thus articulates the total piece of humanness to a degree far beyond a real moaner's moan. Music of grief performs the unusual, almost miraculous, job of articulating certain aspects of the quality and subjective structure of grief without making use of the representation of an objective occasion for that emotion. It retains the dominant indefiniteness of the moan or cry as regards the objective factor, yet it unfolds to an amazing degree of definiteness subjective features such as tone, mood, quality, pattern, rhythm. Emotive music is the emotive cry preternaturally developed in the subjective dimension.

Neither Beardsley's Significance Theory nor his Immanence Theory—the one operating with resemblance and reference, the other with structure and quality—grants a place to this kind of meaning. Hence neither of them is adequate to the understanding of the emotive music of lyrical romanticism. And this is only one example. Beethoven's music is not as close to the moan of grief as Tchaikovsky's or Wagner's. The meaning of his music needs more for its description than what can be gotten at by following out the clues suggested by analysis of the language of lyrical emotion alone. We require a concrete and highly developed notion of artistic meaning for the foundation of artistic hermeneutics, not the abstract, generalized concept of reference or pointing.

I conclude that Beardsley's Significance Theory could not possibly represent the claims of Content Aesthetics adequately, and therefore it cannot stand as the ground of an adequate theory of the hermeneutics of art. And since the persuasiveness of his argument rests on the supposition that the Significance Theory *is* adequate, the whole argument loses its power of conviction.

Hence I do not need to discuss here the further issues he raises. In any event, time does not permit their detailed discussion. I will speak briefly to the two most important of them.

Is Formalism, as represented by Beardsley's Immanence Theory, indeed able to take care of the whole of artistic phenomena, as he claims it can, so that it proves itself to be an aesthetic theory equally competent with the best Content Aesthetics? In my view, it is not adequate. It does not even begin to recognize the genuine presence of artistic meaning in the very field, we have just seen, where it seems to have the strongest claim to applicability, namely, pure music. It does not see how such so-called pure or abstract art can have genuinely concrete content that is more than a matter of structure or quality alone. Hence it cannot provide the categories for an adequate understanding of art. A satisfactory aesthetics of content has to include a valid theory of artistic form, since artistic content is content that is formed. But there can be no satisfactory aesthetics based on form alone that is isolable from content, since it will not include a valid theory of artistic content. To show this would, of course, take a lengthy argument.

Is the choice between Form Aesthetics and Content Aesthetics essentially and at root a matter for normative decision rather than theoretical-factual determination? In the first place, I do not accept the distinction between normative and factual as ultimately valid, especially where we move into the domain of the spiritual. But leaving that point aside, and allowing the distinction a contingent validity, in my view the choice between the two kinds of aesthetics is theoretical rather than normative. At any rate, normative elements are by no means as predominant as Beardsley's essay would like to make out. We must indeed ask which type of aesthetics is best calculated to lead, not to aesthetic value or to value generally, but to truthful understanding of art works; and this already implies certain normative considerations. I recognize the need to use words like "proper," "adequate," "best calculated," "desirable," "effective," and "true" in discussing the claims of the contending theories. But the decision is based largely or wholly on grounds of evidence regarding the presence and character of artistic meaning—just as in the foregoing remarks I have tried to point to some evidence. And here I think the evidence is all in favor of an adequate Content Aesthetics, which recognizes the indispensable role of form, in a number of senses, in art; and it is all against Formalist Aesthetics, which at most is an attempt to justify theoretically a certain aesthetic ideal associated historically with movements like the Parnasse and the Pure Poetry phase of Symbolism, and with mistaken interpretations of the intentions of the nonobjective arts of the twentieth century—intentions which, by and large, are intensely expressive in character.

NOTES

1. *Truth and Art*, Ch. 4, "Language as Articulation of Human Being" (New York: Columbia University Press, 1965).

C

Types of Interpretation

STUART HAMPSHIRE
Princeton University

I AGREE with Mr. Beardsley that we cannot interpret the critic's role as an interpreter without raising an underlying question of how art is to be approached. I agree also that this is in part a pedagogical question and a question of desirability (sometimes called a question of value). How are people best introduced to the enjoyment of art? Secondly, why is it to the highest degree desirable that they should be? We are today postponing these larger questions. We are also leaving on one side the doubts that might be felt about the wide, inclusive use of the term "work of art." Are we justified in assuming a unity here? What is the interest that is distinctively an interest in things as works of art, an interest that is the same whether we are concerned with novels, quartets, the Bible, or the Parthenon?

Postponing these larger questions, I shall be concerned only with interpretation. Mr. Beardsley says two things about interpretation: (1) "that it is essentially connected with meaning, in a broad sense"; (2) that he who offers an interpretation "tacitly claims correctness for it." I shall examine these two statements.

What do we understand by the word 'interpretation'? For we are, I think, concerned here with a word rather than with a distinct concept. Our starting point must in such a case be the typical circumstances in which we put this word to a serious use. I shall therefore give a few selected examples of types of interpretation, which I hope will not be taken to be different senses of the word interpretation. Since we have no defined concept of interpretation, we are not justified in speaking here of different senses of the word. We would be justified in speaking of different senses of the word if we had provided some rules for its correct applications. So far we have no such rules. But the word is not a homonym in the different employments now to be cited.

1. "What is your interpretation of the recent events in Russia?" A contemporary interpreter of the news might be asked this. He offers the type of interpretation that a historian would offer of political events in the past. Mr. Beardsley's word 'meaning' is not out of place here. But of course our problem is to distinguish as specifically as we can the different kinds of meaning. What does the deposition of Khrushchev "mean"? This is the "mean" of "the clouds mean, or are a sign of, rain." What does Khrushchev's fall indicate or portend as likely to happen? Of what is it a symptom (or sign)? For symptoms are interpreted.

The historian puts the facts together and he offers his interpretation of an event in British eighteenth-century politics. Distinguish this kind of interpretation from the interpretation that a Marxist is committed to offer of British eighteenth-century politics. Distinguish also "The Whig Interpretation of History," the title of a once famous book. These last two are systematic interpretations, which find a meaning behind the events in accordance with some principles or guidelines. The news interpreter need not go as far as this. He puts the facts together in an arrangement which indicates the dependence of one event, or state of affairs, on another. Why should history, the whole sequence of political events, have a meaning (or direction or sense), as Marxists and some theists and Macaulay might be thought to have thought?

The news interpreter and the historian's interpretations can be assessed as "wild," "perverse," "unplausible," "does not fit the facts," and even as "correct." So far Mr. Beardsley has not erred. But the "meaning" that we have here, uncovered by interpretation, is not the type of meaning that the Significance-

Theorist is interested in. He is not interested in natural signs, nor in weak causal dependencies.

The word that might be substituted in some of these contexts, without too great a change of sense, is explanation. But in none of these cases *is* interpretation explanation, except for the Marxist, when he is a strict historical determinist.

2. In the above examples, or in some of them, to interpret entails filling in more of the story. So we think of an ordinary case of imputing motives to a person as a case of interpreting what he does. Here interpreting again comes near to explaining: but not for all types of motive. Some typical epithets of assessment here are 'far-fetched,' 'strained.' When we find *ulterior* motives, then we interpret, and we hope that it is a *possible* interpretation. But we will usually admit that it is not the *only* possible, the only plausible, interpretation; if it were, the motive would not be ulterior.

3. An interpretation is something that a psychoanalyst gives of the imagery that occurs in free association, or of parapraxes, or, above all, of a dream. A psychoanalyst is par excellence an interpreter. He interprets people to themselves. He therefore exhibits one part of a person trying to communicate with another. A dream is singled out among all natural phenomena as something that is taken to have a meaning, an ulterior meaning, a deeper meaning. It has always seemed to men, long before psychoanalysis existed, that dreams call for interpretation. As soon as one remembers a dream one almost unavoidably wonders what it could possibly mean. Remembering a dream even seems a way of asking oneself this question. The interpretation of a dream is an interpretation of symbols, which are neither exactly natural signs nor the conventional symbols of a language. ("The sea is *usually* a symbol of libido, but perhaps not in *this* dream.") What is the meaning beneath the surface, masked by the manifest content recalled? There is also the interpretation which a psychoanalyst offers of a passage of free association and of the patient's conduct during analysis, and of features of his conduct generally. This kind of interpretation again comes near to explanation; but it is a

special kind of explanation. He finds meaning (motive, purpose) in behavior and in words that seem insignificant or that seem to have some different significance. He even interprets acts as having a symbolic significance, and thereby explains them. He finds a deeper theme in details, which the ordinary observer, attending only to the plot, would have overlooked. "What was I really saying when I made that absurd mistake?" "What was he really doing when he did that otherwise inexplicable thing?" I shall recur to the interpretation of dreams. It is a plausible candidate for a possibly illuminating analogy.

4. "How do you interpret this passage in Aristotle's *Metaphysics*?" Here interpretation comes nearer to "read" and to "translate." Questions of interpretation are sometimes left open when all questions of translations, strictly speaking, are settled. But the interpretation and the translation can also be fused. In the latter case "interpret" nearly, or entirely, coincides with "read"; but it is a strong, artificially reinforced sense of "read." An interpretation is something that a passage in Aristotle may *bear*, or permit. Here we are evidently concerned with meaning; but sometimes with ulterior meaning, the meaning beyond or between the lines. It is a failure of Aristotle's, the failure to be clear, if the reader has too often to read between the lines. But it might be—and has been—held that all imaginative writing requires the reader to read between the lines, that the writing must, if it is imaginative, suggest more (mean more) than appears in the print. The Significance-Theorist will be satisfied with this type of meaning.

It is worth noticing that he who translates spoken, but not written, words is an interpreter. Is this because one interprets a person? He who interprets not a passage in Aristotle, but Aristotle the philosopher, or has his own interpretation of Aristotle, is not someone who finds the meaning of Aristotle, at least in the plain and satisfying sense of "meaning" just mentioned. Of any great writer, who is also a philosopher, there can be several interpretations. There is the phenomenalist Kant and the empiricist Aristotle. These interpretations differ from the usual ones in laying the stress on one of the philosopher's doctrines rather than on another. They say, "This is what he was really interested in." They do uncover a moving face behind a fixed mask of prose. They purport to discover something ulterior. The bland surface of, e.g., Spinoza's writing calls for an interpretation. Where would he have placed the stress? Which of these propositions would he have been least willing to doubt? Interpretation requires skill of a peculiar kind, namely, an attention to that which does not lie evident on the surface. He who translates must stay on the surface. He who reads carefully is often intermediate between these two positions.

5. Oracles are things that have to be interpreted. More even than dreams they demand interpretation. They exhibit proudly a gap between manifest content and real meaning. A fortune teller, I think, has a choice between interpreting the cards and just reading them. An astrologer reads my horoscope; for he has signs with allotted meanings, a dictionary. A palmist reads the lines of my hands, though he may also interpret some features of them. The archetypal interpreter was Hermes who brought messages to and fro as a go-between between gods and men. The gods often speak in riddles, or at least with grand obscurity. One interprets the Old Testament and the prophets.

I hope that no Significance-Theorist would claim that the interpretation which is in question in the criticism of art is interpretation guided by a rule, least of all, a rule that allows one to infer the deeper meaning from the manifest content. The interpreter of a work of art, who is a crtic, is not a cryptographer, who *translates* the work. The work is not an oracle or a riddle. This would be a theory of literature, and of art generally, as essentially allegory. Yet critical interpretations that come nearer to allegorical interpretations have been sometimes enlightening; e.g., Mr. Wilson Knight seems driven to find concealed meanings, usually morals, in Shakespeare or in Byron; and he is often a critic who tells us what we hope to learn from critics; but one may subtract the criticism and keep it as a by-product of the discovered allegory. Poems, novels, and works of art generally do not covertly convey propositions, and novelists and poets are incidentally, not essentially, prophets. The works do not typically constitute messages; and if the critic finds *the* message, we expect that another critic will find a different message in the same work.

6. An actor interprets a role or part. A pianist or violinist interprets the piece of music that he plays. Apart from criticizing his competence and technique, we may criticize his interpretation. Once again, the work will not permit or bear this or that interpretation. The piece of music is susceptible of being interpreted in more than one different way. For some types of music one might intelligibly and truthfully say that it is of their nature to be susceptible of a great variety of different interpretations. Even the best interpretation of these romantic works might not be counted as a perfect and final interpretation, leaving nothing for any future performer other than exact reproduction. Some operas are in this way particularly indeterminate. Interpretation of this kind closely resembles the interpretation, not of a specific passage in Aristotle or in Kant, but rather the interpretation of Aristotle or Kant. We assume that music and doctrines are, as far as accuracy is concerned, correctly reproduced. But a role in a play, or in an opera, a song, a whole philosophy, require an interpreter; there is a penumbra of uncertainty about where the stress should be laid, about which elements in the whole should be made to stand out prominently, and where there is a connection and where there is a disconnection.

We have now, I think, the two most plausible candidates for an illuminating analogy to critical interpretation. They are the interpretation of dreams and, secondly, the interpretation that an actor or musician gives. They are widely different types of interpretation, and different types of criticism will show an analogy with one rather than the other. It is plainly not an accident that art and dreams have commonly in history been assimilated. He who interprets a dream knows that he looks for a meaning which was not intended and which was not purposefully put there. Yet he attributes the meaning to the dreamer, who, in a sense, had these thoughts and wishes, and found a way at once to comunicate them and to communicate them with a disturbing indefiniteness. Many works of art do have a mysterious power to disturb. Many do convey, without the intention to state, a wish for an ideal and impossible form of life, and a sense of loss that has to be discovered. Many works of art therefore require interpretation, and require that the interpretation should be uncertain and not exclusive of different interpretations. The critic, like the analyst interpreting a dream, cannot altogether disregard his subject's intentions and conscious purposes—what he thought he meant—as a sign that itself needs to be interpreted, and a critic may hope that his interpretation will be accepted by the artist as (for him) a surprising discovery; but a strong denial of the interpretation may sometimes not be a refutation.

He who interprets a role or a piece of music has narrow limits within which he must move. He must stay as close as he can to the text, and only then can he find different shades of emphasis, different phrasings, which he may choose, or which come naturally to his temperament. There are several kinds of art, and several kinds of works of art, which allow very little space for the interpreter to move. But a shade of emphasis may make all the difference in bringing out what is there in the text. The critic as parodist comes near to the actor in his role. In delineating a style, and making it visible, and in all questions of pure aesthetic quality, the critic has to be minutely exact. He makes one see (hear, notice, while reading) the exact calculation of intervals, the pauses, transitions, juxtapositions, omissions.

These observations about serious uses of the word "interpretation" only indicate negative conclusions. First, that we must not too simply say that interpreting is a weak kind of explaining. It sometimes is, and sometimes it isn't. In any case, there are many very different types of explanation. Secondly, we must not say that interpretation "is essentially connected with meaning in a broad sense." It usually is, but not always and necessarily. More important, the sense of "meaning" is not only broad, but too broad. It would be easier to discover why we use the word "interpretation" in the great variety of different contexts in which it occurs than it would be to discover why we use the word "meaning" as broadly as we do. The verb of activity is usually more easily understood, in a philosophical sense, than the undifferentiated noun; for we can usually delineate the purposes and the social setting which are normal for the activity. The third negative conclusion is: critical interpretation does not always "tacitly claim correctness," and usually it does not claim to be guided by a rule. If correctness is taken to imply finality, then I see no reason to accept this as the right epithet of praise for a critical interpretation. Some interpretations are impossible, absurd, unplausible, farfetched, strained, inappropriate, and the object does not permit many of the interpretations that have been suggested. But the epithet of praise is more likely to be "illuminating," "plausible," even "original," also "interesting." "True interpretation" is an unusual form of words in the context of criticism. "Correct interpretation" does sometimes occur in these contexts; but it isn't standard and even less is it universal. In general aesthetics it has sometimes been remarked that it is typical of works of art that they should normally be susceptible of some interpretation and not susceptible of just one interpretation. They are open, and they are published, exhibited, or left about, for scrutiny. Works of art typically *require,* or at least invite, criticism. To look at something with great care, and attentively, is already to be on the verge of appraising it. The critics may be parasites on the body of literature and of art; but there are creatures which can only remain alive as long as they have their appropriate parasites. Perhaps there are types of art, and types of works of art, which do not *require* interpretation, in the way which music requires to be interpreted or in the way in which dreams require to be interpreted. But even they do need to be read, or seen, intensely and carefully, and one kind of interpreting critic sets himself to make this possible.

1

Viable Meaning in Literary Art

OSCAR CARGILL
New York University

FOR TOO LONG scholars and critics have earnestly but blindly sought an author's meaning in their desire to know absolutely what he meant when he composed a literary masterpiece. The primary error in this approach is the assumption that the author has achieved what he intended to achieve, that the development from the "germ" of his creation to his finished work has been in a simple straight line. Both his intent and his conscious vagaries, his admitted falterings and new insights may have left their marks upon the finished work, but their sum is not necessarily the work itself. Subconscious associations of language and ideas produce effects of which it is fair to assume the author is not wholly aware; mythologists and psychoanalysts reveal patterns not disclosed to the creator himself; and these and other imponderables give force to the ancient assumption of the author being led by his genius in composition or to the modern assumption, voiced by Proust in his attack on Sainte-Beuve, that the man of verifiable biographical fact is not the person who created the masterpiece. To the degree in which either view has any validity, the fashionable "interviews" in the *Paris Review*, or the equally earnest responses of Faulkner to students in Japan, at West Point, or at the University of Virginia (all faithfully recorded), are misleading as to the meaning of the author in any given literary work of art.

The further search of diaries, letters, and other personal materials for the author's ultimate meaning may compound the errors of interpretation, for such searches are based on inferences that, in composition, the author never avoided embarrassing topics, or was never deliberately evasive or ambigious; that he has remained unaffected by what others have said about his work; and that the totality of creation remains, amidst other efforts, a clear reality for him. The Prefaces of Henry James, who published 75 books and 576 contributions to periodicals in his lifetime, can be shown to be inaccurate in many instances in regard to time, place, and other factors in composition, even incorrect in regard to the "germ" of some of his fictions. Yet James made as earnest an effort to set down the creative circumstances and intent of his fiction as a writer has ever made. The common whimsical evasion of an artist about his work ("Young lady, when I wrote that only God and I knew what I meant; now only God knows") is possibly the fairest summary of all that is involved in composition. Shakespeare, summoned from beneath the admonitory stone in his Stratford church, could be discredited as an expert witness as to the meaning of his plays by some of the current experts on Shakespeare.

Still, the author is a witness, even if from the legal point of view a prejudiced one. If his testimony can be substantiated by other witnesses and other proof, it has some credibility. Hence the wide-ranging effort to elicit all of the surrounding circumstances of an author's life and thought: the views of his companions and competitors, the meanings possibly affixable to his vocabulary, the prevailing political, economic, social, and philosophical conventions to which he may have ascribed, the literary models and methods he may have imitated, the probable significance of the symbols he may have used. The ingenuity of this probing is extraordinary, but it is based on an assumption that the author is what Emerson has called "a representative man," by which he meant a person who epitomized an epoch. One's personal experience of authors, however, is that they are not "representative men." In any contention as to which was the representative man in Mississippi in our time, Sheriff Rainey or William Faulkner, Rainey would win a consensus hands down. Genuine artists appear representative of no one but themselves. Hence all of the objective methods of scholarship combined produce merely a hypothetical meaning which can never be confirmed as absolute, though it may be an acceptable meaning for a while. Whenever an interpretation receives this kind of endorsement, interest in the author wanes, and the hypothetical meaning degenerates into what may be called "gross meaning"—the meaning apprehended by the lazy generality, the stuff frequently found in textbook headnotes.

Quite apart from its creator, a work of art has a life of its own. But also legends grow up about it and its author; indeed, wed to legends of the author, they sometimes swamp the gross meaning of the work with revelations of the personal history of the author, vaguely drawn from the more dramatic episodes of his life. Adopting or starting such legends has been a favorite diversion of some literary journalists: failing to contribute to acceptable meaning, they may nevertheless revive an interest in the work. At the vulgar level there is the illustration of the charge of the *Edinburgh Review* that Poe had murdered his wife so that he might have a fitting theme for "The Raven." When Mary McCarthy recently sought to adapt and improve on some of the legends which have grown up about *Madame Bovary,* including such a dazzling item as the "fact" that Pradier, the husband of one of the originals of Emma, "died suddenly, like Charles Bovary, killed by the discovery of his wife's character," she got a hard lesson from Francis Steegmuller who pointed out that it took seven years for Pradier to make up his mind. Nevertheless, legend, in the decay of gross meaning, may, if not too extreme, outlast the verifiable elements in that meaning.

Noting that an unread work has no meaning, noting the frustrations of an objective approach to absolute meaning, certain critics have felt it wise to abandon the effort to achieve a definitive historical interpretation. "A work of art means whatever it means to you," is the essence of the position taken by T. S. Eliot, and there is no gainsaying this. The chief virtues of this impressionistic, subjective approach are (1) its abandonment of absolute for relativistic meaning; (2) its recognition that a work of art may serve another age as well as, if not better than, its own, as in the case of the poetry of John Donne recently; and (3) its reliance on imaginative reconstruction and intuition in interpreting a masterpiece. These virtues are offset by obvious defects. Meaning patently becomes personal and private, in part influenced by the content and limitations of the reader's psyche when engaged with the masterpiece. The reader becomes a datum in the interpretation. Yet because he creates a relation with the work of art that others in his time and place with similar qualities would have to that work, he may fortuitously seem to be a better interpreter than a host of better scholars and critics. If he does so succeed in making his criticism viable, he has no method to vend or transfer, and his success is frequently attributed to his personality or position, to the group or clique to which he belongs, rather than to his acumen or penetration, and his adjustment to his audience.

Yet a comparison of the objective against the subjective goals—an unrealizable absolute meaning against a relatively assimilable one—confers the palm on the impressionist. The problem is to make a contemporary approach—one that takes account of the reader relationship in his time and place—regularly viable. If intuition and imaginative reconstruction are joined to objective methodology (for something of its history lives on in every work of art) a "viable meaning" may be achieved. But it is necessary to distinguish "viable meaning" from "gross meaning." "Viable meaning" is that reading of a work of literature which satisfies the best literary intelligences of the critic's times. It is a reading which employs as many of the highly developed techniques of objective criticism as seem pertinent to a result that does no violence to a simultaneous imaginative reconstruction of a work of art. Not only must the objective methods agree with the impressionistic interpretation but they must confirm each other for a viable meaning. General acceptance by the best critical minds does not imply that a definitive meaning has been reached, for meaning is obviously as much governed by the expert reader's sensibilities and interests as by the author's uncertain intent, and alters with time and place, as does the text. Ultimate meaning is not assured by any technique of criticism, not even of anything as simple (I should not use that word) as one of Grimms' fairy tales. Viable meaning is the proper aim of criticism.

2

What Is the Quarrel About?

VINCENT TOMAS
Brown University

AT THE BEGINNING of Part III of his paper, Mr. Beardsley asks, "What is the fundamental character of the dispute between the Significance Theory and the Immanence Theory?" In what follows, I shall address myself to this same question and will answer it in my own way. I believe that some of what I will say will be in agreement with some things that Mr. Beardsley says, and possibly nothing I will say will be in disagreement with anything he says.

According to Mr. Beardsley, two of the claims made by the Significance Theory are the following: (1) *Every* work of art has a "significance"; i.e., every work of art refers to, points to, signifies, symbolizes, copies, imitates, represents, expresses, or in some other way "means" something other than itself. This is a factual claim. (2) People ought to approach *every* work of art as if it had significance and to appreciate it for its significance. This is a normative claim. In contrast, two of the claims of the Immanence Theory, according to Mr. Beardsley, are the following: (3) *No* work of art has a "significance." (4) People ought *never* to approach *any* work of art as if it had significance, but always as if it were something that "wants all our attention on itself."

According to the above, the dispute between the two theories consists in the fact that whereas the Significance Theory asserts (1) and (2), the Immanence Theory asserts the contrary of each. Therefore, not both theories can be true. But both theories may be false. I submit that both theories, as formulated above, are false.

For, consider Mr. Beardsley's example I, 1, "The painting includes a mauve elliptical area," and his example II, 1, "The painting represents a Conestoga wagon." Now imagine yourself to be looking at a nonobjective painting, like one by Mark Rothko, say, in which one can see a "mauve elliptical area." This area does not refer or point, in any usual sense of "refer" or "point," to anything "beyond itself." It only invites our attention to itself, namely, to a "mauve elliptical area." Therefore, assertion (1) of the Significance Theory is false. Therefore the Significance Theory is false.

Next, imagine the sort of painting Mr. Beardsley must have had in mind in Part III, the one that he says is probably entitled either "O Pioneers!" or "The Last Stand on the Prairie." It is, of course, a *representational,* not a nonobjective or an action painting. It is the sort of painting in describing which one might well say that one can see in it a Conestoga wagon. One might point to a mauve elliptical area and say, "See, there's a Conestoga wagon." One might then point to a green rectangular area, below a blue rectangular area, and say, "See, there's the prairie." In this representational painting, one can see both "a mauve elliptical area" and "a Conestoga wagon." I doubt that one can see both of them at the same time. But it seems clear that at one time, when looking at the painting, one can attend to "a mauve elliptical area," and that at another time one can attend to "a Conestoga wagon."

Be this as it may, it seems certain that there are *some* works of art that have a significance. When we contemplate them, we behold "a Conestoga wagon," "a vase of flowers," "a bowl of fruit," "a nude woman," and so on. This is enough to refute (3). Therefore, the Immanence Theory, as formulated by Mr. Beardsley, is also false.

If we qualify (1) of the Significance Theory so that it will read, (1′) "*Some* works of art have a significance," and if we qualify (3) of the Immanence Theory so that it will read, (3′)

"*Some* works of art do not have a significance," there will be, so far as their factual claims are concerned, no dispute between them.

We are then left with the conflicting normative claims: (2) People ought to approach *every* work of art as if it had significance and to appreciate it for its significance. (4) People ought *never* to approach *any* work of art as if it had significance; they ought always to attend to the work "itself."

To a dispassionate observer, this may seem to be an odd sort of conflict, given that (1′) and (3′) are both true. Why not appreciate the significance of those works of art that do have it and why not appreciate those works of art that do not have it "for themselves?"

Furthermore, is it not a sufficient rebuttal of the extreme normative claim of the Significance Theory to say, "Ought implies can. But how can one appreciate the significance of a work of art that has none?" A similar rebuttal, it should be noted, cannot be made of (4), for it is possible to contemplate a work that has a significance and yet not attend to its significance. One may look, for example, at "The Last Stand on the Prairie" and see in it not "a Conestoga wagon on a prairie" but only "a mauve elliptical area against a predominantly green and blue background." One can, that is to say, see representational paintings as two or three dimensional patterns of lines, shapes, and colors. The question is, how does the Immanence-Theorist justify his claim that we ought to cultivate this way of seeing representational pictures?

The fundamental argument—so far as I know the only argument—the Immanence-Theorists have given in support of (4) is the one summed up in Ortega y Gasset's remark that "preoccupation with the human content of a work is in principle incompatible with aesthetic enjoyment proper." The essence of the argument appears at least as early as 1885, in James McNeill Whistler's "Ten O'Clock" lecture, in which he attacks John Ruskin's version of the Significance Theory. In *Modern Painters* (1843) Ruskin had written:

> Painting, or art generally as such, with all its technicalities, difficulties, and particular ends, is nothing but a noble and expressive language, invaluable as the vehicle of thought, but by itself nothing. . . . It is not by the mode of their representing and saying, but by what is represented and said, that the respective greatness either of the painter or the writer is to be finally determined. . . . The picture which has the nobler and more numerous ideas, however awkwardly expressed, is a greater and better picture than that which has the less noble and less numerous ideas, however beautifully expressed.

Whistler believed that if one subscribes to a doctrine such as the one above, one will take a work of art "to point beyond itself to something else," to use Mr. Beardsley's words. One will then attend not to a work of art itself and to its aesthetic value but to the something else it points to. A picture will then be "more or less a hieroglyph or symbol of story," and we will acquire "the habit of looking, as who should say, not *at* a picture, but *through* it, at some human fact." We will then consider the arrangement of shapes, lines, and colors the painter creates "absolutely from the literary point of view." We degrade the art of painting, he continues, by "supposing it a method of bringing about a literary climax." It then "becomes merely a means of perpetrating something further, and its mission is made a secondary one, even as a means is second to an end." For Whistler, a picture "as a picture" is not a vehicle of thought or story, and the entire mission of the painter is to "put form and colour into such perfect harmony, that exquisiteness is the result. . . . As music is the poetry of sound, so is painting the poetry of sight, *and the subject-matter has nothing to do with harmony of sound and colour.*" (My italics.)

When he protested against the habit of "looking through" a picture, then, Whistler was protesting against the use of a picture as a device for conveying to the spectator the thought of the *subject* of the picture. A picture "as a picture" is for him the configuration of lines, shapes, and colors adhering to the canvas. A picture "as a hieroglyph or symbol" is a likeness, or representation, of something "outside" the picture. When his famous painting in the Louvre is seen as Whistler thought it ought to be seen, "as a picture," it is seen as "an arrangement in grey and black," not as "Whistler's mother" nor as "a serene old lady seated in a chair."

The defense of (4), then, amounts to this. The aesthetic value of even those works of art that have significance can be appreciated only by ignoring the significance and attending to the work itself. If one attends to the significance, one's attention is drawn away from the work, one's aesthetic appreciation is disrupted by irrelevant factors, and one's aesthetic judgment is warped by nonaesthetic considerations.

How good a defense is it?

The weakness of it was shown up as long ago as 1909 by A. C. Bradley in "Poetry for Poetry's Sake." There Bradley considers such locutions as, "What is the subject of the poem?" and "What is the poem about?" and he convincingly shows that the content or substance (Mr. Beardsley's "significance") is "in" the poem, is distinct from any subject "outside" or "beyond" the poem, and can be attended to without attention being paid to anything outside the poem. In other words, a poem can be "about" something, "mean" something, without being about or meaning anything external to the poem.

When Mr. Beardsley distinguishes between "depicting" and "portraying," he is following Bradley. Rightly so, I think. It is ironic, however, that at the end of Part III of his paper he should write (italics mine):

> The Immanence-Theorist, then, sees works of art as variegated wholes, more or less coherent and complete complexes of elements and qualities, which present themselves for absorbed contemplation. *Their apparent references are pseudo-references; they are, so to speak, transformed into qualities.*

The irony is that Mr. Beardsley gives the credit for this insight to the "Immanence-Theorist." Bradley was a "Significance-Theorist." Maybe this shows something as to what the quarrel is about.

PART III

Art and Reality

A

Art and Reality

JOHN HOSPERS
Brooklyn College

ANY DISCUSSION of so wide a subject as art and reality should probably begin with definitions of the terms "art" and "reality." But to embark on this preliminary project in one paper would undoubtedly mean getting involved in the definitions of these terms for the entire allotted length of the paper, without ever coming to grips with the substantive issues into which they are supposed to lead, so I shall not stop over definitions at the outset. Suffice it to say that under the heading of "art" I shall discuss works of painting, sculpture, architecture, music, and literature, without implying that these are the only arts and without attempting to delineate the limits of the concept "art" by discussing borderline cases. By "reality" I shall mean simply "that which (in some sense or other) exists," with the following qualifications: (1) Although works of art themselves are surely a part of reality (of the totality of that which is), I shall mean by "reality" that which exists *apart from* works of art; and (2) since my main concern will be with the relation of art to *external* reality, I shall (unless otherwise stated) also exclude the artist's state of mind (which is also part of reality), and discuss the relation of works of art to the world apart from both works of art and their creators.

Not all ways of construing the term "reality" accord with mine. For example, Max Eastman in his book *The Literary Mind* argues that the function of poetry is to "heighten consciousness" (Edith Sitwell's term) by an "intensification and vivifying of the felt quality of our first-person experiences."

Whether or not this is the function of poetry I shall not argue here; but, going on to inquire what then is the relation of poetry to reality, Eastman says that our "first-person experiences" are "about all the reality that we will ever grasp." If he means by this merely that works of art evoke experiences in us and that these experiences are a part of reality, his point may readily be granted. But if he means that the experiences themselves are all the reality that we can ever grasp (as he apparently does), most philosophers from Aristotle on will rise to refute him; for experiences are experiences *of* something, and of what are they if not of reality? For example, if literature helps to give us insight into human nature, it is human nature as it exists apart from works of art into which it gives us insight, and moreover of human nature itself, not our *experiences* of human nature (the latter are only the consequences).

I

The theory of art that was current from classical times until the Romantic movement did indeed allege that there was a relation between art and reality: namely, that art is an *imitation* (Greek, mimesis) of reality. The term "imitation" is not a very fortunate one, for we use that term today in a somewhat narrower way. Thus, we say that one work of art may imitate another work of art, or, more precisely, that its creator was imitating in one work of art another work already created by someone else. If the term "imitation" is thus reserved for the relation of one work of art to another, the term "*representation*" will serve as a name for the relation of the work of art to reality. Works of art, then, represent reality. But, of course, not all works of art do this: music certainly does not, nor do nonrepresentational paintings and many other types of art such as architecture; but in many works of art, both literary and visual, there are people and scenes and situations and actions depicted which resemble to a considerable degree those which we find in the life outside art. We shall, for the moment, restrict our attention to these, and only inquire later in what respects music and other nonrepresentational arts have a relation to reality.

What, then, is the relation of representational works of art to reality? One thing is clear: art is not a carbon copy of reality, although critics have sometimes written as if it were. Those who praised a painter's still life by remarking on the detailed accuracy of the painter's representation of a bunch of grapes, and went on to use the fact (if it is a fact) that the birds flew down to peck at the picture of the grapes, thinking them to be real ones, as grounds for *praise* of the painting, were certainly using the criterion of "art as a copy of reality" in assessing the work of art in question. Yet it surely requires no argument today that art is no such thing: if visual art ever had any such aim, the invention of photography has certainly relieved it of the dismal responsibility. Art is not simply life-over-again, and if art were merely a carbon copy of life, one would do well to say, "Leave the copy, and give me the original."

But if art is not a carbon copy of life, what *is* the relation between the two? It is usual to say, "Art is a *transformation* of life." But this, while it may be true, is singularly unhelpful: for how exactly does art "transform" life? The landscape paintings by Cézanne do not look very much like the actual French landscapes from which they were modeled, and when we examine the books in which the photograph of a certain French landscape is shown on one side of the page and Cézanne's painting of the same landscape is given on the other side, we are always more struck by the great differences between them than by any similarities, even though the latter are recognizable. How is Cézanne's representation of the landscape different from what we find in the photograph? At this point one is inclined to take the easy way out and say simply that he has "transformed" it, and if asked how art transforms reality, to say that one cannot specify this further because every work of art transforms reality in its own unique way. All this may well be true, but it does not provide us with any specific answer to the question. What exactly is the relation of art to reality?

Obviously, if our discussion is to be fruitful, we must break it down to make it more specific. Since each art has its own distinctive medium and mode of presentation, I think it would be most fruitful to trace the relation of art to reality in each of the major art-media separately. We shall begin with the art-medium in which it is most obvious that there is a relation of art to reality (though the nature of the relation may not be obvious), namely literature, and then see whether any conclusions that may emerge therefrom can also apply to visual art. Only later will we take up the more difficult case of music.

Literary art does not represent objects, scenes, situations, and people in the same straightforward way that visual arts do; for visual art can directly present for our vision patterns of color and shape which could hardly be taken by any observer as anything other than representations of trees, houses, people, etc., whereas literature can present us only with *words*, through the reading of which we can then reconstruct in our imagination the situations and events being described.[1] But whether we choose to call it "representation" or not, there is no doubt that we find in works of literature descriptions of human beings and their actions, together with the physical setting of such actions, and that these described people and situations resemble to a considerable degree the people and situations that are to be found in the world outside of art. In the case of descriptions of historical personages, there can be a very close relation; but even when the characters are fictitious, they are recognizable as being *like* the people that we meet in real life—like enough to them to enable us to identify with them as with other human beings and care about what happens to them.

We are thus led to a consideration of the closest relation that exists between art and reality: the relation between characters in literature and people in life. The test of "fidelity to human nature" is as old as Aristotle, who set forth a test for determining such fidelity. With a bit of sharpening, the test comes to this: Consider any character in a work of narrative literature, who is described as performing a certain act; *would* a person—not just anyone, but a person such as has been described thus far in the narrative—act (or think, or feel, or be motivated, etc.) in the way that the author describes him as doing, *in* just the circumstances that the author has shown us? Schematically, would a person of type T, in circumstances C, do act A? If so, the character-portrait (so far as this act is concerned) is true to human nature; if not, it is not. It is often very difficult to decide this question, either because our knowledge of human nature is not sufficiently complete, or because the novelist has not provided us with enough clues in the present case. But once a reader is convinced that the character in question would not behave as the author describes him as doing, he will condemn the characterization as implausible, as lacking in fidelity to human nature, in short, as wanting in the required relation between art and reality.

This test of fidelity to human nature is, however, a tricky one which can easily become empty; for, one may say, "If the character of type T does not, in circumstances C, perform act A, then this shows only that he is not after all a character of type T as we thought he was." With this built-in loophole, the test could never have a negative result, and there would be no way of distinguishing a plausible characterization from an implausible one. There is, however, a way to get round this: namely, by making sure that his being a character of type T is determined quite independently of his doing act A; in this way, certain kinds of actions would count against fidelity of characterization. Thus, if he is a character of type T, as shown by the previous incidents in the story, and still he does not perform act A under the given circumstances C, then the characterization (at least with respect to act A) lacks the required correspondence of this aspect of the author's art (characterization) to reality. If, for example, a character is described as spending a lifetime attempting to achieve a certain goal, and suddenly without explanation deserts this goal when he is within sight of its attainment, then (following Aristotle) he did not act as a person of the kind described would "probably or necessarily" act. Now it is true that there are people who do things of just this kind; but if that is to happen in this case, the writer must have made clear through prior characterization that this particular character is one such character. If the writer has not made this clear to us, we condemn his characterization (or at any rate this part of it) as implausible and unconvincing—and it is of its correspondence with reality (truth) that we must be convinced.

The fact that somewhere, sometime, there might have been an actual human being who did perform the kind of act which is condemned as implausible in a characterization, is not what counts in the test of "fidelity to human nature." Some people *would* desert their goal at the crucial moment and some would not, and even the same person might do so in one situation or at one time in his life-span but not in another. The single isolated act tells us nothing; everything depends on the *context* in which it is presented. We must be convinced that, not just anyone, but *this* character, as characterized for us by the author, *would* in fact do what this character is presented as doing, *in* the precise circumstances given. It does not matter how unusual, statistically, the act in question may be. Even if the character in question does a totally unexpected thing—such as a person who to all his friends seems normal and well-adjusted suddenly joining a sect devoted to flagellation and devil-worship—the novelist must have prepared the ground for us by characterizing him as the kind of person who is subject to such sudden characterological changes, as opposed to other people who are not. Otherwise the event is left totally unexplained, the reader is left baffled, and the required tie between art and reality is broken.

With respect to human characterizations, then, the relation of art to reality is a close one: human beings in fiction (which also includes drama) must behave, feel, and be motivated as actual human beings behave, feel, and are motivated. Aristotle's test of a characterization, or something very like it, is in fact employed constantly by literary critics in evaluating works of literature; the moment they feel that the author has not convinced us that a character of this kind would behave or feel in this way, they condemn his characterization as "untrue to human nature," and in this condemnation I believe they are right. There is thus a much closer tie between art and reality in the depiction of human nature than there is in other aspects of literary art. Thus, the author may ignore or flout fidelity to truth in the realm of geography (as when Shakespeare gives Bohemia a seacoast, or Swift populates the earth in *Gulliver's Travels* with islands and continents that never existed) and do so with perfect impunity; the events need not even take place on the earth but on some distant planet, but the people must still be real people. The fidelity to reality of the author's astronomy does not matter either: Milton employed the Ptolemaic astronomy in *Paradise Lost* with deliberate intent, while knowing it had been superseded by the Copernican. Nor need a novel or drama reproduce any of the facts of human history; in this respect the account may be entirely fictitious. But the author cannot tamper much with the facts of human nature. Even when the human beings take on the external form of animals, as in children's stories, they still retain the human psychological characteristics: they are imbued with the same desires, passions, motives, and impulses as those which animate the human beings in the real world. If they did not, we would not be able to recognize or understand them; they would not be "within our ken" and we would not be able to fathom why they behave as they behave. As Hawthorne said, the one kind of truth which novelists dare not violate is "truth to the human heart."

Not only the characters themselves, but the actions they engage in (by means of which we understand them), must be credible in the circumstances given. But it is important for us to distinguish two very different reasons why an author may depart from "fidelity to reality" in his depiction of human actions. One reason is strictly a *formal* reason having to do with the formal requirements of a work of art: unity, balance, development, climax, etc. Thus, Shakespeare (in *Henry IV,* Part I) shows us Prince Hal dying at a later time than he did in history because, if he was to be the main character in the first Henry IV play, he had to survive until the action of that play had been virtually completed, and could not have been eliminated from the scene in Act I as fidelity to history would have required; the play must be brought to a climax by means of its principal character. On the other hand, an author may also depart from fidelity to history for reasons of truth itself: that is to say, he may neglect or distort some aspect of the total facts (reality) of a situation in order to emphasize another aspect. An author cannot do all things at once, nor deal with all aspects of even one situation or chain of events simultaneously; he must select, and his selection must be of one thing at the expense of another. Part of the total history of King Henry IV may have been that he had breakfast promptly at seven every morning; but the omission of this and countless other details was necessary if the important line of action was to be pursued unswervingly in the play. Nor is it only by omission but by commission that an author must forsake some aspects of total fidelity to a person's actual history. If Macbeth had been a historical person, it would not only have been necessary to omit some of the facts about his life (such as the time of his breakfast), but also necessary positively to distort some things in order to bring out others: if Shakespeare wanted to illustrate (among other things) in his play the final consequences upon the agent of a course of action motivated by ambition and power-lust, he would have had not only to omit those aspects of his character not related to this theme, but also to recast and reorganize some details of the principal character's life in order to achieve the same goal: some things that occurred earlier would best be depicted as coming later, and some series of events that took a long span of time would best be depicted as occurring comparatively suddenly (e.g., some idea germinating in his mind over a period of years would best be telescoped into a few days). All this would be for the sake of bringing out some important (real or alleged) truth, not only for the sake of a tighter or more pleasing formal arrangement of the events in the drama.

An interesting question arises at this point: how does our insistence upon fidelity to human nature square with the usual characterizations of "the aesthetic way of looking at things" as "detached from reality," "in a world apart," and in general indifferent to matters of truth (which in this case means correspondence with reality) because it is absorbed totally in concentration upon the artwork alone and not at all upon the *relation* between the artwork and anything outside of it? It is precisely at this point that formalistically-minded critics (such as Clive Bell) would say that literature differs importantly from the other arts, and that the appreciation of literature does involve considerations of correspondence with reality, whereas appreciation of the other arts does not, and that the appreciation of literature is not primarily aesthetic at all. (They would admit that there are elements of characterization in some works of visual art, e.g., self-portraits by Rembrandt, but they would not admit that such characterization plays the slightest role in our aesthetic appreciation of such works, since in their view aesthetic appreciation is of pure form alone.) But others would reply that the appreciation of literature, though different, is still aesthetic, and does not violate the requirements for strictly aesthetic appreciation, so long as we do not have to become distracted from the work of art during the appreciation-process itself by consciously comparing the character presented with actual people in the world outside. Knowledge of human nature, they would say, is something we bring with us to the work of art, just as we bring with us the ability to recognize trees, houses, and people in representational paintings, and this recognition is no more inimical to aesthetic appreciation in the one case than in the other. As long as we do not have to take time off for comparison-purposes while reading the work of literature itself (as opposed to an earlier time, when we learn facts about human nature, or a later time, when we sit back and reflect about what we have read), the aesthetic attitude can still easily be sustained.

To what extent does this requirement of fidelity to human nature occur in visual art? In many works of visual art, such as most works of architecture and all nonrepresentational painting, it does not occur at all; many paintings, such as pleasing combinations of colors and lines by Mondrian, do not call for that type of response. But some works of visual art do: the appreciation of a portrait of a human being does require on our part an elementary acquaintance with how people look, as well as an ability to recognize on the human face signs of various emotions such as grief, fear, joy, terror. Without such knowledge a work of art of this type could not be understood. Again, this does not imply that the face in the portrait must be the face of any historical person, but only that the representation (however distorted) must be recognizable as that of a human being, and that the outer signs of inner states be recognizable as such. Just as in literature, a representation in visual art may be distorted: the effect of ferocity in certain Egyptian statues can best be conveyed by having the head be larger than life in relation to the body, and the nose more elongated; this is what the artist often calls "necessary distortion," and it is distortion in the interests of fidelity to certain "life-values"—one type of depiction must be suppressed or altered in order to emphasize another. But distortion may also be motivated by strictly formal reasons: for example, normally a human being has five toes on each foot, but a painter may show a human being as having three rather than five, if the formal requirements of the painting seem to him to demand it, e.g., if the effect in question would be "too cluttered" if the full ten toes were shown; indeed, the painter could show no toes at all but only a foot with no differentiation of digits at the end of it. There must always be some point in the distortion, but the point can be either in the interests of form or in the interests of fidelity to reality, or preferably, of both at the same time.

In music, so far as I can see, this criterion does not apply at all, since there is no representation in it of people and situations; in it there can be no fidelity to human nature because there is no depiction of human nature, and characters in it cannot be said either to possess fidelity to human nature or to lack it, for the simple reason that no characters occur in it at all. Music does not represent or describe. To describe something, a work of art must be *about* something, namely that which it describes; and in music there is nothing for it to be about. Even what is called "descriptive music" does not literally describe, nor does music that is called "program music" describe whatever is indicated in the title as being the "program." There is no way in which musical compositions can depict human beings or human actions. All that the title does is to channel our associations (not always for the better) so that we think of or are reminded of Don Quixote, or the sea, or a domestic quarrel, or whatever is indicated by the title, while listening to the music; and even this is usually a distraction from the music rather than an aid to listening. To think of Cervantes' character, Don Quixote, while listening to Strauss's tone poem with that title, is very different from Strauss's tone poem being *about* the Spanish knight; and the latter is impossible in the medium of music. Music cannot possibly be about a Spanish knight in the way that Cervantes' novel is. Music cannot depict the Don and his adventures with fidelity to reality or without it, for the simple reason that it cannot depict them at all.

If, therefore, we are seeking some way in which art is related to reality, and we want this to be a way in which *all* art can be related, we must start exploring a different vein from the one we have thus far been mining.

II

Let us, accordingly, pursue the theme of art and reality from another and perhaps more interesting aspect. There are many theories of art which do not pretend to state any relation of art to external reality at all, but only the relation of the work of art to the artist's inner states. Traditionally, the *expression* theory of art has held that in a work of art some feeling experienced by the artist is "expressed" through the artistic medium, and that the outcome—the art-product—is (again) an "expression" of this inner state. So far as theory of art is concerned, a work of art need not "say" anything about reality (nor be about it, nor be concerned with it)—its primary function is to "express" the inner state of the artist at or prior to the time of creation. If incidentally during this process the work of art represents things in the external world, or says anything about that world, there is no objection to this, but its primary function is to "express" the artist's inner states. Such a theory of art may seem to be, of all possible theories, most inimical to the view that art has any relation to external reality but, as we shall see, it is not. However, a number of misunderstandings and ambiguities must be ironed out before we shall be in a position to state this clearly.

The formula is, first of all, ambiguous: its meaning depends on whether the word "art" refers to the art-process or to the art-product. It could mean "The process of creating art is the process of expressing feeling," or it could mean "The product that results from the art-process is a product which (in some way) expresses feeling." Since the traditional expression theory of art is primarily concerned with the first of these two, I shall focus attention upon it first and deal with the far more interesting second interpretation thereafter.

1. "The process of art-creation is a process (on the artist's part) of expressing feeling." But what is it to express feeling? What is it to do this? R. G. Collingwood, a representative of this type of view, writes as follows in answer to this question:

> When a man is said to express emotion, what is being said about him comes to this. At first, he is conscious of having an emotion, but not conscious of what this emotion is. All he is conscious of is a perturbation or excitement, which he feels going on within him, but of whose nature he is ignorant. While in this state, all he can say about his emotion is: 'I feel

> . . . I don't know what I feel.' From this helpless and oppressed condition he extricates himself by doing something which we call expressing himself. This is an activity which has something to do with the thing we call language; he expresses himself by speaking. It has also something to do with consciousness: the emotion expressed is an emotion of whose nature the person who feels it is no longer unconscious. It has also something to do with the way in which he feels the emotion. As unexpressed, he feels it in what we have called a helpless and oppressed way; as expressed, he feels it in a way from which this sense of oppression has vanished. His mind is somehow lightened and eased. (R. G. Collingwood, *The Principles of Art,* pp. 109–110.)

This account is unclear in several respects. To take one point only (though a rather crucial one): what is meant by saying that "he is not conscious of what the emotion is"? It surely does not mean (a) that he does not know its name or general classification: for example, that it is sadness or terror or exhilaration, for he may often know these things. (Even if he did not know them before, and knew them afterwards, one might say "So what?") Perhaps then it means (b) that he does not know what particular kind, or subclass, of one of these emotions he is experiencing: e.g., is this terror of type 250 or type 251? And is this the same as not knowing the *name* of this subclass? Most of these subclasses have no names at all. Or perhaps it means (c) that though he knows all the relevant words, he does not know the "nature" of the emotion he is experiencing. But what does this in turn mean? (c–i) In one sense he is the supreme authority on what he is experiencing, since he is the one who is experiencing it; he knows it in the sense of being acquainted with it, of *having* just this unique and induplicable feeling, even though he does not know any names for it. (c–ii) Perhaps he knows (is acquainted with) what he is feeling but not with its causal connections or other relations. But is this something which the creative artist (as opposed to his biographer or psychiatrist) during the process of creation needs to know about?

The whole passage—and, I might add, countless passages like it—bristles with vagueness and ambiguity; but, however it is to be construed, there is one problem I want to raise about it which is of central importance. The artist feels something that is in some way unclear to himself, and this bothers him; after he goes through the process which is called expressing himself, he now feels clear about it, and consequently relieved and eased. Let us suppose that this occurs. Now comes the crucial question: what has all this specifically to do with the creation of works of art? One would have thought that the creation of a work of art consists at least in this, that the artist is working *in a medium:* if he is a poet, he is evolving in his mind new combinations of words (not emotions—words!); if he is a composer, he is doing the same with tones; if he is a painter, he is doing it with combinations of colors and shapes in paint. But in every case, he is exploring new combinations of elements in a medium. *This* is his creative activity as an artist. Now where, in all this, is the transition made from *emotions* which bother the artist, and which in some way he is supposed to "express," and the *medium* in which he is working? What is the relation of his emotions to his artistic medium? The creation of art consists, surely, in devising new combinations of elements within the artist's chosen medium; and it is this, quite regardless of what emotions the artist has during the process, or even whether he has any emotions at all.

When composers compare notes with one another about the compositions they are creating, they usually talk about what combinations of tones are "right" at this or that point in the composition—*not* about what emotions they passed through during the process of devising these combinations (the emotions they do talk about are the ones they attribute to the musical composition itself—but of this more shortly). Could one seriously suggest that if no emotions are being "expressed," these composers are not creating works of music? What if the creator is not disturbed in mind at all, and has during the entire creative process no emotion that he could name or recognize? What if he just goes ahead and composes? Suppose that an intriguing scrap of melody floats into his mind one day and, fascinated by it, he develops it bit by bit until he has completed a concerto that satisfies him? What emotions has he had or expressed in doing this? Surely he *is* engaged in musical creation, since music is the medium he is handling; and surely the product of his labor *is* a musical composition, again because this is the medium in which the art-product exists. What has emotion to do with all this? How can one say that art-creation *is* the expression of emotion, when that which makes it the creation of art is the invention of new combinations of elements in his chosen medium?

Perhaps an expression-theorist might wish to say, by way of amendment, that the expression of emotion (as described, e.g., by Collingwood) always *accompanies* the creation of works of art. I doubt whether even this is true: sometimes the artist is in an utterly emotionless state, feeling nothing whatever, and perhaps his composition-process can go ahead best when he is quite undisturbed by emotions. Richard Strauss wrote in his autobiography: "I work very coldly, without agitation, without emotion even. One must be completely master of oneself to organize that changing, moving, flowing chessboard, orchestration. The mind that composed *Tristan* must have been as cool as marble." Will the expression-theorist deny that Strauss was an artist, or say that Strauss's report of his creative experience is untrue?

But even if it *were* always true that the expression of emotion (in whatever sense) always *accompanies* the creation of art, it would still be the fact that the emotion only *accompanies* it; it is not what art-creation *consists in.* Instead of saying, "Art is the expression of emotion," we could only say, "*When* art is created, one finds that there is *also* the expression (clarification to oneself, or whatever) of emotion." And even if this is true (which I doubt), it does not contribute in the slightest degree to a conception of what art is—not even "art" in the sense of art-creation. The creation of art consists in the creation, or invention, of new combinations of elements in a given medium, regardless of *what* (emotions, or anything else) may accompany this process.

Emotion may, to be sure, accompany the creation of works of art, just as it may accompany the creation of anything. But there is no necessary connection between emotion of any kind and the creation of art. Emotion accompanies the process of scientific creation, mathematical creation, technological creation, etc., and there is doubtless something that can be called the expression of emotion in each of these (experiences inchoate at the outset of the process, becoming fully formed and clearly articulated, tension being worked off followed by a feeling of release). Yet we do not say that mathematics is the expression of emotion. Rather, mathematics is (in the process sense) the discovery of hitherto unknown mathematical relations; and this is so regardless of the emotional state of the mathematician. I submit that the same should be said of art-creation.

Instead of talking about *expression*, we should talk about *creation;* and instead of talking about *emotion*, we should talk about the artistic *medium*. Thus altered, much of what expression-theorists say about artistic activity is true. It is true, for example, that there is no means-end relation in art, in the sense that there is nothing that the artist can use as a means toward the creation of a work of art as an end, as there is in a craft such as copying or bridge-building. That is to say, there is no means-end relation for artistic *creation* (rather than, as in Collingwood's formulation, for the expression of emotion). It is only when our talk about creation gets mixed up with this talk about *emotions* and their expression that confusion ensues. That art is creation in a medium is true, and that *when* art is created emotion is expressed is both dubious and irrelevant.

2. We come now to the product sense of "express": "The product that results from art-creation is a product which expresses emotion." But what does this mean? Paintings and poems do not express emotion—only sentient beings do so. But what products *can* be is *expressive of* emotion. Here, one may say, there *is* a special relation of emotion to works of art:

that emotion is *embodied* in works of art, and not in works of mathematics or natural science. Here we are discussing, not the nature of the art-process but the qualities of the art-product, and emotional expressiveness can be one of these qualities.

One of the most pervasive features of all art is this, that in it *percepts are suffused with affect.* A certain painting may be predominantly suffused with a mood of gloom and foreboding; so may a melody, and so may a passage in a poem. These, or at any rate so every critic believes when he ascribes such qualities to works of art, are qualities that the work of art *has,* quite regardless of how they got there or what were the experiences through which the artist had to pass in order to infuse the work with these qualities. (A natural object, such as a piece of driftwood, can have them too.) Among the qualities of works of art, these *affective* qualities are at least as important as strictly formal qualities—indeed the former are conveyed to us by means of the latter. I believe that the expression theory of art, as an attempt to provide us with either a necessary or a sufficient condition of art-creation, is an unfortunate blunder; but that theories concerning the expressive qualities of works of art may be true and important, and may give us a clue to a relation between *all* art and reality.

But what does it mean to say that a painting is gloomy, or that a dance is joyous, or that a piece of music is sad? Clearly these attributions are metaphorical, for in the literal sense only sentient beings, capable of feelings, can experience these states. How can music be sad, or have, or contain any other affective quality?

a. One answer to this question is extremely simple, but quite surely mistaken: it is simply that "The work of art has (affective) quality A" means "The work of art causes me (or others, or most people, or a selected group of people) to feel A when they see (hear, read) it." But this is a most unsatisfactory analysis. A person can recognize the feeling-quality of a work of art without having that feeling himself. If hearing the music really made him feel sad, he would probably not wish to repeat the experience. In any case, recognition of the quality of the work of art is quite distinct from the emotions one feels when he is in the presence of it. One may hear happy music and be bored by it, or be joyous at hearing sad music. What a person feels and what quality he attributes to the music are two different things: the felt quality of the work of art is (in Professor Beardsley's terminology) phenomenally objective, or "felt as being in the work itself," whereas a person's state of feeling is quite distinguishable from this—it is felt as "phenomenally subjective," belonging to him and not to the artwork, and only *evoked* in him by the artwork. There is no reason why the two should always accompany one another.

b. When we attribute an affected quality to a work of art, we attribute it to the work of art itself, unable though we may be to analyze what such attribution means. The difficulty is one of explicating what is meant by a true view, not of confusing it with a false one. It is easy to see how people may express grief or joy in their overt behavior; but how can works of art have these expressive properties? Granted, "The music is sad" is a metaphor, but what does the metaphor mean?

That percepts *are* suffused with affect—that lines, colors, sounds and combinations of sounds—can be (in some sense) expressive of attitude, feelings, emotions has been widely held by aestheticians and universally assumed by critics. But not everyone has agreed either on what it means to say that percept X is expressive of affect Y, or on how this expressiveness is acquired. It may be that a consideration of some views on the latter subject will help us to arrive at some views on the former one: Let us consider the elements in visual art first, beginning with colors:

(1) The most obvious view is that colors acquire expressiveness by association with experiences we have had in conjunction with them; and that, consequently, "Percept X expresses affect Y" means merely "X is associated in my experience with Y." For example, if I have had a traumatic experience on seeing something colored violet, seeing the color

on later occasions reminds me of this experience; and this is what expressiveness is—a mental connection of A with B by virtue of past associations. There is no doubt, of course, that this kind of thing occurs, but there must be a closer connection than this between sensory and affective states. How could an artist possibly know what colors or sounds would be suffused with what kind of affect if the nature of this affect depended on thousands of such incidents in each person's history, varying from case to case?

(2) Another view is that the associations that determine expressiveness are culturally conditioned and depend on social conventions of various kinds, varying not from person to person but from culture to culture. Again, this phenomenon occurs, but I doubt that expressiveness in works of art can be accounted for on the basis of it. Nor is the phenomenon as widespread as is sometimes thought. When different colors are used to celebrate the same type of occasion—e.g., white is the color of mourning, appropriate to funerals, etc., in the Orient, whereas black is with us—this in no way shows that the same color-percepts are expressive of different affects in the two cultures. Rather (the point is not a new one), the Orientals do not share our belief that the symbols connected with a funeral should be such as to express negativity, destructiveness, and despair of death, which black does for us (and presumably for them also); they consider different colors appropriate because they consider a different mood appropriate on such occasions. There seems to be no evidence that culture determines color-affect, but only that color-evaluations differ in different cultures. (Two people may both find a melody sad but one may like sad music and the other not.) There is, I would contend, a uniformity of affect (connected with different percepts) which is much greater than the uniformity of evaluation of this affect.

(3) I turn, then, to the third (and I hope correct) view, that there is a "natural expressiveness" of certain colors and other sensory items which is invariant from person to person and culture to culture. I shall give some examples, beginning

with the realm of color, before stating the view more precisely.[2] (a) Green is the color of the normal foreground of landscapes, and is not usually of significance as food or danger or other conditions important to life. The green coloring of grass and trees is simply the normal fact of existence, harmless and agreeable. Green, consequently, has as its affect the feeling of quiet cheerfulness. (b) Blue is the color of the sky, the source of light and the realm of illumination; there is also the blue of distant hills, bordering on purple. But the sky and the distant land are not objects of important reaction—usually the only thing to do about them is to pay them no attention. There is, therefore, a lack of insistency or aggressiveness about blue; it "takes a back seat" in paintings, tending to recede. (c) Red is the color of blood, and apart from vegetation few things have this color—blood is almost identifiable by its color alone; it is, moreover, the life-fluid of organisms, vital to life, belonging to success in the hunt, raid, combat, danger, thus courage in battle. Red is the most dramatic and stirring of colors: it does not have the gaiety of yellow (the color of sunshine), or the cold intensity of white (snow and clouds), or the quiet cheerfulness of green; it possesses more than any other color the quality of excitement, drama, activity. (The full truth of the matter will probably not be known until neurology has had its say on the subject; I suspect that part of the dramatic character of red lies, not in these universal associations, but in the way in which the color itself impinges upon the retina of the eye.)

I submit that the affect with which each of these color-percepts is suffused is universal—with regard to human beings, at any rate—being rooted as it is in the most primordial reactions of human beings to conditions of nature which all human beings confront. The same considerations apply to lines and shapes. Horizontal lines are expressive of restfulness, quiescence, peace; the horizontal position, being the position of rest and sleep, is naturally felt as quiescent, and moreover it is a position of safety and security from which we cannot fall. Jagged lines are by contrast disturbed, excited, restless. If we were not gravitational beings who could fall or feel insecure, all such expressiveness would be absent; but nature has not yet produced any nongravitational beings, though it has produced many creatures who do not lie down to sleep, and for such creatures, presumably, horizontality would lack the affective character which it has for human beings. But for human beings the affect in question is universal.

This "natural expressiveness" of lines and colors is so great that we normally sense the expressive quality of shapes in a painting even before we have traced in detail the geometrical configuration of the shapes themselves. As Rudolf Arnheim writes in his book *Art and Visual Perception:*

> If I sit in front of a fireplace and watch the flames, I do not normally register certain shades of red, various degrees of brightness, geometrically defined shapes moving at such and such a speed. I see the graceful play of aggressive tongues, flexible striving, lively color. The face of a person is more readily perceived and remembered as being alert, tense, concentrated rather than as being triangularly shaped, having slanted eyebrows, straight lips, and so on. This priority of expression, although somewhat modified in adults by a scientifically oriented education, is striking in children and primitives. . . . The profile of a mountain is soft, or threateningly harsh; a blanket thrown on a chair is twisted, sad, tired. . . .
>
> If expression is the primary content of vision in daily life, the same should be all the more true for the way the artist looks at the world. The expressive qualities are his means of communication. They capture his attention, through them he understands and interprets his experiences, and they determine the form patterns he creates. . . .

Professor Arnheim goes on, however, to hold that certain shapes and patterns are *intrinsically* expressive:

> People normally deal with and react to expressive physical behavior in itself rather than being conscious of the physical experiences reflected by such behavior. We perceive the slow, listless, "droopy" movements of one person as contrasted with the brisk, straight, vigorous movements of another, but do not

necessarily go beyond the meaning of such appearance by thinking explicitly of the physical weariness or alertness behind it. Weariness and alertness are *already contined in the physical behavior itself;* they are not distinguished in any essential way from the weariness of slowly floating tar or the energetic ringing of the telephone bell. . . . Nor is expression limited to living organisms that we assume to possess consciousness. A steep rock, a willow tree, the colors of a sunset, the cracks in a wall, a tumbling leaf, a flowing fountain, and in fact a mere line or color or the dance of an abstract shape on the movie screen, have as much expression as the human body, and serve the artist equally well. In some ways they serve him better, for the human body is a particularly complex pattern, not easily reduced to the simplicity of a shape and motion that transmits compelling expression. Also it is overloaded with non-visual associations. The human figure is not the easiest, but the most difficult, vehicle of artistic expression. . . .

Expression is an inherent characteristic of perceptual patterns, and its manifestations in the human figure are but a special case of a more general phenomenon. The comparison of an object's expression with a human state of mind is a secondary process. A weeping willow tree does not look sad because it looks like a sad person. It is more adequate to say that since the shape, direction, and flexibility of willow branches convey the expression of passive hanging, a comparison with the structurally similar state of mind and body that we call sadness imposes itself secondarily. . . . (Rudolf Arnheim, *Art and Visual Perception.*) (Italics mine.)

What is one to say of this view that colors, shapes, and visual patterns are *intrinsically* expressive? How would one defend the view that, e.g., a color is by its own intrinsic nature expressive of some particular affect? My own view of the matter is that the expressiveness of these perceptual elements *is* rooted in association, but an association so universal in the experience of human beings, and so primordial in the history of the human race, that the percept is suffused with the affect for all human beings alike, and perceived as such by primitives as well as by the most sophisticated, and by the artist himself, who not only feels the percept as having the affect in question but can rely on this universality of affect in creating his works. So deeply rooted is the connection that we do not consciously make a step from the percept X to the affect Y; we take in the two together, as one—we are immediately aware of the color as expressive, i.e., we feel that the color *has* the affective quality, not that it is merely associated with it. (Red is experienced as *being* warm and dramatic, not merely associated with these qualities.) Professor Arnheim's account is correct as a phenomenological description of how the color is *experienced* by us, but not, I think, as an account of how this particular color came to acquire this particular kind of expressiveness. But for aesthetic experience, of course, the way in which it is experienced is all that matters. I believe that the expressiveness of perceptual elements is ultimately the product of association; but this fact is no part of our *experience* of the color, any more than light waves are a part of our experience of it although they constitute its "physical basis"; the color is experienced as itself *having* the affective quality.

Accordingly, I would contend (as against Professor Arnheim) that the weeping willow tree is experienced as "droopy" only because we have prior experience of human beings and their behavior in various moods (and a person without that prior knowledge would not be able to experience the affect): it is because people when in a depressed mood often sit in a hunched position that we are able to recognize the similar geometrical configuration of the willow tree as droopy or depressed. We are not consciously aware of this connection, of course, when we experience this affect on seeing the tree—we simply perceive the tree as having the quality in question. But if we go on to ask, *Why* do we see it as having this affective quality? I do not see how we can account for its having *this* particular affect, among the thousands of other possible ones or none at all, except by exhibiting the similarity of visual pattern between the depressed human figure and the willow tree. In a similar way, I would contend that the line in a painting is not intrinsically graceful, but that the imputation of gracefulness derives from its similarity to the lines of living human bodies, as in the dance. It is when we want to explain the experience, not when we want to describe it, that we must have recourse to these deeply rooted associations, based on similarities in the percepts.

What relevance have these considerations to the art of music? It is quite certain that our auditory percepts (on hearing music) are just as suffused with affect as our visual ones are: music is felt as being sad or joyous, graceful or awkward, disturbed or serene, melancholy or sprightly. Yet there is one great difference between music and the visual arts: colors, lines, and shapes do occur in nature, and because of our experience of them in nature they become invested with affective significance. But though we find sounds in nature, we seldom or never encounter musical tones. As Hanslick said, "Where does one find a chord of the sixth or seventh in nature?" The building blocks out of which visual art is made—color, line, shape—are to be found in nature, but the building-blocks of music—the tones and tone-combinations produced by the various instruments—are man-made. How then in the life outside music can tones acquire an expressiveness?

The expressive character of indvidual tones is, I suspect, virtually nil. C, C sharp, and D by themselves are expressive of nothing, and most people when they hear them singly cannot even tell the difference among them as they can among individual colors. But the case is quite different when we come to *patterns* of tones, e.g., melodies. Here we do find our musical percepts to be strongly suffused with affect. Even those writers on music who stick most closely to musical terminology in writing about music cannot suppress a reference to this strong affect. Consider for example, this brief passage (on the Prelude to Wagner's *Meistersinger*) by the composer Ernst Toch in his fine book *The Shaping Forces in Music* (p. 162):

> A constant undercurrent of moving contrapuntal voices, often supported by or resulting in massed, tension-charged harmonies, keeps driving, urging, rolling the masses like molten metal in the process of founding, and constantly build-

> ing, building, building. Each of the mounting fragments marks the achievement of a higher level, until, in a broad, last, irresistible sweep (bars 158–211), a gigantic, crushing climax is reached, triumphant like the hoisting of the victorious flag in conquered territory. From this peak, the piece plunges to its end in a few bars.

What account are we to give of the way in which this complex series of musical percepts becomes suffused with affect? Part of the answer, at any rate, is to be found along lines similar to those we have already explored in visual art, allowing for the great difference in medium. Music is essentially *kinetic:* being a temporal art, it flows in time—surging, bounding, wavering, driving, soaring, hesitating, dying away, but always moving. The patterns of human feeling, like the rhythmic patterns in music, occur in temporal succession, and this fact makes possible a certain *parallelism* between the two; or stated differently, the temporal patterns in music are *iconic* with (similar to) those of certain psychological processes in life—hence the felt connection between music and man's inner life. Thus, the pattern of rising and falling (in both pitch and dynamics), rising to a higher point each time and then falling again, and finally reaching a climax and suddenly concluding—such as we find in the "Liebesnacht" music from Wagner's *Tristan und Isolde*—possesses a close structural similarity to the rhythm of the sexual act in man. Or again, the rhythmic patterns of the slow movement of Beethoven's Quartet No. 16 (Op. 135) is similar to the inflection of the voice of a person asking profound questions, receiving answers, then asking again.

Whether *all* musical passages are iconic with human psychological processes is a controversial question; and whether their value as music depends on this iconicity is another (one which we shall not undertake to answer here). There is a vast variety of rhythmic patterns in Bach's Preludes and Fugues; can one say with what psychological processes each one of this great variety of rhythmic patterns is iconic? One may, of course, assert that each one is, but that we have no names for the vast variety of affects with which each of the series of musical percepts is connected, and therefore we cannot identify each one by name. But what proof is there of this? It is true enough that language contains but a comparatively small number of names for a vast variety of feeling-states; but this of course does not show that every musical passage is iconic with some such feeling-state. How is one to show that it is?

A further difficulty arises here also: it seems that many psychological processes in man have very similar kinetic qualities, so that a single musical passage may be iconic with many kinds of psychological processes at once. "A long crescendo, as in Ravel's *Bolero,* might signify bursting with joy or blowing your top." (Monroe C. Beardsley, *Aesthetics,* p. 336.) Hanslick tried to show that the sequence of tones constituting Gluck's aria "I have lost my love" could equally well accompany the words "I have found my love," since the kinetic qualities of the two processes are, in his opinion, quite similar, and the kinetic aspects of psychological processes is all that music can give us (Edouard Hanslick, *The Beautiful in Music,* Ch. 3). This could, of course, be disputed, using other passages as counter-examples. In any case, it is quite safe to say that not just *any* musical passage is iconic with just any psychological process; the sequence of tones in a quickly rising melody that after a dozen exciting bars comes to a crashing climax is not compatible with the psychological state of peace, quiescence, tranquillity.

But I believe we can be somewhat more definite than this, in our imputation of affects to musical percepts. Let us remind ourselves of the most basic sense of the term "expression," namely that of outer behavior manifesting or reflecting inner states.[3] When people feel sad, they tend to exhibit certain types of behavior: they move slowly, they walk softly, they talk in hushed tones, their movements are not jerky and abrupt, nor are their tones strident and piercing, and so on. Now music can truly be said to exhibit at least some of these same qualities: music that we immediately identify as sad is normally slow; the interval between the tones is small, with few large tonal intervals; and the tones are not strident but hushed and soft. There is, then, a considerable similarity between the qualities exhibited by the sequence of musical tones and the qualities of people when they are in a certain psychological state, e.g., sadness or grief. Whether these same musical qualities are iconic with *other* psychological processes as well is a moot question; at any rate they do characterize this one sufficiently for people to identify certain passages as sad, quite independently of how they feel when they hear them and of whether they like the music that has this quality. In general, then: a work of music has feeling-quality X when it has features (the more the better) that human beings have when they are in feeling-state X. Here we find a bridge between musical qualities and human qualities, in answer to our original question about how affective qualities can be attributed to music when in a literal sense these qualities can be possessed only by human beings. Moreover, it is possible to put such claims to the test: if someone were to insist that a fast, sprightly waltz was really sombre or melancholy, we could refer him to the behavioral features of melancholy people and show him that when people are in a melancholy state of mind they do exhibit the qualities in question (qualities also shared by the music we characterize as melancholy), rather than speed or sprightliness.

I do not wish to follow some writers by calling music a *language* of the emotions; for a language has a grammar and a syntax, and music entirely lacks these features. To call it a language in these circumstances seems to me a slovenly use of words. Nor would I wish to call music a *symbol* of psychological processes, for, as Professor Beardsley has pointed out, the iconicity, or resemblance between musical structures and emotional structures, does not give us sufficient warrant to call the first a symbol of the second. One tree may resemble another tree, yet the first tree is not a symbol of the second. If iconicity is all we are referring to, then let us for the sake of clarity say that and that only.

All I am insisting on is that there *is* a relation between

music and reality, and specifically between the temporal patterns of tones and the patterns of certain processes that occur in the human psyche. First and foremost, music presents us with endlessly varying patterns of tension and resolution—so constantly that music could almost be defined by reference to this feature. Accompanying these constantly shifting patterns of tension and release we find many other features of human processes—rising and falling, increasing and decreasing intensity, surging and dying away. Indeed, we could say that in the temporally ordered patterns of music we find an analogue of the struggle of the human spirit. In this we find ourselves very close to Schopenhauer's account of music as an expression of the striving of the will—without, however, his metaphysical thesis about all of reality being itself an expression of an underlying will, striving and failing and striving again.

But all this, I fear, is only a part of the picture. We have been speaking exclusively of temporal patterns of musical tones; yet music consists of more than this. A melody that ends on an A flat may have exactly the same rhythmic pattern as one that is identical with it except that it ends on a B flat; and yet the felt affect of the two melodies may be utterly different because of the difference in one tone. One may contend, of course, that it all depends on the key in which the melody is written: a B flat tone provides a natural ending if the melody is in the key of B flat, whereas it provides no resolution if the key is a different one. But this too does not complete the story. I have said earlier that a single tone carries with it virtually no affect at all; but I must now mention that a single chord does, and in a chord there is no temporal sequence. Yet one chord may have a very different affect from another: e.g., a chord of C-E-G-C is very different in felt quality from one in D-F-G-B. It would seem that no reference to the rhythms of life-processes can explain the difference in affect between these two—the first, easy and restful, the second somewhat disturbed and tense—since no rhythmic progression is here present. It may be that we can account for some of the affective difference between the two by showing the *future* chordal patterns that each of these two leads us to expect; thus the first is comparatively self-sufficient, being a resolution-chord, and with it we rest and expect no more, whereas the second one is unresolved and leads us to expect future ones to resolve it—a tension is set up until the chord is resolved. Still, I am not satisfied that this kind of suggestion is sufficient to take care of the entire affect attendant upon musical chords. Why it is, for example, that the C-E-C chord is felt as serene whereas the C-E♭-C chord is felt as somewhat melancholy (quite singly, and without anticipation of tones to come), I cannot explain on the basis of any expectation of future chordal patterns.

We enter here upon a very profound and troublesome issue: [4] why is it that certain combinations of tones in a work of music immediately produce a powerful affect, and can be heard again and again without diminution of their power, whereas other combinations of tones quickly become wearisome to the ears and indeed may be felt to be trivial or pretentious the first time they are heard? Even one single tone may make the difference between the one kind of melody and the other: e.g., a change of one (or at most two) tones in the surging main theme of the last movement of Beethoven's Symphony No. 9 would have reduced this stirring and powerful melody to a rather insipid lullaby. How can one melody be such a delicate and intricate structure that a slight alteration in one single tone can annihilate it? Every musician is familiar with the fact (hence Beethoven's repeated and labored attempts to arrive at just the right combination of tones in the melody just referred to), but how is one to account for it? Are there any principles by which we may determine which melodies are which, and why? I know of no such set of principles which are usable when we come down to specific cases, and am almost content to take Clive Bell's description of music as "sounds combined according to the laws of a mysterious necessity" as the most we can say on the subject. We may be inclined to laugh at Bell's unhelpful formula, but before we do so we should ask in what way we could improve upon it. Why is it that any of the numerous arias from Mozart's *The Magic Flute* is profoundly moving and can withstand endless repetition, whereas other melodies, far more ingenious and many of them very similar to Mozart's, move us not at all? Why is one melody felt as profoundly sad, whereas another very like it has no discernible affect whatever? "Sounds combined according to the laws of a mysterious necessity"—and what more can one say;

Roger Fry, a contemporary of Bell, who was equally dedicated to the proposition that the secret of the greatness of a work of art lies in its form, believed that both in music and in visual art the only criterion of excellence in art had to do with form. He did not set forth any specific principles of form such as other aestheticians (such as DeWitt Parker and Stephen Pepper) have done, but held simply that certain combinations of colors and lines in paintings, and of tones in music, have great aesthetic power because of the nature of these combinations, and other organizations of elements in the medium (however similar to it) lack it entirely. Why the difference? In one fascinating passage Fry tries to hint at some explanation of why one combination of forms has the required quality and other ones do not, by probing behind the forms, as it were, into the nature of the deeply-rooted life-experiences which (Fry suggested) lie at the basis of our appreciation of form, and determine why some combinations of forms, but only some, possess this extraordinary power to move us.

> In art there is, I think, an affective quality which . . . is not a mere recognition of order and interrelation; every part, as well as the whole, becomes suffused with an emotional tone. Now . . . the emotional tone is not due to any recognizable reminiscence or suggestion of the emotional experiences of life; but I sometimes wonder if it nevertheless does not get its force from arousing some very deep, very vague, and immensely generalized reminiscences. It looks as though art had got access to the substratum of all the emotional colors of life, to something which underlies all the particular and

> specialized emotions of actual life. It seems to derive an emotional energy from the very conditions of our existence by its relation of an emotional significance in time and space. Or it may be that art really calls up, as it were, the residual traces left on the spirit by the different emotions of life, without however recalling the actual experiences, so that we get an echo of the emotion without the limitation and particular direction which it had in experience. (From "The Artist and Psychoanalysis," in *The Hogarth Essays.*)

Here, then, is a suggestion that the moving power of some combinations of elements in artistic media can be explained by means of "the residual traces left upon the human spirit" by life-experiences common to all human beings. True, we have here only a hint of the direction in which we should search, rather than a full-fledged theory; we cannot use it in specific cases to contrast one melody with another in such a way as to predict which future melodies will carry the same powerful affect. But at least it is a beginning: it indicates a possibly fruitful direction in which a solution is to be sought to one of the most baffling problems of aesthetics: the precise character of the relation of certain combinations of tones of music, and colors and lines in visual art, to the nature of the reality that lies outside it.

NOTES

1. I shall not take the time here to distinguish the various modes of representation, e.g., depiction vs. portrayal. See Monroe C. Beardsley, *Aesthetics,* pp. 270–80.

2. Some of these examples are drawn from Charles Hartshorne, *The Philosophy and Psychology of Sensation.*

3. I shall be brief about this here, since I have discussed this issue elsewhere: see "The Concept of Artistic Expression," *Proceedings of the Aristotelian Society,* 1954–1955.

4. Professor Leonard Meyer has dealt ably with this problem in his book *Emotion and Meaning in Music* and in a subsequent article in the 1959 *Journal of Aesthetics.* His most distinctive con-

tribution to the problem, however, lies in his presentation of "information theory" as an explanation of why some musical passages are superior to others; and, brilliant and fruitful as this discussion is, it is concerned primarily with "musical syntactics"—the relation of tones to one another—rather than with "musical semantics," the relation of musical tones to reality, and it is the latter with which we are here concerned.

B

What Reality? A Comment

RENÉ WELLEK
Yale University

"ART AND REALITY" is such an all-inclusive subject that Mr. Hospers wisely chose only small fragments for his discussion. Unfortunately for me as a commentator, he chose primarily problems from music and painting and discussed a question of literary theory only briefly at the beginning of the paper. I feel properly prepared to comment only on literature, but agree that it would be a mistaken insistence on specialization to refuse commenting on other problems of aesthetics and on a central question of all the arts.

Mr. Hospers' paper makes, if I summarize it correctly, several main points. In literature there is a close relation of reality, as we require fictional characters to behave in a manner called "true to life." Psychological coherence and probability must not be violated. Historical truth, however, may be distorted for specific purposes of emphasis. Mr. Hospers then drops literature and argues against the expression theory in music. The composer need not express emotion or his emotion: he embodies it in his medium. Music is not, for instance, sad or cheerful. It does not necessarily even induce sadness or cheerfulness in us. It has merely the quality of sadness or cheerfulness. Mr. Hospers then moves to a third subject, that of colors in painting, and argues that colors have affective qualities due to associations which are, however, not merely personal but so widespread that they can be called universal. He then returns to the topic of music and accounts for its emotional effect by its similarity to psychological processes of tension and release. At the end Mr. Hospers raises the problem of the effect of nontemporal chords and digresses on the question of artistic value: how is it that a specific group of sounds affects us very powerfully while a very similar group may leave us completely cold? He points to a solution suggested by Roger Fry. Art calls up "the residual traces left on the spirit by the different questions of life."

I submit reluctantly that Mr. Hospers has not faced the problem of "art and reality" but rather argues about specific subject matters and theories which have little to do with it. He constantly abandons his original laudable resolution of being concerned with the problem of art and external reality either by dismissing, for instance, the problem of descriptive and program music or by raising the problem of artistic value. Disappointingly enough he seems to embrace an obscure theory of Roger Fry as a final gesture toward the unknown.

On music Mr. Hospers agrees with the theory of divorcing the composer's feelings completely from the feelings embodied in his work. The quotation from Richard Strauss, however, cannot convince. It ignores the distinction between conception and the technical working-out of a composition. It hardly touches the age-old problem of the share of the unconscious in creation, the role of what traditionally is called "inspiration." It reflects Strauss's preoccupation with awareness and detachment in the process of orchestration, with effect rather than the composer's emotional participation. Wagner was not, as Strauss gratuitously suggests, "cold as marble" when composing *Tristan und Isolde*. We have a letter to Matilde von Wesendonck which speaks of his weeping profusely when composing the third act. The composer's emotional involvement in his work is obvious in many periods and styles, particularly of course in romantic music, which nowadays is oddly enough called "classical." The immediate expression of emotion by a dancer or singer, the emotional participation of instrumentalists playing, for instance, a quartet seems to me undeniable. Both extreme theories are mistaken: music (and all art) is not a release of raw emotion nor is it merely deliberate cold calculation. Mr. Hospers seems to contradict an earlier paper of his "Implied Truths in Literature,"[1] which recognizes that a writer implies or suggests truths and hypotheses in his work. Why could not he and the composer suggest feelings and attitudes which he will have shared and experienced, at least imaginatively, in most cases himself?

All this is quite remote from our topic "art and reality," at least if we put it in terms of the relation of art to external reality, in terms of *mimesis* as Mr. Hospers professes to do at the outset. For literature he selects only one problem: that of characters in fiction and answers it by accepting the traditional standards of psychological probability as obligatory. This standard, no doubt, has been observed or implicitly recognized in one important current of modern literature: the novel of manners, the middle class drama, and related kinds. But this is a standard inapplicable outside of that tradition. The farce, or the fairy tale of the German romantics, surrealist art, even much of Dostoevski and Kafka, who outwardly observe many conventions of the realist novel, cannot be held to an observance of probability. In many good works of literature there are unexplained events: the reader may be left "baffled," the "tie between art and reality may be broken." But is it a "required tie," as Mr. Hospers claims? Does characterization "untrue to human nature" necessarily deserve condemnation? Surely not under all circumstances, nor in all contexts. I admit that even the most outrageously improbable farce, or fantastically weird fairy tale is, in some way, still related to external reality. Even the inner life of the most self-centered, most subjective artist could have been developed only in encounters with the external world. Language as such and a tonal system are social facts. That much must be granted to such monists as Georg Lukaćs who in his new, prolix, but highly ingenious and perceptive *Aesthetik* argues that all art is "Widerspiegelung" of reality. But the metaphors of "mirroring," "reflection," and even "imitation" are quite inaccurate in describing the process of artistic creation which is not passive as a mirror is not imitative in any sense in many art forms:

"absolute" music, ornament, architecture, etc. Art is, of course, part of reality and concerned with reality if we include everything in it: inner and outer life and all of nature. Saying then that "art is imitation of reality" is the kind of statement like "life is a dream." If everything is a dream what is not a dream? If all art concerns some aspect of reality, nothing is said of any real consequence except possibly that reality excludes transcendence, or the creation out of absolutely nothing. I am quite prepared to accept such a very broad "realism" but the actual problem of aesthetics emerges only after we make some discriminations and distinguish among kinds of art. It is the advantage of a theory of art not committed to the dogma of realism to allow multiple relations between the work and reality and to emphasize other relations in the aesthetic transaction: those between creator, work and audience, or between the expression, the structure of the work, the purpose, the address, etc. It allows us to describe the whole gamut of relations of art to reality, from copying to the most fantastic dreamy art. Mr. Hospers has not touched on these urgent problems of our time, the debates on realism, on socialist realism, on abstract art, etc. I must refer to my paper "The Concept of Realism in Literary Scholarship" [2] for an extended discussion of some of these questions and books devoted to them. Mr. Hospers' paper is, I know, resolutely unhistorical and unconcerned with the concrete questions debated today. But "art and reality" should be discussed in terms of such problems as art's slow emancipation from magic and religion and mainly with "art and society" and "art and history."

NOTES

1. *Journal of Aesthetic and Art Criticism*, Vol. 19 (1960), reprinted in M. Levich, *Aesthetics and the Philosophy of Criticism* (New York, 1963), pp. 352–68.

2. 1960, reprinted in *Concepts of Criticism* (New Haven, 1963), pp. 222–55.

C

Art and Being

WILLIAM BARRETT
New York University

I. ART AND NON-ART; ART AS A PART OF "REALITY"

Professor Hospers is to be applauded for his boldness in undertaking a subject so broad as the relation of art to reality. Discussions of narrower issues, while they may permit tidier and more conclusive results, are usually not so stimulating or provocative as his paper turns out to be.

We begin without definitions. Art is not defined—which may be all to the good—but taken as recognizable in works of painting, sculpture, architecture, music, and literature, etc. Reality, on the other hand, will be taken as all that is that is not art. Professor Hospers adds a further specification—which could be misleading—that he will deal with the relation of art to "external" reality. Do not novels, plays, and poems deal with the *internal* thoughts, moods, and feelings of people, and are these internal data to be excluded from consideration? Of course not; by "external" Professor Hospers means to refer to what is outside the work of art itself as well as what is outside the mind of the artist.

Thus we start with a simple schema—art on one side in its compartment, and reality set over against it in another compartment. On a subject so broad as the present one I suppose one must begin with some simple schematic distinction or other, simply, as Professor Hospers puts it, to get the discussion going; yet this initial bifurcation of art and reality raises some troubling questions and also conceals, I believe, more philosophical presuppositions than at first meet the eye.

First of all, the distinction between art and what is not art has shown itself to be a shifting and uncertain matter. We should be particularly aware of this today when we have experienced the anti-novel, anti-drama, anti-easel painting, music of chance, and a recent oratorio (like Stockhausen's *Originale*) in which the audience itself may be drawn into participation. These works, of course, could be dismissed out of hand as not really being "art." But then, if art is an open rather than a closed concept (in Wittgenstein's sense), we have to ask: Where do we choose to draw the line and why? These experiments of modern artists have been of varied and unequal success and integrity; yet as a positive principle behind all these efforts is a struggle to escape from a dualism between art and reality that the artist himself finds sterile. The assignment of art to a compartment of its own usually leads to the sterility of official salon art. And the philosophy that usually accompanies such art is usually not any more fruitful.

Secondly, and perhaps more significantly: works of art themselves have become, in a new and extraordinary way, part of the reality of the contemporary artist. A Buddhist sculpture, relic of a vanished empire, dug out of the rotting jungle, becomes a datum of man's fate. Art itself becomes to some degree its own subject matter. Thus pastiche, parody, deliberate and ironic deflation abound. An odalisque by Matisse is a tongue-in-cheek reminder of Delacroix; Proust imitates and deflates the brothers Goncourt; and there are the numerous parodies by Joyce in *Ulysses* and *Finnegans Wake*. Some works of Picasso's so-called classical period suggest figures from the museum that have escaped into the contemporary nightmare. "All those dead voices" (Samuel Beckett) never cease murmuring and continue to haunt our actual historical landscape.

The sculptor Noguchi once told me: "The work that haunts my imagination the most, and the one to which I would like my own to aspire is—Stonehenge." This example cuts, in several different directions, across all neat compartmentalizations. Stonehenge, we now believe, was a monument to the Sun (or Sun-god), but at the same time a practical instrument to regulate the calendar by measuring the risings and settings of sun, moon, and stars. Through the wear of time and weather, and the random depredations of later men, Stonehenge has now become—at least in Noguchi's view—a great work of sculpture. Thus it has become a work at once of man, nature, and history all together. By becoming historical —which means, by entering into human history—this object now cuts across the bifurcations between the utilitarian and the aesthetic, the artificial and the natural. But however we eventually classify it, it is decidedly a part of Noguchi's reality.

What emerges from all these illustrations is a philosophical issue so elementary and traditional that I would hesitate to bring it up except that it obtrudes everywhere in Professor Hospers' paper. He speaks in one place of "the totality of facts (or reality)," and this apparently passing phrase seems to me telltale of the basic philosophical conception under which his thinking proceeds. Reality as the aggregate of all facts is a piece of metaphysical atomism that is unacceptable for reasons too copious to enter into here. For the Leibnitzian God surveying his monads the world may be just such a totality; but this is not the world in which we live, think, and even carry out scientific research. Any significant new scientific theory may cut up and parcel out the facts differently. One modern scientist has remarked aptly that reality for the scientist is simply what the contemporary state of science says it is. Of course, there is that *noumenal* sense of reality in which we say that the universe would be what it is even if all scientists were to disappear; but that reality is hardly a datum in a discussion of art and its reality. Even more markedly than for the scientist, reality for the artist can never lose its *phenomenal* roots as a human reality, therefore historical through and through, and consequently shaped—among other things—by great works of art, past and present. There is no experience not formed by imagination, and the quality of experience differs with the imaginative forms under which we take it in. Kant showed that we never encounter an experience that has not already been structured to some degree by mind; accordingly, we shall never find an artist confronting a reality that has not already been pervaded and moulded by the style and vision of other works of art to which his imagination has been receptive, which he may wish to transform, or against which he may rebel.

This reality is not a matter of the artist's purely "subjective" states of mind (which Professor Hospers wishes to eliminate altogether from consideration). On the contrary, it is a trans-subjective reality, as is shown by the fact that the audience that grasps the work enters—immediately, without inference or construction—into that world and inhabits it side by side with the artist. On the other hand, this reality—or world, as I should prefer to say—is trans-objective (at least as objectivity has commonly been understood)—in the sense that it could not come to be unless man, in all the dimensions of his being, had come to be.

II. REPRESENTATION

In the case of literature, Professor Hospers asserts, there is a definite relation between art and reality: namely, representation. That literature is in some sense representative of life would seem to be beyond doubt; the difficulty, however, resides in how this representativeness is to be analyzed; and I am rather surprised that Professor Hospers is satisfied to revive the old Aristotelian theory of probabilities, which used to be a cherished pillar of neoclassicism, but which I imagined had crumbled long ago. A character, it is alleged, is "true to life" when he behaves in accordance with his type. Where human beings run predictably true to type is usually in the more normal, commonplace, routine, and external portions of life. Accordingly, this doctrine of probabilities might cover one kind of literature—realism—and then only a certain kind of realism. The classic case here would be Tolstoy's famous diatribe against *King Lear*. From the point of view of Tolstoy, the great poet of the normal, *Lear* simply abounds in absurdities. We seem to have more taste for the absurd these days, and in any case Shakespeare's play has survived the Russian novelist's blast. (During most of his life, by the way, Tolstoy also thought that the characters of Dostoevski were not "true to life.") What is involved in *Lear* is a world strained to its breaking point, on the edge of ruins; and when things are falling into chaos, the stable routines of the typical and normal may vanish, and thus "normal" probabilities can be violated.

Consider Kafka's *Metamorphosis.* One day a man wakes up and finds that he has been transformed into a bug, though still retaining human consciousness. Now, what could typical behavior in that situation mean?

A work of art, according to Professor Hospers, is truly representative when it is faithful to "the truths of human nature." Earlier, he had rejected carbon-copy realism by remarking that if we have the original why should we want the copy? A perfectly analogous point might be made about his present theory: If we already have the "truth about human nature," why do we need the work of art? Perhaps merely as a pleasant pedagogic illustration of a general truth already known. In that case, all literature will resemble Aesop's fables, designed to illustrate some general maxim.

Moreover, the model of artistic creation that this theory would suggest seems to be singularly impoverished. We have here the picture of the writer knowing exactly the "truths of human nature" he wishes to advance and then searching for some pretty finery with which to clothe them. Even Kant, who was a neoclassicist in his tastes, had a doctrine of the spontaneity of the imagination as a faculty that can surprise its owner by the novelty of its product. And artists repeatedly testify that the process of creation is a surprising adventure in discovery.

"The truths of human nature," I must confess, is a phrase that makes me slightly uneasy, and I almost expect it to be followed by a plea for "fiscal integrity." I do not deny that there may be such truths. I am not sure, however, that I possess any myself; and yet I continue to read novels and plays with some degree of appreciation, and, I hope, understanding. These truths, whatever they may be, are—I have a strong suspicion—ritual formulae by means of which mankind strives to exorcise its utter confusion about itself. Human nature would seem to be, as Irving Babbitt observed, like a Chinese box with an endless series of false bottoms. Even a casual reading of those human-interest fillers in the afternoon papers could shake the neoclassicist's faith that any behavior could be described as typical of our amazing species. What, for example, would the proper Aristotelian, armed with his doctrine of probabilities, make of the following passage from Jack Douglas, a far-out comedian defending the credibility of his material?

> All my professional life, both in writing and performing, lots and lots of experts have told me that I'm too wild.
>
> For instance, I have a story about a girl getting raped on top of a sixty-two-foot flagpole. The way I tell the story: a certain Mr. William M. Pettit, thirty-three, a flagpole sitter, today faced charges of statutory rape of a fifteen-year-old girl atop a sixty-two-foot flagpole. According to the charges, the incident took place while Pettit was spending sixty-five days on the pole, as an advertising stunt. . . . There was no ladder, and apparently the girl was raised by a rope that Pettit used to haul up food.
>
> The incident came to light when a relative of the girl spotted Pettit on the street later, and beat him severely about the head. The girl signed a statement admitting she consented to relations with Pettit. However, in cases of statutory rape involving a minor, consent is not an issue. Her parents said they knew she had been seeing Pettit on the flagpole and had ordered her to stay away from him. Sounds like a pretty wild, far-out story, doesn't it? But it isn't. This story appeared on the front page of the New York *Journal-American,* datelined El Paso, Texas, October 22, 1958 (UPI). So you see, no matter what *some* people might think, I'm *not wild.* At least, not to the people in El Paso.

Let Scaliger, Boileau, and the other neoclassicists field that one!

III. EXPRESSION AND EXPRESSIVENESS

Passing beyond representation, Mr. Hospers finds that another relation with reality may lie in the fact that art is expression; and here I am in substantial agreement with his principal contentions, though I should like to suggest some qualifications as well as directions in which his own conclusions might be developed further.

I follow Mr. Hospers in dispensing with art as the expression of the artist's emotions as being a concern more for biographers that aestheticians. Shakespeare may have been passing through "a perfect hell of time"—a phrase from the *Sonnets*—when he wrote his tragedies, but for all we know some of them may have been done while he was having a ball. The important point is the expressiveness of the work, and here I would agree with Mr. Hospers that the work of art is objectively expressive—viz., that feelings are "phenomenally objective" within it.

I would also agree with him that the sensory materials—lines, shapes, colors, chords and melodies—with which the artist works are objectively expressive in the same sense, though the matter of colors seems to me far more complex than Mr. Hospers allows.

Green, for example, he says, is the color of quiet cheerfulness. Now, there is a particular green used by the German Expressionists that is harsh, clanging, disquieting, and even sinister. Again, blue as the color of the sky is the color of spirituality—Mary's color, as the medievals put it. But it certainly does not always "take a back seat," as Professor Hospers avers; as used by the French Impressionists, it can be very much in the foreground, and the effect of this color of spirituality is rich and voluptuous. Yellow (the color of sunshine), he tells us, expresses gaiety. Yet the yellow sky in Tintoretto's "Crucifixion" is sulphurous, lurid, and sagging—as if the sky itself were sick with what had just been perpetrated on earth. And the yellow in one of Van Gogh's self-portraits is eerie, frightening, and ominous—as if already portending madness.

These variants are not cited to prove relativism or subjectivism; the affect in each case is, I believe, phenomenally objective in Professor Hospers' sense. But these instances do show that the modalities of color are multitudinous, and that the affect in question may very well depend on the concrete context in which the color appears.

We come now to the subject of music, on which Professor Hospers makes some of his most fertile suggestions. Certain melodies (and rhythms) are suffused with affect because they resemble the movements and rhythms of our "psychic processes" (or the movements of our bodies when we are in the grip of any of these affects). Here is a new relation of art to reality: *iconicity*—i.e., the musical work contains ingredients (Professor Hospers does not speak of the work as a whole, but that would not be excluded) that are icons, or likenesses, of real processes. Resemblance is usually taken as a symmetrical relation: if A is like B, then B is like A. But I wonder whether we might not consider a relation here where the emphasis went in one way—as when medieval philosophers attempting to interpret the Biblical statement that "man is made in God's image" could say that man in some very imperfect way does reflect the being of God, but God in no way reflects man's being. Or, to take a possibly more concrete example: a quite plain girl at a certain moment, in a sudden shaft of sunlight, might shine in the eyes of her lover with the immortal beauty of Helen of Troy, but it would be wrong to say that Helen resembles her. Let us take the words "approximates to" as an expression of the kind of relatedness I have in mind here.

This qualification may appear a trivial matter, but I think it cuts to the center of Professor Hospers' basic philosophical orientation. His discussion proceeds, it seems to me, within a framework of neorealism: reality is there, and is what it is, and the work of art is to be justified when it *corresponds* part by part to the details of reality outside it. (Now we do not expect such literal and point-by-point correspondence in a scientific theory: the single concepts of a physical theory, and the theory as a whole, are not mirror images of nature.) I should suggest, rather, that the significance of art is that life occasionally does "approximate to" it. This is not a declaration of preciosity à la Oscar Wilde, but a point implicit in John Dewey's contention that art carries forward and intensifies the rhythms, tensions, and resolutions found in ordinary life. (Analogously, though perhaps the analogy should not be pushed too far, nature "approximates to" a physical theory; the spray of points "approximates to," and often with a fairly wide margin of variation, the mathematical curve that the physicist constructs.)

To return to *King Lear:* the significant thing about Lear is not that he represents accurately a type already found in reality, or that the actions of the play are typical of what happens every day. The significant thing, so far as art is concerned, is that Lear *lives in the imagination,* where we may roam the earth and howl with him against the indignities of life. The significance of Mozart's music is not that his melodies, part by part, resemble our psychic processes or bodily movements, but that amid the banal frustrations of life there are fleeting moments of harmony whose consummation we can imagine only in his music. Yeats said of art: "a super-human/ Mirror-resembling dream"; and each of his words here can be profitably reflected on. Art resembles, but is not a mirror; it is a dream, not a literal transcript of reality; superhuman, because even the most modest work of art carries us beyond the sheer banality of the everyday.

IV. BEING VS. REALITY

We come now to the more substantive points in this comment, which are indicated in the shift of my title from "Art and Reality" to "Art and Being." Is this change from "Reality" to "Being"—both of which words might make some philosophers equally uncomfortable—merely an idle verbal shuffle? I think, rather, it brings us to the core of the problems that Mr. Hospers' discussion evokes.

In discussing the Expression Theory of art, Mr. Hospers is

drawn into the question, originally provoked by Croce and Collingwood, whether the work of art exists only in the imagination or whether it has real existence as a physical object in a sensuous medium. In a work of plastic art—a painting, for example—there is the original copy, which plainly has a spatiotemporal physical existence. Yet one observer, with a perfectly adequate pair of eyes, may "see" nothing in it, while a second may be enthralled by what he "sees." Clearly, this "seeing" is not ordinary seeing. Seeing is normal visual perception of a physical reality—here, colored paint spread on flat canvas—while "seeing" definitely involves something more. What is this something more? Croce and Collingwood profess to tell us; but their theory seems too uncomfortably subjective, and abandons the physical work of art, which seeks by all means to assert its sensuous immediacy and resistance, as almost irrelevant, or at best incidental to its imaginative (or ideal) reality.

What is involved in this quarrel, clearly, is a subjective-objective split, which can be overcome only by a radical phenomenological remedy.

To begin with, the degree of physicality—or thingness—in the work varies from art to art. It is clearly more pronounced in painting than in literature. To be sure, the sounds and rhythms of language are sensuous elements in the literary work, but they are subordinate to the images and meanings that the writer is trying to create in our imagination. Figures represented on a canvas have an immediate physical existence that the characters of a novel or play do not have. And even from artist to artist—within the art of painting—the canvas' insistence upon its physical reality may vary considerably. Thus Bonnard holds us persistently to a richly colored surface, even while evoking the whole world of French bourgeois life; in some of Picasso, on the other hand, we are immediately plunged past the picture surface into a fantastic and imaginary world. The painted or drawn figure is almost a symbol of a mysterious reality beyond it. And if we come to a painter like Jasper Johns, the painting as a sheer physical fact seeks to go far beyond Bonnard. For in these paintings—of flags, targets, or colored numbers like the page of a calendar—we seem to have no world at all expressed, but only the sheer self-assertion of a flat surface.

This variation from art to art suggests that one trouble of aestheticians is a tendency to oversimplified and too-comprehensive generalizations. Some years ago Morris Weitz made the fruitful suggestion that the attempt to seek a definition of art, as if one were eliciting some homogenous universal essence, should be properly replaced by an application of Wittgenstein's notion of "family resemblances." Art, that is, would be taken as an *open* concept linking various objects and activities, some of which resemble each other in some ways, others in others. Indeed, the phenomenon of art, it seems to me, makes necessary a more radical use of this Wittgensteinian device than Weitz appears to have in mind.

Consider, for example, Wittgenstein's example of the question, "What is number?" We do not answer the question by a defining statement of a common essence to all numbers. Rather, we indicate the different members of the family—natural numbers, fraction, real numbers, etc., etc. The Greeks considered only the natural numbers beginning with 2 as numbers, since they had a definition of number as a plurality of unities. Thus number was a closed concept. Since there are practical advantages to it, modern mathematicians keep the concept open, and without the necessity of a common definition it suffices that resemblances can be shown among the members of the family.

Consider, now, the question "What is art?" so earnestly asked by so many aestheticians. Obviously this presents many more ambiguities and difficulties than the same question about number. Number—the thing intended—is not directly a historical entity though there have been changing historical conceptions of number. But art, profoundly and directly historical in its very being, changes from epoch to epoch. Here we have to compare not only different members of the same family actually coexisting but members of vastly different epochs whose secret life can scarcely be guessed. Were the creators of the cave drawings artists or magicians? Certainly they were not artists in the manner in which some of our contemporaries are. We, of course, have performed the historical act (not yet possible for the nineteenth century) of incorporating their works into what Malraux calls the imaginary museum, which is to include all the works produced anywhere and any time on this planet. So we have turned those unknown creators into "artists." But this imaginary museum—an expression of the global civilization of the twentieth century—would have been ununderstandable to those primitive creators.

So historical in its being is the work of art that one is rather amazed that aestheticians, with the exception of Hegel, have done so little justice to this dimension. Hegel, indeed, in his *Lectures on Art,* virtually suggests that aesthetics be replaced by the philosophical history of art. The geometry of the beautiful, as it were, is to be replaced by a reflection on the historical morphologies of the human spirit embodied in art. Several facts about the history of aesthetics slyly reinforce Hegel's suggestion. Aestheticians usually have slanted their theories in the light of a particular historical form of art to which they were especially attached. And aesthetics itself as a separate field within philosophy—which it most remarkably is not with the ancients and the medievals—emerges only in the eighteenth century with the rise of the museum as a social institution that marks the separation of art from life.

But most strongly corroborative of Hegel's proposal is the uniquely temporal character of the work of art itself. No work of art is ever repeated. Repetition of a past style, where it is significant, always produces something new. Renaissance sculptors who took the Greeks as models produced something as different from the ancients as the North from the South pole.

This temporal dimension of art brings us now to the notion of Being. I use the term "Being" here in its phenomenal concreteness—with all the particularity and density of the historical moment—as well as in its phenomenal simplicity—as the realm of openness directly accessible to prereflective experience, which does not so much reconcile subject and object as first makes that distinction itself possible.

Thus the dichotomy between the work as existing in the imagination and the work as a sensuous physical object is possible only within Being. A clue to this unifying unity is provided by our ordinary perception of objects. Such perception is possible only because our sensibility is immediately, persistently, and prereflectively structured by imagination. Here imagination—in however rudimentary a form—is self-projecting transcendence. But is not such transcendence only possible through, indeed identical with, Being as self-projecting and enveloping presence. The object is always within the world, and as such points beyond itself, but in such a way that the world contracts about it in its thingness. This diastole and systole movement of expansion and contraction—here one speaks metaphorically—takes place in our perception of the most ordinary objects, but the tension between the two moments is heightened in the case of works of art. The more immediately sensuous the work the more strikingly it brings into being a world within which it finds its proper place.

Even those works—like the ready-mades of Duchamp, Rauschenberg's combines, or the flat paintings of Jasper Johns—that insist on their sheer reality as objects to the point where they seem to escape "art" altogether have to be grasped by this sensuous-imaginative unity in duality. Such objects are not representative, in the traditional manner, of any world, nor are they meant to be expressive like the shapes and colors of the Abstract Expressionists. 'I do not want to express anything,' Rauschenberg is reported saying, 'only to cooperate with the things in my environment.' (Presumably, to cooperate means here: to let those things be, or become, what they are.) Yet we see these objects in galleries and museums, which are very significant parts of a world. These works point beyond themselves to the whole tradition of art that they would seek to abolish, but without which they would be, quite literally, pointless. They refer negatively beyond themselves, but negative referring is referring. They are witty, ironic, and surprising comments on a tradition that they would jostle out of its routines. They are also highly complex comments on an industrial civilization, whose products they would seem to embrace benignly, though by tearing these objects from their usual context, they usually show them as absurd. All of these references —and many more, if there were time to spell them out—are present within these objects that are supposed only to be themselves. The man who does not "see" a Jasper Johns's picture —though he sees it in a physical sense well enough—is unable to feel it immediately as a bold, bouncy, light-hearted rejection of a tradition, without which in fact it would be nothing. Indeed, so heavily dependent upon the past is this kind of painting, that it could not exist without Abstract Expressionism, and all the reference to tradition that has gone into *that* style.[1]

V. ART AND THE ARCHAIC

Professor Hospers concludes with the interesting speculation that the expressiveness of certain elements in the work of art—tones and colors, for example—as well as combinations of these elements, like certain melodies, is the result of certain deep traces left in the human psyche. Yet it is not altogether clear how far his speculation would reach. He has previously discounted individual association as explaining such expressiveness. But if not individual association, would it be racial? In that case, Mr. Hospers would be offering us a version of Jung's Collective Unconscious—a very interesting hypothesis, to be sure, but one perhaps a little too strong for Mr. Hospers' stomach. In any case, these questions do not lie within the ken of the philosopher, and their decision must be left ultimately, if at all, with the psychologists.

However, if we turn to art itself rather than its sensory elements exclusively, there is a speculation that the philosopher may properly and soberly reflect upon: namely, that art as such lives only by making contact with a more archaic and primordial stratum of the human psyche. Hegel, as you know, predicted in the nineteenth century that art was on the way out because it was becoming too bland, too much a mere part of "culture," and that it would be replaced by a more sophisticated and clever consciousness that had lost touch with the power of myth. Recently, Edgar Wind has advanced much the same position very plausibly in his *Art and Anarchy*. Though we have today vast quantities of art in the form of museums and concerts, though there is much knowledgeability and much talk about art, yet, Wind argues, art has nevertheless become much more "marginal" in modern life. A gallery-goer may now see five shows in an afternoon; if art really had an impact on him, he could not go immediately from, say, a Picasso to a Klee exhibition. That he does do so, suggests that the works have stirred up no turmoil of the spirit for him to contend with.

But if art is indeed becoming a more marginal phenomenon, is it not because imagination itself has a declining role and power within modern life?

> Shakespearean fish swam the sea, far away from land;
> Romantic fish swam in nets coming to the hand;
> What are all those fish that lie gasping on the strand?

But how if imagination as the synthesizing unity of sensibility is the place where Being projects itself? Would not the fact, if it be a fact, that art is becoming more marginal, mean that Being itself, as Heidegger has suggested, is receding for modern man—going up in a thin vapor, in the words of Nietzsche?

We leave all such speculations as questions.

Meanwhile, we may observe with some relief that art has not altogether succumbed to Hegel's prophecy. However, it has had to achieve survival by a prodigious return to its sources back beyond the bourgeois phase of its history: Realism. Modern artists have projected a world of the imagination in which their own works live, or struggle to live, beside Easter Island and Stonehenge, as well as Ingres or Courbet. The history of art is thereby reopened to new vistas and has to be rewritten. Realistic works are only some members of the vastly extended family, and the crucial family resemblances to be observed will be different from heretofore. Perhaps aesthetics has to begin all over again.

NOTES

1. Along these lines, Heidegger has given a much more extended analysis of Van Gogh's painting of a pair of peasant shoes ("Vom Ursprung des Kunstwerkes," *Holzwege*):

"The painting is of a pair of peasant's shoes—and nothing else. Just a pair of shoes; yet around and through them emerges the world in which the peasant traces his furrows, watches patiently for the wheat to bloom, or trudges tiredly at evening back from the fields. The cycles of time—Spring, Summer, Autumn, Winter—enfold these simple boots, which, as serviceable and dependable, find their place in a world. Being, as presence, emerges through the painting of the shoes; yet in such a way that it enfolds them in their concrete thingness—just a pair of shoes, and nothing else—as the simple, serviceable gear that they are."

But Van Gogh's painting is a work of representative art. It is to be expected, therefore, that it would evoke a world. I have chosen to consider, instead, works that, neither representative nor expressive in their aims, would seem to assert only their own identity as sensuous objects, and nothing more. Yet here too, if we are right, the object cannot work upon us without generating its own enveloping context. In this sense, art never escapes being expression, though we might add that it is never the expression of anything "subjective." The Expression Theorists, who hold that art exists only in the imagination, are thus partly right and partly wrong, as are their critics, who insist that art is *essentially* the activity of combining sensory materials. The reconciliation of the two points of view comes through understanding the Thing in its relation to Being.

1

Is Art Really More Real than Reality?

RAZIEL ABELSON
New York University

WHAT I HAVE to say has at best only incidental bearing on works of art, but I hope it has enough intrinsic interest to be worth saying in this volume. Having no pretensions as a critic or historian or even a philosopher of art, I hope only to clear up some verbal muddles that others, who may have such pretensions, sometimes create. In particular, I want to comment on some rather perplexing uses of the words "reality," "real," and "exists."

John Hospers contends that works of art may be judged, in part, by their "correspondence to reality." Against this view, but assuming its intelligibility, William Barrett argues, à la Oscar Wilde, that life imitates art because art is "more real" than commonplace life. At times Barrett deplores the poverty of aesthetic experience in modern life, associating such aesthetic poverty with lack of reality, although at other times and somewhat inconsistently, he claims that modern life and modern art interpenetrate and cannot clearly be distinguished. In any case, it is with the opposed claims of Hospers and Barrett about the relation between art and reality that I shall be concerned. Both views seem to me confused to the point of unintelligibility.

What is reality? Unless one believes with Spinoza and Bradley that there is only one subject of true predication, a unique entity called "reality," this remarkable noun comprehends everything that, in some sense or other of the adjective "real," can be judged to be real. But just about anything can be described as real in some perfectly acceptable sense, as we shall see, so that the substantive, "reality," fails to distinguish anything from anything else.

Hospers seems to believe that his use of "reality" can be made somewhat more definite by defining it in terms of existence: "I shall mean by 'reality' that which exists apart from works of art." But this definition is of little help toward understanding what he means, since his use of "exists" is as indefinite as his use of "reality." In what sense of "exists" does he hold that human nature exists, or that a character's motives and actions correspond to what exists? What can possibly be meant by motives that exist, or actions that exist? Bewilderment increases when we find Hospers agreeing with Aristotle that an action is not real merely because it has actually been performed, or a motive merely because it has in fact been acted upon. Actions and motives in literature, he insists, must conform to what we know of human nature if they are to be aesthetically acceptable. No doubt he is right about this, but what does it have to do with "that which exists"?

It might be helpful to get a bit clearer on the meaning or meanings of "real" before drawing conclusions about the relation of art to reality. I suspect that once we do get clearer, we will find that this profound question has no sense at all.

There are four main grammatical forms in which the adjective "real" or its adverbial cognate "really" does some useful work, as in the following schemata:

1. That is (or isn't) a real X.
2. That does (or doesn't) really look like (sound, behave, taste, smell or feel like) an X.
3. That is (or isn't) really an X.
4. That X is (or isn't) real.

The above schemata are all too frequently treated as equivalent, although the grammatical differences alone should warn us against such cavalier treatment. Initial caution is further justified as soon as we consider the kind of information conveyed by each type of locution, particularly in the negative form. Replace "X" with "apple": (1′) "That isn't a real apple" informs us that an object that looks like an apple is only a facsimile, made perhaps of wax. (2′) "That doesn't really look like an apple" informs us either that someone did a bad job of painting an apple or making an artificial one, or that whoever mistook a certain object for an apple should have his eyes (or head) examined. (3′) "That is really an apple" conveys, so far as I can see, no more and no less than "That is an apple," except that the former locution is likely to be employed when a person is in doubt and needs reassurance. However, the adverb "really" does more substantial work when used to distinguish superficial from informed classification, as in "A whale is not really a fish; it is really a mammal." (4′) "That apple isn't real" *may* be understood as equivalent to (1′), but it may, on the other hand, serve to stamp a presumed apple (such as the golden apple of Atalanta) as mythological, hallucinatory, fictitious, illusory, or otherwise unreal. The service performed in such case is of considerable philosophical interest, but for our purpose we need only note that, when used as a predicate, "real" has an ontological ring; it distinguishes reliable from unreliable conditions of perception and further predication.

Returning now to our search for Hospers' elusive Reality, is there any class of things that comprehends all these uses of "real"? I believe there is no such class, because in each of these uses, "real" can be both affirmed and denied of anything. An apple is a real apple, but not a real candlestick, although it can double for one. It does not really look like a rubber ball, although small children may need convincing on that score. It is not really a preventative for all diseases, despite the old cliché to the contrary. And the apple that, in a drunken stupor, I see growing from the chandelier is not real.

But perhaps there is some one favored use of "real" or "really" that will serve to mark out the class of things to which

Hospers wishes to compare works of art. Let us then take a closer look at each of our four schemata to see if we can find that remarkable class.

1. When we say that a Y is not a real X, we can mean either of two things. We may mean that the Y in question is an artificial or counterfeit or otherwise deceptive surrogate for an X, or we may mean it is simply a very bad X. I shall call these two uses the contrastive and the normative uses of "real," respectively.

Now clearly the contrastive meaning of "real" depends on what it is being contrasted with. We frequently contrast real flowers with artificial flowers, real people with mannequins and puppets, real money with counterfeit or play-money, real numbers with imaginary and transcendental numbers. When it is asserted of an apple in a painting that it resembles a real apple, is any more information conveyed than if we merely assert that the object in the painting looks like an apple, thus leaving out the ponderous word, "real"? If not, then this use of "real" can hardly serve Hospers' purpose. If "real" is additionally informative, then the statement must be contrasting real apples with some contrast-class, such as wax apples: "That apple in the painting doesn't resemble a wax apple; it resembles a real apple." But this statement could just as well be a ground for criticizing a painting as for praising it. For suppose the painter had been trying to paint a wax apple and not a real apple? Clearly, the contrastive use of "real" will not help us to catch our elusive Reality.

Where we do not recognize contrastive sets, the adjective "real" can still serve a normative function, by which I mean a function served equally well by the expression, "very good." "Here's a real apple for you!" informs us that an apple is a fine specimen of its species. But this use of "real" is always *within* a class and cannot serve to compare two different classes. It has been said that while *Oedipus Rex* is a real tragedy, *Death of a Salesman* is an unsuccessful attempt at a tragedy. In this mode of speaking, any very good work of art is a real work of art, but we cannot, on pain of vacuity, *explain* its goodness by its reality. Furthermore, its reality has nothing to do with what lies outside the work, so this sense of "real" cannot be the object of our Hosperian quest.

2. Can the Reality to which good works of art correspond consist of all the things that elements of such works might really look (or sound or act) like? This class of entities would seem a promising candidate for the lofty post in question, since we often do say, "That's a fine portrait; that face really looks like the model's face," or "Dostoevski's story, *The Double,* is a great story; his character really behaves like a madman," etc. Reality would then be the general reference class for comparisons. But two considerations prevent coherent discourse about such a class. First, there may always be something that even the most poorly drawn element of a work resembles. A badly drawn orange may correspond to a grapefruit; an ineptly described lover in a dime novel may resemble the village idiot. Shall we say, on that account, that they are well drawn after all? Secondly, qualitative resemblances of shape, color, sound and behavior serve only to identify a particular style of art (naturalistic style), but not to evaluate a work within its style. It would be absurd to criticize Picasso's "Woman Looking into a Mirror" on the ground that it doesn't look like a woman looking into a mirror. Hospers explicitly disowns any such vulgar criterion of artistic excellence, so he cannot mean, by "Reality," the class of things that elements of works of art might really look like.

3. Perhaps Reality is what things *really are,* rather than what they might really look like? This may be what Barrett has in mind when he claims that certain characters of fiction are more real than our neighbors, on the ground that great writers like Cervantes and Homer discover and reveal to us essential types by which we may measure ourselves, as when we call a person quixotic, or when a lover compares his sweetheart to Helen of Troy. But again, the class of types is far too fully packed, too bulging at the seams to constitute Reality, since,

as Parmenides argues in Plato's dialogue, there is always some type that anything instantiates, so that, in this sense, everything corresponds to *some* type of reality.

In any case, this notion of reality serves the purposes of science far better than those of art. It was in this sense of "real" that Plato described his Forms as more real than sensible objects, identifying knowledge of the former with science, and knowledge of the latter with opinion. I spoke earlier of a nontrivial use of the adverb "really," when we say that a whale is really a mammal, not a fish. "Really" serves here to distinguish what things look like from what they are: the very reverse of our previous sense (2). But just as sense (2), "really looks like," was appropriate to naturalistic art, sense (3), which repudiates the way things look, is inappropriate to art altogether, for there is surely no work of art that does not involve sensual appearances. Platonism in art criticism would seem as close to a self-defeating view as one could get, and it was for good reasons that Plato concluded that art is the least reliable mode of knowledge and the furthest removed from Reality. Plato was wise enough to be an anti-Platonist when it came to art.

Barrett makes the interesting point that resembling or looking like is an asymmetrical relation when asserted to hold between objects in life and objects in art, and he seems to hold that Hospers has pointed the relation the wrong way. Our neighbors resemble or approximate to characters in great works of fiction, but not vice versa, according to Barrett. Now it is true that we sometimes say, "That landscape resembles a Corot," or "Sadie reminds me of Madame Bovary," but we could just as well say the converse. In fact, the latter way of speaking is preferable where any doubt arises, since the former can become ludicrous. I recall a newspaper story about the defense of Bataan during the war in the Pacific, in which American soldiers were reported to have performed heroic feats in conscious imitation of Robert Taylor's actions in a movie about Bataan. Some people I know try to model themselves on characters in novels. But their imitation of characters in fiction is ludicrous because (and to this degree Hospers is more right than Barrett) one cannot imitate what does not exist. To try to act like a fictional character is to confuse fact with fiction. One may of course try to develop certain traits that an author ascribes to one of his characters. One may aspire to be a saint like Alyosha, a charming rogue like Raffles, or a tough guy like Sam Spade. But this is hardly imitation of a *person* except in a figurative sense. Literally, it amounts to cultivating traits that one realizes to be desirable when reading about them. Surely the fictional status of the character described as possessing such traits is not a necessary condition of their desirability.

4. We are left with the use of "real" in schema (4) as the sole surviving candidate for the Reality we seek. "That X is real," when meant, not as synonymous with the contrastive "That is a real X," but as what might be called ontological predication, reassures us that we are not hallucinating or misperceiving and seems, more than any of the other schema, to point toward something called "Reality." But if we expect to reach that ineffable goal, we are going to be disappointed.

J. L. Austin (to whom, it need hardly be said, this essay owes a great deal, if not everything) described the predicate "real" as a trouser concept, pointing out that its contrary, "unreal" wears the trousers (he might more aptly have called it a spouse concept). We do not have, nor do we need, criteria for being real, but only for being unreal in some specific sense, such as illusory, hallucinatory, fictitious—in some way the object of false belief. Now there is only one way of being real, so these different kinds of unreality must be features, not of the object of belief (the object, after all, does not exist), but of the process by which we arrive at our belief. An illusion is a product of abnormal physical or physiological conditions of perception, a hallucination the product of mental derangement, a fictitious entity the product of false information. Now, is the Reality in relation to which art is to be evaluated simply the totality of things about which our beliefs are not products of illusion, hallucination, or false hearsay? Surely no one would ever dream of maintaining *this* thesis, for the simple reason that, to the degree that it is true it is trivial, and to the degree that it is nontrivial it is obviously false. To take the latter case first, when a writer (e.g., Dostoevski in *The Double*) describes hallucinatory experience, it would be manifestly silly to criticize his description for not corresponding to normal perception. That would be like criticizing a doughnut for having a hole in the middle. Probably most works of art are not concerned with these abnormal sources of false belief. So the claim that they must correspond to something other than the objects of such abnormal experiences is too trivial for anyone to bother to make.

Summarizing our results, it would appear that there is no genuine issue of the relation of art to reality because (a) there is no thing or class of things called "reality"; (b) the only ground of comparison between elements of a work of art and things outside that work is the relation of "looking like," a relation that goes more naturally from art to non-art than the other way, but which is a criterion only of naturalistic style and not of aesthetic excellence; (c) in each of the other senses of "real" (namely, the contrastive, the normative, the scientific, and the ontological), it is either trivial or senseless to compare a work of art with anything outside it that, for some entirely different purpose, may be said to be real. Thus in none of these *façons de parler* can we make clear sense either of Hospers' claim that a work of art is good to the degree that it corresponds to external reality, or of Barrett's claim that life is real to the degree to which it resembles works of art.

2

Taste, Meaning, and Reality in Art

C. J. DUCASSE
Brown University

ANY DISCUSSION of the relations between art and philosophy is likely to be hampered by confusions unless notice has initially been taken of the ambiguity of the word "art," which alike figures in such expressions as "the fine arts," "the liberal arts," "the industrial arts," "decorative art," "the art of self-defense," etc. In its generic sense, "art" means *skill;* and a "work of art" is therefore correspondingly anything intentionally brought into existence through the exercise of skill. During the sessions of the New York University Institute of Philosophy devoted to *Art and Philosophy,* however, "art" was tacitly taken to designate specifically what is called fine art; this, according to Webster's Dictionary, being "art which is concerned with the creation of objects of imagination and taste for their own sakes and without relation to the utility of the object produced." Hence a work of fine art is "that which is produced, as paintings, sculpture, etc., by the application of skill and taste."

The patent fact, which these two definitions simply register, is that in a work of fine art the artist's taste was one of the factors that determined his creating precisely what he did create rather than something slightly or greatly different. And, in view of this, it is strange that Professor Schapiro's account of the grounds for positive or negative judgment of excellence in works of fine art makes no mention at all of the taste of the judge and of its similarity or dissimilarity to that of the artist.

I submit, however, that such judgment ultimately does depend on the particular taste of the individual judge: his evaluation of the aesthetic merits of a given work of fine art is ultimately a matter of whether *he* likes or dislikes what he experiences when he takes as object of his aesthetic contemplation either the given work of art as a whole, or one or another of the recondite aspects, features, or details of it disclosed by the repeated scrutiny on which Professor Schapiro insists.

Even if this should be granted, however, it might yet be contended that a person's taste concerning works of fine art or particular features of them can *itself* be bad; that is, that he likes some works that are bad and dislikes some that are good. But if this is contended, the question then automatically becomes *whose taste* concerning works of fine art is good, and whose is bad. And the answer, I submit, is that "good taste" ultimately means there *one's own taste*, whether it be shared by many other persons, or by few, or by none; and that "bad taste" correspondingly means taste that conflicts with one's own. For the situation in matters of taste concerning works of fine art is exactly the same as in the case of a person's taste in matters of food or of odors. It is probably true, for example, that the majority of persons have a taste for pineapple—they like the gustatory sensations it gives them. But I have known one person who disliked those it gave him. And obviously there is no possibility of proving either that his taste, in disliking pineapple, is bad; or that the taste of the majority, who like it, is good. There, and equally in the matter of tastes concerning given works of fine art or particular features of them, the ultimate fact is that *de gustibus non est disputandum.* The persons called experts as to the aesthetic merits of works of fine art are expert only in tracing their positive or negative evaluation of a given work to the more or less recondite features of it from which *their* evaluation of it arises; whereas ordinary amateurs of art simply like or dislike the work of art as they directly perceive it. But precisely such personal, purely de facto liking or disliking is the case of the expert himself as regards the recondite features of the work to which he points as bases for his aesthetic evaluation of it: he has no grounds other than his own taste for basing his positive or negative judgment of artistic excellence of a given work on the particular grounds on which he does base it. That his taste is perhaps shared by many does not in the least show that it is good in any sense other than the question-begging one of being shared by many; or that a taste peculiar to one person, or shared by but very few, is bad.

Tastes change, of course—those of "experts" as well as those of amateurs. But one automatically tends to regard change in one's own taste as maturation of it; and as perversion, change in the taste of another that makes it diverge from one's own. It is true that a person's taste may become sensitive to differences in the object concerned, which before made no difference to him. But the question then is whether his taste had before been crude, dull, coarse, and had thus robbed him of beauties he now perceives; or whether his taste has now become finical, precious, morbidly sensitive, thus robbing him of the aesthetic enjoyment certain things had given him before, but which now he no longer gets from them. For there is such a thing as perceiving too little, or too much—only the trees, perhaps, but not the forests; or only the forest, but not the trees.

Professor Beardsley's paper, its title tells us, is concerned with the limits of critical interpretation—that is, of interpretation discerning and judicious—of works of art. But the definition the paper then gives of "to interpret," to wit, "verbally to unfold or disclose meaning," is too narrow; for unverbalized interpretation, whether critical or uncritical, also occurs; and indeed far more frequently than does verbalized.

Leaving out, then, the restriction "verbally to unfold or disclose," the correct definition of "critical interpretation" would be: judicious discernment of the meaning of something; which in Professor Beardsley's paper is specifically works of art.

As possibly throwing light on what the limits of such interpretation are, the paper then addresses itself to the question of the merits of, and the relationship between, two theories as to the nature of art. One of them, which the paper denominates the "Significance Theory," contends that *all* art is "inherently referential," i.e., that "it is the very nature of a work of art to point beyond itself to something else." The other theory, denominated the "Immanence Theory," is most pointedly formulated in the paper in terms of an example—that of music, and more specifically, of the "little snatch of melody" consisting of the first six notes of "The Star-Spangled Banner"; the contention there of the Immanence Theory being that this bit of melody is, "in its own right with its own shape and qualities," *itself* vigorous and forceful, without any need of pointing beyond itself to vigor and forcefulness in human beings or their actions.

Considering now first the Immanence Theory as applied to those six notes, I submit that the only sense in which it is true that they are *in themselves* vigorous and forceful becomes evident if one bears in mind that music is an arrangement of physical sounds in time; and this *even when nobody hears them,* as would be the case if the sounds are caused to occur by a phonograph playing inside a soundproof box or in a closet in some room of an uninhabited building.

For obviously, the music can be said to be even then vigorous and forceful only in the sense in which, for instance, quinine can be said to be bitter even when nobody is tasting it; "bitter" being then the name not of a taste-sensation but of a *capacity,* to wit, the capacity immanent in quinine but not being exercised by it at the time, to cause the particular *taste-sensation* named "bitter taste" whenever the quinine is put on the tongue of a normal human being whose tongue is not at the time being stimulated by any substance causing taste-sensations incompatible with the taste-sensation called "bitter."

Thus, what is likewise immanent in those six notes of "The Star-Spangled Banner," when the phonograph plays them but they are not being heard, is not *feelings* of vigor and forcefulness, since music does not *itself* have feelings, but is the *capacity*—disposition, power—which those five notes have but are not exercising when they are not being heard to cause feelings, or more strictly *mental images of feelings,* of vigor and forcefulness in a human being if and when he hears them; if his attention is not then otherwise engaged (as it would be if, for instance, he were then perceiving his clothes to be on fire); *and* if his interest in those six notes at the time is *aesthetic* interest, i.e., is interest in the feeling-images they can induce in him, not *inquisitive* interest (as would be, for instance, curiosity as to the location of the source of those sounds) nor *practical* interest in what to *do* about them (as, e.g., was his interest in whether to stand up or to remain seated when he heard them on his radio the evening before).[1]

Turning now to the Significance Theory, which holds that the very nature of *all* works of fine art is to point to something beyond themselves, i.e., to have some meaning, a word may be said first concerning the need pointed out at the end of Professor Beardsley's paper for a clear conception of value specifically aesthetic, as distinguished from, for instance, commemorative, or religious, or economic value, or physical utility, etc.

An example of a physical object which can be a work of fine art having aesthetic value, but which can, together with it, have value also of each of these other kinds, would be a bookend made of some precious metal, and consisting of a statue of Moses, seated and recording the Ten Commandments. In its function as a bookend, it is evidently a work not of fine art but of *practical* art, i.e., of engineering skill, which endowed it with the capacity to resist the sidewise pressure which books standing on end exert, but which the books do not themselves have. The fact that the bookend in view is made of precious metal gives it *economic* value, irrespective of such economic value as may derive from its aesthetic merit or its practical utility. And the fact, made patent in one way or another, that the bookend is a statue of Moses recording the Ten

Commandments gives the bookend also both *commemorative* and *religious* value, largely independently of whether its aesthetic value is high or low. No puzzle or problem arises from the object's having, together, aesthetic value and value of each of the other kinds mentioned. And as regards the need pointed out at the end of Professor Beardsley's paper, to "know what aesthetic value is," it is readily met: Aesthetic value, positive and negative, consists in *beauty* and *ugliness;* and these respectively in *pleasantness* and *unpleasantness* of the feeling-images obtained in aesthetic contemplation whether of a work of fine art, or of decorative art, or of practical art, or of some natural object; aesthetic contemplation itself consisting in, as we may say, "listening for," i.e., making the mind receptive to, the feeling-images which, when the object is attended to with such receptive attitude, may present themselves to the mind.

Passing now to statements such as those included in Professor Beardsley's second group, which purport to formulate each a critical, i.e., discerning and judicious interpretation of the particular work of art it concerns, what is needed in order to make evident their relation to statements such as those of his first group is a clear idea of the generic nature of interpretation and of meaning; and of the respective *differentiae* of the several species of interpretation and of meaning concerned in the various statements.

The basic fact in this connection is that interpretation is a psychological operation irreducibly involving the following four factors jointly:

1. A conscious *interpreter P.*
2. An *interpretandum I;* to wit, something which is presented to *P*'s consciousness; which has meaning; and which may be more specifically either a *symbol,* or a *sign,* or a *signal.*
3. An *interpretans M;* which is the meaning (i.e., less ambiguously, the *meant*) of *I* for *P; P*'s consciousness of *I* being what then causes in *P* consciousness of *M.*
4. The *psychological context* in *P,* in which causation of *P*'s consciousness of *M* by *P*'s consciousness of *I* occurs.

"Sign" is used above *not* in the comprehensive sense in

which symbols and signals would be species of signs (and for which comprehensive sense *semata* would be a better name) but in the narrower, ordinary sense in which "sign" designates anything perception of which constitutes *evidence of the existence,* future, present, or past, of something else; as, for instance, approaching black clouds, of future occurrence of rain; a certain odor, of presence of a skunk; a footprint, of a man's foot having stepped there.[2]

In the light of the generic nature of interpretation as set forth above, one of the things which become evident is that *perception of a physical fact,* no matter how trivial, simple, or accidental that fact may be—for instance, visual perception of a line, or a dot, or a smear—is a case of interpretation: to wit, interpretation of one's sensation(s) at the time as being caused by occurrence of some *nonpsychological* event, which, as such, is denominated "physical." For sensations are never proximately caused by psychological occurrences, and hence, as G. E. Moore pointed out,[3] if we had no sensations we would know nothing of a physical world.

But further, the dot, line, or smear, or other physical fact *wholly* present to perception, can be made object of aesthetic contemplation as defined earlier; which *itself* is a case of interpretation—one in which the *interpretandum* is the physical fact present to perception, the *interpretans* is the feeling-images which the contemplator is caused to experience by the physical fact he is perceiving, and the context of interpretation is the rest of his total psychological state at the time.

What is aesthetically contemplated, however, may be not that presented physical fact itself, but instead something which it is interpreted as *representing,* e.g., a Conestoga wagon, or an apple, or a man, etc. And further, what is represented could itself be a representation of something else, as would be the case if a picture of an interior contained, as one of the objects it depicts, a painting of, say, a landscape hanging on the wall of the room depicted—which landscape could then be what the interpreter *P* elects as object of his aesthetic contemplation.

The next thing important to notice is that interpretation may be either verbo-verbal, verbo-real, rei-verbal, or rei-real; meaning here by "real" simply that a real *interpretandum* or *interpretans* is one that does *not* consist of a word or other discursive entity. It follows that both the *statement* of a critical interpretation of a given work of art, and a *statement* simply describing a given work of art, are equally instances of interpretation—specifically, of *rei-verbal interpretation,* i.e., of what is commonly called *formulation.* The difference is that a statement simply describing a particular work of art does not —whereas a critical interpretation statement concerning the work does—report the outcome of the utterer's aesthetic contemplation of what the work of art concerned either actually presents, or as the case may be, represents directly, or indirectly.

In view of the diverse things mentioned, any one of which a person can with complete freedom elect to take as object of his aesthetic contemplation when attending to a given work of art, it becomes evident that *there can be no rules of critical interpretation* which he would be bound to obey. There can be rules to which critical interpretation *statements* must conform, but only because and insofar as such statements have the status of *signals,* that is, are intended by the utterer of them to be read or heard by other persons and to be understood by them. These rules, however, demand only that the language he employs in addressing those persons shall be one familiar both to himself and to them. They have no authority at all wherewith to pronounce right, or wrong, the interpretations and aesthetic evaluations he formulates in that shared language concerning given works of art. The rules, on the other hand, which govern certain games, or team work, are binding on the players or the workers only because one same end is aimed at by the participants, for success in the pursuit of which not only communication but also *collaboration* between them is indispensable. But in judgment of a work of art as aesthetically good or bad, there is no such shared end in view, nor therefore is any collaboration called for.

The statements made by one person about the aesthetic merits of a given work of art may of course direct the attention of another person who hears them to aspects of it he had not yet noticed. But whether he then finds these aesthetically pleasing or displeasing is, once more, solely a matter of his individual taste. The statements made, by "expert" or by amateur critics, about the aesthetic merits of various works of art thus provide information *about the critic's own taste,* but do not show it to be in any objective sense good or bad. Only if and insofar as contemplation of a particular work of art were likely to arouse in the contemplator feeling of kinds that generate socially or personally harmful acts (as, e.g., pornographic art may) could the contemplator's taste be bad or wrong; and this then in an objective, *practical* sense, not an aesthetic sense.

The question considered by Professor Hospers in his paper, "Art and Reality," is that of the relation of works of any of the arts to "reality"; meaning there by "reality" the world apart both from works of art and from their creators.

In the case of works of narrative literature, the paper's contention is evidently sound, anyway concerning works of fiction—novels, stories, dramas—as distinguished from narrations of historical facts, whether of the past, or the contemporary ones reported in the news media. The contention is that in a work of fiction the characters and their actions and experiences must *correspond to reality* in the sense of being faithful to human nature, plausible, convincing, if the story is to be a work of art rather than of lack of art. That is, the actions, thoughts, and feelings which a story depicts a person as performing or as experiencing must be consistent with what a character of the particular type the story has assigned to him would do, think, or feel in the situations he is described as facing; and this even if that type of character be an erratic, or insane, or irresponsible one.

For the consumer of fiction expects, and is expected by the author of fiction, to take while he reads it a vacation from his own life and to live imaginatively that of the persons in the story. The story is a good work of fiction if it enables the consumer to do this easily. He then enters imaginatively in actions and experiences for many of which no opportunities occur in his real life, or which he could not actually perform or undergo without wrecking his actual life.

But although the situations into which he thus projects himself are only imaginary, he may by doing so come to know, vicariously but nonetheless genuinely, emotions—such perhaps as jealousy—for which no occasion had yet arisen in his own life. And, through his reading of fiction, he may also learn various bits of wisdom without paying the price the learning of them has in real life; for example, learn to act cautiously instead of impulsively in kinds of situations he had not before realized were risky.

As consumer of fiction, he does not and should not at the time attend to and contemplate aesthetically the technique of the story, since this would to a greater or lesser extent distract his attention from the story's content. A teacher of story writing, on the other hand, or a literary critic, might, as a matter of occupational habit, attend to and admire or condemn its technique, instead of "consuming" the story; or an actor, sitting in the audience at a play, is likely to attend to the acting, but not to the play.

In the second part of his paper, Professor Hospers comments on the ambiguity of the statement that art is "expression" of emotion, and he rightly points out that to "express" emotion in the sense, for instance, of sighing or groaning when one is sad, is one thing.[4] But "expression of emotion" is quite another thing as designating the *process* by which an artist, who at the time is not himself sad but intent, creates a work of art that "expresses sadness" or is "expressive of sadness" in a yet third sense; to wit, that of *embodying* or *objectifying* sadness.

That works of art do embody or objectify emotion (or more broadly, feeling) is what Professor Hospers means by saying that they have expressiveness and that in all art "*percepts are suffused with affect.*"

This quite correct and important assertion, however, introduces his exposition of a contention which seems to me wholly invalid. It concerns the source of the affective import of colors and of lines.

If their affective import were wholly due to the associations which the color or line has had in the experience of the individual or to the conventions of the particular culture of which he is a member, then, since these vary greatly, the affect with which each of the colors and lines is suffused could not be "invariant from person to person and culture to culture." But, the paper contends, it *is* invariant to a certain extent. For instance, quiet cheerfulness is universally the affect of green; that of red, universally excitement, drama, activity, etc. Hence, Professor Hospers argues, these invariant affects must be rooted each in some association "universal in the experience of human beings, and so primordial in the history of the human race, that the percept is suffused with the [same] affect for all human beings alike."

I submit, however, that the alleged invariance from person to person and culture to culture of the affect of green and of horizontal lines is simply not a fact and therefore cannot need to be accounted for.

That "green is the color of the normal foreground of landscapes," as the paper asserts in support of its contention that green has an affect invariant from person to person, is patently not true. What is true is only that green is the color of the normal foreground of landscapes *at certain seasons of the year in certain regions of the earth.* In others, on the other hand, as in certain parts of New England in the fall, the color of the normal foreground of landscapes is a mixture of vivid reds and yellows. Moreover, even in the case of green, there are many greens, perceivably differing from one another in one, two, or all three of the dimensions of color which textbooks of psychology term *hue, brilliance,* and *saturation.*[5]

Each of the hundreds of distinguishable greens, when it is made object of aesthetic contemplation by a perceiver of it, has for him a likewise distinguishable affect; and the affect of each of the discernibly different greens is a matter partly of the contemplator's individual temperament, partly of the associations the particular green he perceives has had in his past experience, partly of what the color-context of the green happens to be at the time he contemplates it, and partly of what the green may be representing, i.e., be the green *of:* whether perhaps of grass, or of mildew, or of an emerald, or of a frog, etc. And obviously the case is exactly the same as regards the affects of the equally numerous distinguishable reds, yellows, and other colors.

Similarly, the horizontal position of a man may indeed, as the paper asserts, signify that he is resting, is comfortable, and is safe from falling. But it equally well may, and often does, signify instead that he is sick, or is drunk, or is dead. And the affect of what his position signifies will differ correspondingly.

When the various solid facts which have now been pointed out are duly taken into consideration, I submit that they make patent the indefensibility of the contention that given sensory items have an affect invariant from person to person and culture.

Those same facts, however, fully allow as much or as little sameness of affect as those sensory items happen to have among human beings.

NOTES

1. As regards the insistence above that *mental images of feelings,* not actual feelings, are what occur during aesthetic contemplation of music in a person who hears it, see Secs. 5,6, of the present writer's paper, "Art and the Language of the Emotions," *Journal of Aesthetics and Art Criticism* (Fall 1964), p. 110.

2. The writer has discussed at length interpretation and its

various species in Ch. 16, "The Mental Operations," of his *Nature, Mind, and Death* (Open Court, 1951); also, earlier and more briefly, in his address, "Symbols, Signs, and Signals," *Journal of Symbolic Logic,* Vol. 4, No. 2 (June 1939); and the meaning of "of" in the phrase "perception *of* physical facts," in Ch. 15 of the book cited above.

3. *Philosophical Studies* (London: Kegan Paul, 1922), pp. 185–86, 188.

4. In the recent article of mine cited earlier, I proposed to term it *effusion,* or *venting,* of one's emotion.

5. See the definitions of these three terms, and of "the color-solid" or "color-pyramid," in H. C. Warren's *Dictionary of Psychology* (Boston: Houghton Mifflin, 1934); and the color-pyramid diagram of the three dimensions of difference perceptible among colors in, for instance, E. B. Titchener's *Text Book of Psychology* (New York: Macmillan, 1909), I, 62–63; where Titchener concludes (p. 64) that they cannot fall far short of thirty-five thousand.

3

Form and Content in Art

W. E. KENNICK
Amherst College

THE SECTION of Professor Schapiro's paper dealing with the "unity of form and content" in art reminds us once more how easy it is to generate perplexity by a failure or reluctance to be clear about what we are saying. The following remarks are an attempt to clarify the form-content distinction as it applies to (at least some) works of art.

1. Philosophical questions about form and content express what are essentially conceptual problems. To talk about form and content is, in aesthetics, to talk—usually in the 'material mode'—about the logic of certain concepts, e.g., unity, or of different kinds of statements, what Professor Beardsley has called "form-statements" and "content-statements." [1]

To begin with Beardsley's distinction: a form-statement he defines as a description of relations among elements or complexes of elements within a work of art; "a content-statement is a description that is not a form-statement." As a way of characterizing the distinction between form and content in art this is surely wrong. It reflects the mistaken assumption that every feature of a work of art is an element either of its form or its content. Form and content, however, are neither exclusive (see below) nor exhaustive concepts. To describe a song as melancholy or a picture as dark is not to talk—certainly not directly—about either its form or its content, even if in explaining or justifying such remarks we are compelled to say something about the form and/or the content of the song or the picture. To describe a picture as a portrait or seascape, a play as a tragedy or comedy, is not clearly and obviously to make a content-statement about it, i.e., to describe its content as opposed to its form; nor is to describe a piece of music as a symphony, a poem as an ode, clearly and obviously to make a form-statement about it, i.e., to describe relations among elements within the work as opposed to saying anything about its content. Therefore, if we are to attempt to elucidate the form-content distinction in terms of a distinction between different kinds of statements, the distinction between form- and content-statements must be drawn differently from the way Beardsley draws it.

2. The word 'content' (or 'contents') means simply what is contained, and we can begin our elucidation of its aesthetic use with this rudimentary observation. Works of art, we might say, are like rooms or boxes in that they may contain many different things.[2] A content-statement about a room, then, is simply a statement about what is in it.

But this is ambiguous. Consider the following:

> (A) 'The room contains a sofa, three chairs, and a table.'
> (B) 'The sofa is covered with yellow silk, the chair seats with green leather, and the table is mahogany.'

or

> (B′) 'Every piece of furniture in this room cost less than a hundred dollars.'

Both (A) and (B) are *about* what is in the room; but (A) tells us, directly, what the room contains, while (B) is about the things, severally, that are in the room. (A) is about the *room* in a way that (B) is not. Content-statements like (A) may be called 'inventories' to distinguish them from content-statements like (B).[3]

Form-statements, on the other hand, singly or together, describe relations, arrangements, patterns, compositions, designs, structures:

> (C) 'The sofa stands along the east wall. To its left is the table. Across from the sofa are three chairs standing side by side.'

(C) is also, of course, about what is in the room; in the way (B) is, not in the way (A) is—although there are form-statements analogous to (A), e.g., 'The room is awkwardly arranged.' But this does not obliterate, nor need it blur, the distinction in question.

Statements similar to (A), (B), and (C) can be, and often are, made about works of art, and they provide the basis for the form-content distinction.

3. Works of art can be analyzed in different ways so as to yield discriminable elements of content (i.e., contents) of different types or kinds. A picture may be said to contain a table, a jug, some apples in a bowl; soft yellows, muted blues, firm but graceful lines, rounded forms with soft contours; a subtle arrangement of shapes and colors; signs of the painter's morbid preoccupation with the transience of things. A play may contain stock characters as well as declarative sentences; a poem, rhymed couplets as well as ironies. Even the 'same' item of content may be described in a variety of ways: a picture may be said to contain some apples, some spheroid masses, some circular shapes, some red spots. It is surely a misplaced formalism that insists on describing the contents of works of art only in a specialized 'formalistic' vocabulary.[4] Alternative descriptions are applicable, and only if we forget that different descriptions have different purposes are we likely to be impressed by the apparently paradoxical character of this fact; for example, that the same thing can be both an apple and yet not an apple but a circular red spot.

4. We are speaking, of course, of contents of works of art as objects of aesthetic vision or discrimination. Whether there is an 'ontological' distinction between works of art as physical or material objects and works of art as aesthetic objects, there is clearly some distinction. As material object, a statue may

contain so much bronze, so much tin, so much lead. But these metals are not contents of the statue as an object of aesthetic appreciation, though their tints, hues, and textures are.

5. There is another, and related, use of 'content' in aesthetics, and it is correlated with another, but related, sense of 'form.' 'Form' originally meant the shape or look of something (cf. *forma* in Latin), and it still bears this sense, as when we speak of a picture containing human forms or geometrical forms.[5] It was metaphorically extended, like *eidos* and *morphē* in Aristotle, to cover cases where the concept of shape would be literally inapplicable. In this sense, form is correlated with another concept, that of stuff or matter (*hylē*), e.g., the clay that the potter shapes or forms into a bowl. This too can be extended metaphorically, e.g., in logic, to cover cases where the concept of stuff or matter would be literally out of place.

More complex forms or shapes (like the form of a cross) can be construed as arrangements of simpler forms (squares, say), as in the following figure:

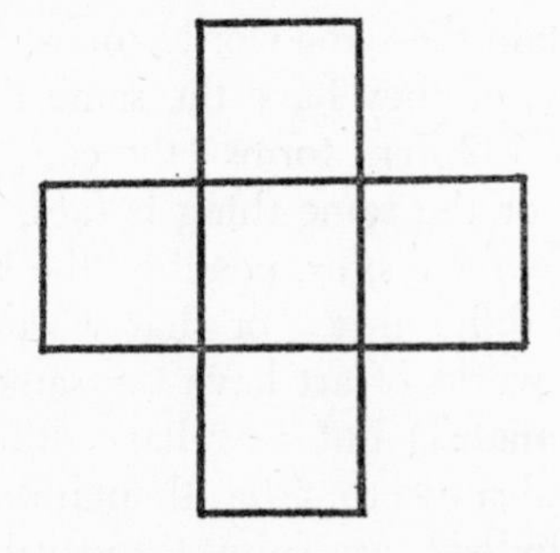

This shows the connection between form in the sense of 'shape' and form in the sense of 'arrangement.' The 'content' or 'matter' of the figure is five squares: it contains five squares; it is made or shaped out of five squares. This is the connection between content, or that which is contained, and matter, or that out of which something is made. But form (shape) and matter (stuff) vary independently. Any number of things may have the same shape or form and yet be made of different stuff, and the same stuff (clay, say) may be shaped successively in a number of different ways. Five squares may be arranged in an L-shape as well as in a cross, and a cross may be formed out of ten suitable triangles. It is also at this point that the distinction between *what* is said, depicted, presented, etc., and *how* it is said, depicted, presented, etc., connects with the distinction between form and content.

Now just as a potter may take a shapeless lump of clay and make a bowl, a pitcher, a vase, or a plate out of it, so the artist is sometimes described analogously as taking the same matter or content—be it the same words, images, colors, figures, tones, or the same story, subject, theme, thesis, or idea—and as working it up in one of a variety of possible ways. The adequacy of this metaphor to artistic creation or to works of art has been challenged—and rightly so, for there are differences as well as similarities—but it does call our attention to at least one feature of our talk about art, namely, that we often want to say that two or more works of art have the same content (they contain the same words, tones, or shapes, or they tell the same story, or they have the same theme or subject) but that they have different forms (the contents are arranged in different ways; or the same thing is said, the same subject depicted, in different ways; or, possibly, the same matter, e.g., bronze, is shaped differently); or that we often want to say that two or more works of art have the same form (they are both sonnets or sonatas) but they have different content(s).

6. Content and subject matter, though related, are not the same thing; nor, indeed, are subject and subject matter. The *Iliad* contains extended similes, but extended similes are not part of its subject matter and are certainly not its subject. The Trojan War is part of its subject matter; its subject is "the wrath of Achilles which, according to the will of Zeus, brought so much suffering to the Achaeans and sent the noble souls of many to Hades." The crucifixion may be the subject of a picture; the Roman soldier gazing up at the dying Jesus is part of its subject matter.

The subject of a work of art is, roughly, what it is *of* or *about*—the death of the Virgin, the sea (Debussy's *La Mer*), the Fall of Man, the harbor at Honfleur, Mrs. Siddons as the Muse of Tragedy. Any object, event, incident, person, or state of affairs, real or imaginary, may be the subject of a work of art.[6] Like contents generally, the subject of a work of art may be identified or described in a variety of way. A given motion picture may be said to be about alcoholism; about a woman who drinks; about a poor girl who is seduced by a rich man and, when he refuses to marry her, takes to drink; about the psychosocial causes of alcoholism; etc. Subject matter, again roughly, consists of discriminable items of content identifiable by natural descriptions, i.e., the sort of descriptions used to identify the objects and events of nature. While every work of art has content(s), not every work of art has a subject or subject matter. And some works of art—Brancusi's "Bird in Space," Debussy's *Nuages*—have a subject but no subject matter, or subject matter but no subject.[7]

7. Form-statements about a work of art are statements about the way(s) in which items of content are arranged or composed, when they are not simply about the way material is shaped. They "describe internal *relations* among the elements or among complexes within the object." (Beardsley, *ibid.*) The emphasis belongs on the word 'relations,' but the character of the elements related must not be overlooked. Relations are relations *of* elements, and sometimes the character of the elements (partly) determines the form. Form, in other words, is not always a function of just the relations considered in abstraction from the elements related. This is especially so where the question is one of the identity or differences of forms. Suppose I take a penny, a nickel, a dime, and a quarter (call them 'P,' 'N,' 'D,' and 'Q,' respectively) and I arrange them successively in the following three ways:

P D   Q D

Q N   N P

N D Q P

The third arrangement is clearly different from the first two, and it is the relations that make the difference; for in the third arrangement all the coins are in a line, and this is not true of either of the first two arrangements. But is the form of the second arrangement different from the form of the first? Yes and no. Insofar as we consider merely that the coins, irrespective of denomination, are arranged in a square, the second arrangement is the same as the first. But insofar as we consider that in the first arrangement P is in the upper left-hand corner and is diagonally across from N, while in the second Q is in the upper left-hand corner and is diagonally across from P, and so on, the arrangements are different.[8]

8. It is not always clear whether a given statement is about the form or the content of a work of art. Apart from the more familiar obscurities of expression, this is due to the fact that the same sentence(s) may be used to make a form-statement or a content-statement or a conjunction of both. Consider the following simple case: 'This Mondrian contains nothing but red, yellow, and blue rectangles geometrically arranged.' We can exhibit the use of this sentence to make a statement about content by rewriting it as follows: 'This Mondrian contains nothing but red-and-yellow-and-blue-rectangles-geometrically-arranged.' This is different from: 'This Mondrian contains nothing but red, yellow, and blue rectangles, and they are geometrically arranged.' Here the first conjunct is about the contents of the picture; the second, about its form.

9. We are now in a position to explain the origin of, and to resolve, what we might call 'Weitz's Paradox': that there is no difference between the form and the content of a work of art.[9] The content of a work of art, says Weitz, is *all* that is in it: "all the elements, expressive characteristics and the relations that obtain among them." This is to move from a truism to a paradox. It is truistic to say that the contents of a box are all that is in it. But notice that Weitz includes the relations too; the relations among the contents are also contents. Hence form becomes a part of content: "there is *no* distinction on

this usage between form and content in art."[10] This is the paradox.

But why include the relations among the contents in the inventory of the contents? If one were asked to make an inventory of a room he would not itemize, in addition to the chairs, lamps, tables, and so on, the relations among them. The relation between a desk and a chair is not part of the contents of a room; it is not *in* the room in the way the desk and chair are. (And, of course, it is not *outside* of the room either.)

What is it about our talk about art that leads to Weitz's paradox? It is, I think, the capacity of statements about content to 'absorb' or include references to relations among contents. Consider the following partial description of Vermeer's "The Cook": 'The picture contains a woman in a yellow blouse pouring milk from a red jug into an earthen bowl. She is sharply silhouetted against a brightly lighted wall.' This can be read as a conjunction of a content-statement and a form-statement: 'The picture contains a-woman-in-a-yellow-blouse-pouring-milk-from-a-red-jug-into-an-earthen-bowl and the woman is sharply silhouetted against a brightly lighted wall.' It can also be read as a complex content-statement: 'The picture contains a-woman-in-a-yellow-blouse-pouring-milk-from-a-red-jug-into-an-earthen-bowl-and-sharply-silhouetted against-a-brightly-lighted-wall.' Anything that can be said to be in a picture can be included in a statement of its contents. But among the things that can be said to be in a picture are 'complexes' (a-woman-in-a-yellow-blouse-sharply-silhouetted-against-a-brightly-lighted-wall). A complex is not simply a conjunction of elements, i.e., something properly described by a conjunction the conjuncts of which may be arranged in just any order; it is an arrangement of elements, something into the proper description of which relational expressions must enter. Hence the presence of relations—between the woman and the wall, the jug and the bowl—in the description of contents.

But the whole picture is also an arrangement of elements and hence can be treated as a complex—the limiting case.

When this is done, we get Weitz's paradox: the relations are now 'in' the picture; they have been absorbed into a description of its contents. But in this, the limiting case, the complex is not *in* the picture, part of its content; it *is* the picture!

10. Form-statements may describe internal relations among elements or complexes within works of art, but at least two things will count as describing a relation. We may say that A and B are in a certain relation, e.g., that A is to the right of B. We may also characterize the relation that A and B are in, e.g., say that A and B are awkwardly arranged. To speak of a sofa as being placed opposite three chairs is one thing; to speak of the arrangement of sofa and chairs as balanced, another. There are thus at least two kinds of form-statements.

The nature of the logical relation between them is a topic of philosophical dispute.[11] One thing seems clear, however: relations between elements of content in a work of art are at least necessary conditions of such formal properties as unity, harmony, and coherence. As Mrs. Hungerland has observed of the concept of unity, it "is restricted in its application to patterns, compositions, designs—that is to say, to elements considered as related by more than mere compresence in a work of art." [12] A single unmodulated tone, a uniform patch of color cannot properly be said to be balanced, harmonious, unified, integrated, coherent, etc. Notice how out of place it is to speak of a typical Arp sculpture—one in which the only relevant form is shape—as unified or coherent.

15. Aesthetic formalism is the view that in art form alone, and content only insofar as it determines form, but not subject or subject matter as such, is aesthetically important.[13] Formalism, however, is of two sorts: (1) the claim that in art only the form, that is, the shape (where that is the only relevant form) or the relations among elements of content (and those elements only insofar as they affect the relations), is aesthetically important; (2) the claim that in art only such second-order properties as harmony, unity, balance, proportion, coherence, and the like (the ancient canons of beauty) are aesthetically

important. Relations among the elements of a work of art, however, have, as such, no inherent aesthetic importance. To say that one admires, is pleased by, or likes a work of art because one element bears a certain relation to (is to the right of, rhymes with, repeats, contrasts with) another is not yet to explain one's reaction in such a way that we can definitely count it as aesthetic. There must be something *about* the relation that prompts the admiration, pleasure, or whatever. The form (in this sense) must, to use Bell's word, be "significant." But to be 'significant' shapes or relations (or elements-in-relation) need not provoke a peculiarly aesthetic emotion; they need only to be characterizable by some such predicate as 'balanced,' 'powerful,' 'delicate,' 'lifeless,' or 'vivid.'

To put the point another way: A work of art may be described formalistically in at least two ways. We may say simply that certain elements or complexes are related in certain ways: this theme follows that; this color contrasts with that; the jug is behind the basket of apples; the figure of the woman is sharply silhouetted against the brightly lighted wall; the third line rhymes with the fifth and the seventh. Such descriptions, *by themselves,* have no aesthetic significance; they cannot, by themselves, fulfill the function of explaining one's reaction to, or experience of, a work of art in such a way that we can count that reaction as aesthetic. They are, we might say, *mere* descriptions. On the other hand, if we describe a composition as unified (tightly-knit), a color contrast as subtle, a tension between two themes as powerful, the relation between two masses as one of delicate balance, then our descriptions have aesthetic significance.[14] They may figure in an explanation of one's reaction to a work of art in such a way that we should have to classify that reaction—at least to that extent—as aesthetic.

But the two sorts of description are not unrelated. The first sort of description may be used, particularly in the presence of the work of art, to make a case for the truth of the second. In this way they borrow or acquire aesthetic significance, and for this reason they play an important part in our talk about art.

NOTES

1. Monroe C. Beardsley, *Aesthetics: Problems in the Philosophy of Criticism* (New York, 1958), pp. 166–67.

2. They are unlike rooms and boxes in that they must contain something. A room with nothing in it is still a room; a work of art with nothing in it, an 'empty' work of art, is no work of art at all. (There are a few exceptions that prove, i.e., test this rule: e.g., Robert Rauschenberg's 'White Paintings' and Jose Garcia Villa's 'poem' "The Emperor's New Clothes"—which consists of nothing but the title on a blank page.)

3. The notion of contents—though not, note, that of content —is intimately connected with the practice of making lists, inventories, and tables.

4. But see Arnold Isenberg's 'Perception, Meaning, and the Subject-Matter of Art,' *The Journal of Philosophy*, XLI (1944), 561–75, for a statement of at least one use of 'formalistic' descriptions of content: "*In the presence of the picture* certain geometrical designations . . . may assist our vision to grasp the unique design where an inventory of subject-matter would leave it fixed on the general type of object or situation."

5. Cf. Professor Schapiro's remark about the Sistine ceiling: "Here the forms have become for us the main content of the work. . . ." The form of some Arp, Hepworth, and Brancusi sculptures is predominantly form in this sense. And where this sense of form is foremost, it is odd to speak of contents—though not necessarily of content.

6. Is the subject 'in' or 'outside of' the work of art? Both. Louis XIV is in Rigaud's portrait of him, but the man in Rigaud's portrait is the same king who built Versailles—which is not to imply that the picture of Louis XIV built Versailles. Whether the Trojan War actually occurred or not, it 'exists' not only in the *Iliad*. It is integral to the notion of the subject of a work of art that whatever it may be it must be *possible* for it to 'exist' outside a work of art—

possible for it to be the subject of something, e.g., a conversation, that is not a work of art.

7. Sometimes the terms 'subject' and 'subject matter' apply to (denote) the same thing. The subject of a Redon still life is a vase of flowers, and that is its subject matter too.

8. I have here discussed only spatial arrangements (forms), but what I have said may be generalized to cover nonspatial arrangements as well. Its application to works of art should also be obvious. Two sonnets, for example, may be said to have the same form insofar as we consider only the rhyme scheme as the relevant determinant. But insofar as we consider the words rhymed and their relations to the other words of the sonnet we may want to say that every sonnet has its own unique form.

9. See Morris Weitz, *Philosophy of the Arts* (Cambridge, Mass., 1950), Ch. 3.

10. Actually there is a distinction, even in this usage, between form and content; form becomes a part of content, but not all of content is form. *Op. cit.*, pp. 47 and 48.

A reverse move is sometimes made by formalists who, like Clive Bell, conceive the form of a work of art as "lines and colors combined in a particular way." *Art* (New York, 1958), p. 17. Here content, or at least part of it (lines and colors), has become a part of the form. But this is justified by the fact that, as we noted above, the form of a work of art may be a function of certain relevant properties of the items related as well as of the relations among them.

11. For two views on the matter, see Frank Sibley, 'Aesthetic Concepts,' *Philosophical Review,* LXVIII (1959), 421–50, and Monroe C. Beardsley, *op. cit.,* 190–209.

12. Isabel C. Hungerland, *Poetic Discourse* (Berkeley and Los Angeles, 1958), pp. 74–75.

13. As Clive Bell puts it (*op. cit.*, p. 27), "The representative element in a work of art may or may not be harmful; always it is [aesthetically] irrelevant."

14. Cf. Frank Sibley, 'Aesthetics and the Looks of Things,' *Journal of Philosophy,* LVI (1959), 905–15.

4

The Dogma of the Work of Art Itself

MORTIMER R. KADISH
Western Reserve University

ONE CALLS a doctrine a dogma if, though unquestioned, its implications are dubious while its alternative is conceivable. I shall urge that doctrine to be a dogma which makes the proper object of artistically relevant controversy "the work of art itself," and a dogma of considerable significance for the philosophy of criticism at that. I shall proceed by commenting generally on the nature of the doctrine and of its alternative and then attempt the principal task of showing specifically how the doctrine affects the three lead-off papers of this volume.

Obviously, a dogma may turn out right. But its rightness is suspect. There will be cause to see why.

I

First, then, for the doctrine and the alternative which, foreclosed, helps define the doctrine:

1. When one critic tells another to pay attention "to the work of art itself" he may pretend that his colleague has suddenly and exasperatingly shifted the discussion to something else than the work of art, but that is for emphasis. Both know that what he actually wants is for the other fellow to say relevant things about the object of criticism; he is convinced that relevant things have not been said; and he hopes to remind the other fellow of the kind of thing that ought to be said if one considers the object of criticism as a work of art.

Usages of this sort must not be allowed to cover the doctrine of the work of art itself with their own innocence.

The *doctrine* of the work of art itself is invoked after one further, if usually unnoticed, step in the argument has been taken: when the appeal to "the work of art itself" occurs not simply as a *reminder* to come back to Erin but to *justify* the relevance and force of a statement about the work of art. For the doctrine takes the work of art as a standard object such that for all artistically relevant questions concerning its nature or value, examining that object with sufficient care and in a standard way will decide the issue. Questions about such matters as the artist's intentions are declared out of bounds because the scanning process cannot decide them. Or, as it is sometimes held, whatever is present in the work of art is relevant, whatever is not, not.[1] The work of art as an object of critical controversy is complete; if not complete, defective.

What kind of object would such a standard, such a complete object be? One very obvious answer is—an "aesthetic object." One considers the work of art itself as an aesthetic object because if the work of art is immediately given in perception as aesthetic objects are supposed to be, then, on examining the work of art itself, one will be able to offer "objective" reasons for one's judgment at once artistically relevant and requiring no appeal to a source outside the work of art.[2]

Since when dealing with familiar works of art we agree, if not in detail, at least on the kind of thing being examined, differences are for the most part resolvable by one party or the other to a dispute *re*scanning "the aesthetic object" under the direction of the opponent. The headache in handling aesthetic objects and, indeed, any version of the work of art as a standard object, is how to resolve disputes over unfamiliar objects or familiar objects for which the rescanning process is itself in question.

2. Accordingly, the work of art itself as an object of criticism does not have for its significant opposite something

other than the work of art, but the work of art in relation. Instead of the work of art as complete, bearing on the face of it, as it were, all that a properly trained critic need know, the alternative doctrine of the work of art in relation holds the work of art incomplete, requiring to be put in proper relation by critics whose qualifications consist in a trained capacity to make decisions on the propriety of relations. Hence the work of art exists for critics who wish their statements open to a possible exception, in "proper" relation.

The assumption is that there may exist legitimate differences of opinion that references to an elite's taste mask rather than resolve—differences over what to contemplate in the picture, over just what did happen in *Hamlet,* what the poem "really" said, how the music is to be interpreted. For if I want to understand the "form" of a picture, I do not merely stare at it. I compare it with this picture or that, consider it in this artistic tradition or that, as a departure from this style or a continuation of that. I consider it as an event in art, in virtue of my knowledge of art. It is not merely that some such procedure describes how I go about reaching my understanding of the picture's form, as though the understanding were consequent upon the procedure as joy upon marijuana. The statement of relations my procedure offers defines the object with which an opposing critic takes issue—for purposes of artistically relevant controversy, defines "what the picture is."

Accordingly, the heart of the alternative doctrine to the work of art itself is that rather than "unfold" or "disclose" the aesthetic meaning of standard objects, we construe what those objects are to be on grounds which *include* scannings and rescannings of the work of art but are by no means exhausted by them. "Aesthetic object" then describes the status of an object of criticism *after* the object's construal has been settled, and the work of art becomes familiar. But the doctrine of the work of art in proper relation does not advance the preposterous view that the appreciations of critics only come after the work of art has been established or that they are irrelevant to the judgmental process of deciding the nature of the pictures being inspected, of the poems read, of the music listened to. One doesn't call important in the Sistine Chapel what one has found in a still life unless one has seen and contemplated both. But merely to have seen and contemplated both is not enough to make the judgment, not when critics differ.

All in all, the doctrine of the work of art in proper relation hangs upon the possibility of an artistically relevant controversy, genuine in the sense that there are rules for making points. Perhaps, indeed, there are no such rules, or if there are any, they are inadequate to the purposes of critical controversy. Let the argument stand, therefore, merely that *if* justification in artistically relevant decisions is possible, it seems likely that some version of the work of art in proper relation is correct and the doctrine of the work of art itself poor metacriticism in significant respects.

II

Now, using the doctrine of the work of art itself and its alternative as tools, we are in a position to assess the papers of Professors Schapiro, Beardsley, and Hospers, all three, as variations of a basic strategy: the strategy which takes the doctrine of the work of art itself as a basic assumption for the analysis of the arts and criticism.

1. Writes Professor Schapiro: "To see the work as it is, to know it in its fullness, is a goal of collective criticism extending over generations. This task is sustained by new points of view that make possible the revelation of significant features overlooked by other observers. In all these successive judgments there is an appeal to the freshly seen structure and qualities of the work."

Over the generations a "collective criticism" uncovers the "significant features" of the work of art itself. At the same time, it is insisted, judgments of coherence and incoherence, completeness and incompleteness, are "often guided by norms of style which are presented as universal requirements of art and inhibit recognition or order in works which violate the canons of form in that style," norms which are "constantly justified in practice by perceptions—supposedly simple unprejudiced apprehension of a quality—which are in fact directed by these norms." Would it not seem that while on Professor Schapiro's metacritical theory, criticism is collective and its results cumulative, his experience of critical practice asserts instead that criticism "extending over generations" is not collective and its results not cumulative? For he has norms of style vary over generations, "disclosures" made in virtue of those varied norms often mutually cancelling and norms themselves, at least in part, self-justifying.

The moral is not some easy relativism that dodges all the interesting problems of criticism. Poker hands are not cumulative either from one hand to another, but each hand has quite determinable better and worse strategies. "Queen's pawn to queen's four" is not an unjustifiable move because it is a good move in one game, bad in a second, and indifferent in a third. The moral is very far from being that the history of criticism, taken seriously, precludes more or less constant rules for the conduct of artistically relevant controversy.

The moral, I suggest, is that Professor Schapiro is much wiser than his philosophy. Dropping the rhetoric of the work of art itself and its unnecessary and misguided commitments to wagers on the future course of criticism, Professor Schapiro, of course, has a good deal to say about the process of construing works of art. The nature of works of art is *not* decided at a glance or even by the most prolonged staring; they are decided in a process of decision-making and argument which may indeed for any given run reach over generations. They *are* built-up decision by decision as knowledge and exploration of past works enlarges and deepens the field in which they exist and as present art lends, as people say, "new meanings" to earlier works. Standards of Perfection, Coherence, and Unity of Form and Content—or, in another version, of Unity, Complexity, and Intensity—are *not* after all for purposes of artistically relevant controversy preset principles which works of art in virtue of their specific characteristics exhibit or do not exhibit in greater or less degree.[3] Such standards are in fact derivative, post hoc affairs; and in a way quite appropriately vague, enable us to allude to certain kinds of previous experience which then function to build further decisions rather than as a court of appeals.

All this is what one would suspect, starting with the work of art in proper relation. The failure of Professor Schapiro to compose his insight within the doctrine of the work of art itself constitutes, on this reading, the chief virtue of the article.

2. Professor Beardsley's problem, he tells us, "has to do with the nature and validity of critical interpretation statements"; and his article lists a series of such statements without any acknowledgment that the construction he places upon them might require some defense. "I am talking about interpreting works of art (not scores or scripts) . . ." he says. "Definition: to interpret is verbally to unfold or disclose meaning." Since the problem of "unfolding" or "disclosing" verbally the "meaning" of finished or totally presented works of art ("not scores or scripts") does not follow immediately from a bare reading of his listed statements, it seems that he has assumed the doctrine of the work of art itself. On the assumption of that doctrine he must both make sense of interpretation-statements as such and (although a difference is not acknowledged) establish the existence of limits within which in specific criticism interpretation-statements might rightly be confined.

A. To achieve these ends he has considered "two general ways of viewing art" as theories of interpretation and compared them: "According to the Significance Theory . . . all works of art have a meaning . . . and therefore all works of art require to be interpreted." According to the Immanence Theory "no work of art, taken by itself (is) interpretable"—"The music is not a sign of anything at all, but simply an object or event in its own right with its own shape and qualities." But the two theories do not differ as he proposes they do:

a. Significance and Immanence Theories cannot distinguish differently, as they are required, artistically relevant interpretation-statements in the class of interpretation-statements. Because every interpretation formulable in the Significance Theory is formulable in the Immanence Theory, and vice versa, they are not "theories" establishing the "limits of interpretation" at all. If the Immanence Theory will have it that a lump of metal being melted down "has" at a given stage "qualities of humility, contrition or perhaps drive or power," it is hard to see why a Significance Theory cannot have the lump of metal representing, expressing, denoting, signifying, meaning—whichever seems most comfortable—those same qualities. If in the Significance Theory the visual design denotes madness, in the Immanence Theory the visual design "has" the quality of madness at least as obviously as the lump of metal "had" the quality of humility. Moreover, what will not work on one theory will not work on the other. If it is difficult to see what evidence could show that the music "refers" to the fear of death, it is no less difficult to see how one could establish that the music has about it the quality of the fear of death. If I cannot state "the object in the painting symbolizes the depersonalization of modern man" in the Immanence Theory with any conviction, neither do I quite know what it means in the Significance Theory.

Therefore, if the Immanence Theory, as formulated by Professor Beardsley, rejects such statements as "visual design denotes madness" the reason may only be that that theory has been defined so that inevitably it throws out sentences in which Significance Theory verbs—like "denotes"—occur. The strength of the rules for reaching agreement on such sentences has nothing to do with it.

b. Beardsley would have it that the two theories are "at bottom, not descriptions of what in fact prevails, but recommendations about how works of art are best apprehended." Assuming the truth of (a) this must mean not that the two theories justify different interpretation-statements, as Professor Beardsley thinks, but at most a second thing, which he also believes: that offering an interpretation-statement on the Significance Theory we look "away" from the work of art (towards what it denotes, etc.) while offering one on the Immanence Theory we keep focussed on the work of art as such.

But even this much will not wash except, perhaps, as an empirical generalization based on what appear to be the tastes of people who prefer the Significance Theory: they are suspect of being interested in other things than art. Recommendations to look "at" the work of art or "through" it to something else are not entailed, in some required loose sense of "entail," by *either* theory. Even if it be true that in some sense "the visual design denotes madness," the Significance-Theorist may quite consistently reject the recommendation "On seeing the design, consider the nature of madness!" He may and, in fact, will, if a real, live Significance-Theorist concerned with art rather than an alienist seeking symptoms, prefer to say, "See that design denoting madness and how it does it!" And while the Immanence-Theorist no doubt will enjoin us to "See the humility of that partially melted down statue," he may nonetheless, and consistently then, go on to direct our attention to the quality of humility.

Hence, whatever the ultimate logical and metaphysical commitments of the two "theories"—and I am far from urging that such commitments do not exist—in the context of metacriticism those "theories" function as alternative languages for expressing the same informational and decisional content, not as theories at all.

B. Why does Professor Beardsley think otherwise? Finally, I would suggest, because of a basic predicament: As an observer of critics he knows that critics actually do interpret works of art and that not all interpretations hold water—while simultaneously, having accepted the doctrine of the work of art itself he also knows that what is not "there" in the work of art itself is no part of the work of art.[4] In consequence, though critical *descriptions* stay in the logical clear, critical "interpretations" become problems in principle. How explain the relevance of interpretations? How determine *which* are relevant? Since all sorts of statements are clearly justifiable, which are irrelevant to a controversy simply distinguishing interpretation-statements by the degree to which a hope exists of their justification does not suggest the criteria in virtue of which such statements become relevant to the artistically relevant controversy. Hence distinguishing critical interpretations which are acceptable from those which are not requires shoring—the intervention of general "theories" of art to do the job, in this instance the Significance and Immanence Theories. These, it is hoped (mistakenly, as argued in A, a), will furnish the distinctions in principle necessary to sustain an opinion on the kind of interpretation-statement that might be relevant. And then, finally, since one is dealing with the work of art itself—that complete, hard object with no edges on which to hang an "interpretation"—we are required to weigh the two theories by the strength of our preference for *approaching* the work of art itself in one way or another. Since, even in Professor Beardsley's view, as I would suppose, the question of whether we are interested in works of art or what they somehow indicate or point to depends upon decisions made outside the artistically relevant controversy, the inclusion or exclusion of interpretation-statements, not covert descriptions, ends as arbitrary a matter as one would expect on the doctrine of the work of art itself.

C. That it is by no means apparent that it must so end, assuming the alternative to the doctrine of the work of art itself, is the nub of the argument. If the characteristics of the object of criticism are not simply there to begin with for anyone with eyes to see, if that object exists in proper relation, then construing the (non-familiar) work of art actually *demands* interpretation. The critic as interpreter has a vocation: to propose and justify decisions to take the work of art in one field of relations or another. And significant interpretation-statements in the context of the critical controversy are seen to be neither those statements over which controversy is finally superfluous ("The painting includes a mauve elliptical area") nor those over which it is silly, like those cloud interpretations Hamlet proposed for Polonius. Indeed, the interpretation-statements which will be worth discussing will be those which, like the more workmanlike books on *Hamlet,* set themselves to *deciding* (not "unfolding" or "disclosing," as though Hamlet were in *Hamlet* like a homunculus) what happens in *Hamlet* —the "nature" of the play.

Interpretation-statements, then, are sensible when there is a specific need for them. Granted that in these lines there has been at most a pointing to that need rather than an analysis of it. Still, they suggest that if Professor Beardsley's paper missed considering such statements in relation to their function, that was not the consequence of the nature of works of art or criticism but of a choice of doctrine.

3. Professor Hospers' problem of the relationship between art and reality may, perhaps, be regarded as a special case of Beardsley's problem of interpretation: to explain how statements placing the work of art in a certain relation to "reality" may be explicable in terms of characteristics of the work of art itself. The strategy is to seek "the distinctive medium and mode of presentation" of the major art-media for the sake of some code or set of rules of universal scope through which the reality relations of specific works of art become intelligible; and success depends upon the possibility of transcending any local or historical or "external" considerations in interpreting the work of art. Is the strategy successful?

A. Professor Hospers essays his question, "What exactly is the relation of art to reality?" by beginning with the "art-medium" in which it is most obvious that there is a "relation of art to reality," literature, and seeks to determine what there is distinctive in the relation of literature as such to reality. And it turns out, of course, that literature as literature exhibits the "closest relation between art and reality: the relation between characters in literature and people in life." Surely, whether a work of literature exhibits "fidelity to human nature" depends upon no conventional patterns, no relation of one play to another, of one novel to another, of novel to history and the like, but upon whether a person "of type T, in circumstance C, [would] do act A." There is but space for the following brief observations:

First, observe that whatever the fate of "art" in general, "literature" has become a "closed" concept. Just as to understand and appraise "comedy" and "tragedy" you need to know the rules of "comedy" or "tragedy" as such, so to understand and appraise the reality relation of specific literature you need to know the principle of that relation for literature as such. Establishing literature in its "distinctive" character according to fixed rules rescues the *poem itself* or the novel itself or the play itself from an arbitrariness of interpretation otherwise as inevitable as it is unacceptable.

The first point, then, is that Professor Hospers' strategy for handling reality relations in literature does not happen by accident; the second is that for a variety of reasons, it won't do. The principle fault is the consequence of the strategy. Literature once taken as relatively fixed in a prime characteristic, a crucial failure to appreciate the resources of the artist in doing literature follows. There is, in this short space I can only repeat, nothing inherently implausible about a non-Hosperian,[5] non-Aristotelian plot in which a "mad" (gratuitous?) act is performed at the beginning by a person carefully established as a routine, conventional chap, whose reason and purpose remain a mystery, however the other characteristics seek to plumb it, throughout the book. It requires only a touch of imagination and an acquaintance with contemporary literature to see that the acceptability of the story depends upon *how* the author writes it, not upon the "facts" of human nature [6] —and that the same psychological burden may be made by an appropriate writer totally "credible" or totally "incredible." In short, in showing the relationship of literature to reality it does seem as though Professor Hospers overlooks the literature in order to hand us a conception of literary credibility more appropriate to a psychoanalytic case study.

I think it fair to say, therefore, that while critics do indeed object to "tampering much" with "human nature," the judgment "X has tampered with human nature" is not to be taken as a straight factual charge such that if the writer is guilty he has done an unliterary act, but rather as a kind of summary judgment summarizing whether a person who writes about human beings does well: whether he has said the "important" things, whether he has done so convincingly, what the whole thing adds up to, etc. Hence the command "Thou shalt not tamper with human nature" is no test or criterion unless the person who utters it intends to read his preferences of style and content into the nature of literature as such.

B. Turning to the nonverbal arts, Professor Hospers wonders how they may have the "expressive properties" they undoubtedly do. His answer is (for painting) that "there is a 'natural expressiveness' of certain colors and other sensory items which is invariant from person to person and culture to culture." "Associations universal in the history of the human race" now become the code or rules for determining the affective significance of the work of art itself; and once again, an artistically independent rule set will not do, though required for the same kind of reason a rule was worked up for literature.

For, first, there seems something as wrong with the notion of perceptual elements in art possessing expressiveness prior to art, as there did with a literary criterion which in itself had nothing to do with art. Perceptual elements do not possess independent weight, as Professor Hospers seems to suggest, *in art,* even though it be the case (*if* it be the case) that people find red "intrinsically" dramatic, or horizontal lines restful when confronted with red blotches or horizontal lines. It would seem obvious that the dramatic or recessive character of a color depends *in painting* upon what the painter does with it, that the "restfulness" of the horizontal line, if we approach the picture fixed in our attitudes to find the line restful, may throw the entire picture out of joint. Hence it is false that the artist "can rely on . . . universality of affect in creating his works." Only the need to rely on the work of art itself makes it seem otherwise.

Next, it seems clear that the effort to show how the percepts of *art* are suffused with affect ignores the possibility that even if the elements of painting are determined by "associations" in their affective quality, the problem of determining the affective quality of works of art is the problem of determining that quality for total works of art not for elements. Even if there exists a kind of vocabulary of paint and line, where's the syntax, the pragmatics? Surely one can not reason from the vocabulary to the message. Indeed, it is notorious that line and color may be used in a relation which leaves an *affective* void. Professor Hospers' hope here would no doubt be to seek syntax in media, as has been done before; he is himself, by confession, exploring art-media. Yet an "art-medium" the requirements of which are set up independently of the traditions for the use of media surely places too much hope upon the sheer possibilities of physical things settling practical decisions for their own use.

Hence, even to explain the relationship of painting to affect seems to have as a necessary condition some account of the existence of painting in a matrix of art—in proper relation.

III

We may count the doctrine of the work of art itself a dogma, then, because (a) a plausible alternative exists, which is the work of art in proper relation to other art; (b) because its acceptance leads to commitments which, as was seen in the specific cases of Professors Schapiro, Beardsley, and Hospers are at the least dubious; and (c) because in all instances the doctrine seems to be taken as a mattter of course, quite as though there were neither alternatives nor difficulties.

The way in which it threads three papers selected independently and in a more or less random way may perhaps measure the prevalence of the dogma.

NOTES

1. Cf. Wimsatt and Beardsley, in "The Intuition Fallacy," p. 4 of *The Verbal Icon,* W. K. Wimsatt (Noonday). "Poetry is a feat of style by which a complex of meaning is handled all at once.

Poetry succeeds because all or most of what is said is implied or relevant; what is irrelevant has been excluded, like lumps from pudding and 'bugs' from machinery."

2. See M. C. Beardsley, *Aesthetics* (New York: Harcourt, Brace and Co., 1958), Ch. X, Sec. 24.

3. See Beardsley, supra, Ch. X, for an illustration of an attempt to take such "principles" as canons or standards to which critics can appeal in justifying their opinions.

4. See Footnote 1, supra.

5. Writes Hospers, "Aristotle's test of a characterization, or something very like it, is in fact constantly employed by literary critics in evaluating works of literature. . . ."

6. What are the facts of human nature? For writer and critic alike, those "facts" may be precisely what is at issue.

5

Imagination, Reality, and Art

ARTHUR C. DANTO
Columbia University

I

When F and G are what I shall term *contrasting predicates,* then, whenever F is predicated of a, it is implied by a rule of language that a is *non-G,* and conversely. Contrasting predicates must each have sensible application to all the same things, so it is sensible, if false, that a is G in case it is true (and *a fortiori* sensible) to say that a is F. But care is required when a predicate points multiple contrasts. Thus we contrast "is real" both with "is fake" and "is imaginary." But since nothing which could sensibly be called "fake" could also sensibly be called "imaginary," the predicate "is real" must range over distinct classes of things according to the contrast we are pointing through its use.

In each of its contrasts (and there are perhaps many), "is real" has a *rectifying force.* It serves to allay suspicions of inauthenticity or of fantasy. But this suggests that it is possible always to mistake for its opposite whatever "is real" applies to sensibly: one may mistake a real for a fake flower, or a real for an imaginary animal. But the latter mistake is logically distinct from the first, inasmuch as the world contains fake entities but not imaginary ones. A false friend, to be sure, is not a friend, but he remains flesh and blood when his perfidy is revealed, while an *imaginary* friend is constituted of the stuff that dreams are made on. But if a real friend, in contrast with an imaginary one, is fleshly, do we want, by the principle of our first paragraph, to say that "is imaginary" has sensible application to material bodies? If we do, then the claim collapses that nothing may sensibly be called both "fake" and "imaginary," and it becomes sensible (as it is not by a rule of usage) to say that the world contains imaginary entities. We restore linguistic (and ontological) propriety by restricting "is imaginary" to such things as have referential properties, i.e., to pictures, descriptions, images, and the like. And it is these which "is real" will range over when it is used in contrast with "is imaginary." Once more, mistakes are possible as between the real and imaginary, but they are mistakes in reference: an imaginary *i* is an *i* which lacks in the space-time world the sort of counterpart which a real *i* has. It is in this respect that Oz is an imaginary country and the hippogriff an imaginary beast: they respectively lack, in contrast with Ghana and mandrills, counterparts in space and time.

It is perhaps convenient to think of "real" and "imaginary" on the model of "true" and "false," though that latter pair is doubly ambiguous, since "true" will mean different things according to whether "false" is synonymous with "fake" or not. There are false fronts and false eyelashes, and hence true (read "authentic") ones as well: but a false sentence is not a bogus sentence: a sentence must come up to the mark as a sentence before we can sensibly raise the question of its truth or falsity. The real is distinguished from the factitious by some intrinsic difference which serves as a criterion for telling them apart. We differentiate between true and false objects by examining the objects themselves. But we do not, special instances apart, differentiate between true and false sentences by examining the *sentences* themselves. And similarly with the real and the imaginary: a picture of a hippogriff seems no less likely to have counterparts than a picture of a coelocanth. Nothing intrinsic marks an imaginary from a real idea unless one believes in ontological arguments. This was recognized by Descartes who knew that by the mere scrutiny of the images in his mind he could not otherwise infer to counterparts. We distinguish real from imaginary *i's* by external criteria, just as we distinguish true from false sentences. Only one already familiar with the world, as children are not, can effect a differentiation with any promise of reliability. The strong sense for the imaginary, which we ascribe to children, is more correctly diagnosed as a weak familiarity with the world.

Now if the real *i* is the *i* with counterparts, and if the *only* difference between a real and an imaginary *i* is the existence of a counterpart for the former, then, if it is always the case that real and imaginary *i's* are intrinsically indiscernible, it should follow that imaginary *i's* are not utterly out of correspondence with the world. A false sentence should sound plausible or it could not deceive anyone who is familiar with the world: it must sound as though it were true. This means that imaginary *i's* must resemble real *i's* sufficiently, or we should be able to distinguish between them on *intrinsic* grounds, e.g., we could tell that there *could not be* a counterpart for these. This, to be sure, presupposes once again a familiarity with the world: if we were not familiar with the counterparts of the real *i's*, we would have no criterion of implausibility to be traduced by framers of imaginary *i's* (e.g., arch-Cartesian deceivers).

Consider in this regard imaginary portraits. These will be portraits stylistically indiscernible from real portraits, only lacking counterparts in the world of depictables. It ought to be impossible, by the mere inspection of their surfaces, to tell imaginary from real portraits.[1] This means that imaginary portraits must satisfy all the same criteria of mimeticity as real ones, i.e., at most two eyes to a face, distributed bilaterally, etc. And no less important, any *aesthetic* predicate which applies to real portraits will apply equally to imaginary ones, for these are, as it were, syntactical rather than semantical features of pictures. Both real and imaginary portraits may be lifelike, vivacious, hard, soft, moving, well-composed, and the like. A crude portraitist is no less heavy-handed in depicting real than in painting imaginary persons, while Rubens is no less master of illusionist device when portraying Semiramis than when painting Helen Fourment.

But conventions of mimesis shift. Someone unfamiliar with

the recent history of art—an aesthetic Rip Van Winkle, say—might, in supposing the same conventions to apply to Picasso's Dora Marr portraits as to Rubens' portraits of Helen Fourment, regard the former as not only imaginary but as intrinsically discernible from the latter since, by *those* conventions, there *could be* no counterparts (in the world as we know it) to the Picassos. But within the same set of conventions, indiscernibility once again becomes the case: an imaginary cubist portrait will, from the surface alone, be indiscernible from a real cubist portrait of Apollinaire or Kahnweiler. If we move a step further to Demuth's "Poster Portraits," or (say) Brancusi's celebrated portrait of Joyce—a spiral suggesting an ear—the amount of independent information required for appreciating the resemblance, as well as the conventions of mimesis which must be tolerated for this even to be considered a resemblance, makes the very notion of a discernibly imaginary portrait in this idiom virtually inconceivable. *Any* doodle might relate to a subject by means of a sufficient elastic set of correspondence rules. Finally, when we abandon mimetic intentions altogether, as in pure abstraction, paintings have no longer any referential purport, and in consequence, the predicates "real" and "imaginary" have no longer any sensible application. Or, if you like, an imaginary abstraction will perhaps only be something —a description, an image, an idea—which has no counterpart abstraction in the art world. A real abstraction then will be comparably one which *does* have a counterpart.

These schematic and preambulary remarks might sustain a good deal of philosophical criticism, but they will serve my purposes here. I want, before going on, only to stress that nothing I have said about imaginary things has anything whatever to do with such predicates as "imaginative" or "shows imagination." For these are aesthetic predicates, which cut across the distinction between the real and the imaginary. Portraiture as such, independent of whether real or imaginary, may show imagination or fail to show it, as might any human activity: cooking, talking, bookbinding, lovemaking. The contrast we point with "imaginative" is "routine," "uninspired," and the like. Finally, nothing I have said about "real" has much bearing upon the aesthetic predicate "has reality" when this is applied to portraits or to characters in fictions. For once again, this will have application as much to imaginary as to real characters: When we deny it of a character, we are saying that he has not been brought to life. And we may say this though the character satisfies whatever rules of projection the prevailing conventions of mimesis demand. Thus "is real"—in *this* sense—is perfectly compatible with "is imaginary."

II

There cannot (logically) be abstract or nonobjective fiction (though there might be abstract or nonobjective writing). Moreover, fiction is imaginary in the specified referential sense. Fiction may employ real characters, but then only in imaginary situations, otherwise it passes over into history. The hybrid case of historical fiction has either real characters in imaginary situations, or imaginary characters in real situations. Pure history has only real characters in real situations, as pure fiction has only imaginary characters in imaginary situations. On this account, historical and fictive writing ought to be indiscernible on the basis of intrinsic criteria, the difference between them being based upon semantical, hence external criteria. But then, in order for this to be so, fictive characters must *resemble* real ones: it must be the case that there *could* be counterparts to them in the time-space world, so that fiction *could have been* history, and vice versa. To the extent that this does not hold, then, conventions of mimesis remaining constant, the fiction in question is implausible, and, as such, aesthetically defective. This, cast in my own terms, is Professor Hospers' theory of the correct relationship between fiction and reality (the world). What is interesting about it is its suggestion that a referential failure may constitute an aesthetic blemish.

Let us say that the relationship is *quasi-semantical,* i.e., a fictional characterization must be *true to* human behavior without necessarily being *true of* the behavior of any specific personage in the world. It is *true to* human behavior if actual human beings would behave as described, were they in the situations specified, and if the situations themselves could arise. Historical characterizations then are *true of* as well as *true to* actual human behavior: and I suppose they must be the latter if they are the former. For no matter how *outré* may be the behavior of an actual personage, the description of him must, if true, be *true to* human nature. Should someone, for example, object that a history of Rasputin is implausible, we must reply that it is Rasputin himself who is implausible: the fault lies in history itself and not in the historian: *e vero si non e ben trovato.* What is true of only *one* man must be *true to* human nature, for our species has exotic specimens. And it cannot be Hospers' claim that fiction must restrict itself to the typical and the *moyenne.* Rather, given only that a type of personage becomes the subject of fiction, then the work must be *true to* that type, however wayward the type itself. If a fictive character K is of type T and behaves in a manner B, then Hospers' criterion demands affirmative answers to the questions "Could there be a type T?" and "Would a member of T behave in manner B?" Negative answers entail aesthetic demerits.

Since the relation is quasi-semantic, reference being to types, it might be thought that fiction has a wider relevance than history. This would be the basis for a famous invidious remark of Aristotle's, that poetry is more "philosophical" than history—"since its statements are of the nature rather of universals, whereas those of history are singular." Taken as marking a syntactical difference between poetic and historical sentences, this, of course, is false, and in the looser sense intended, it is misleading, badly confusing *truth to* with *truth.* For a historical description, if *true of* x, must be *true of* the type of which x is a member, and, in the widest application, must be true to human nature quite as much as fiction. The important question, however, is whether the type, to which a fictional characterization is true, can be an empty one. Or, for the sake of an argument, suppose the type were empty so far as we knew. Then the question really is whether, in view of the fact that we ourselves had had no experience with the behavior of members of that type, we could say whether or not the characterization was plausible or not? And must we postpone a final aesthetic appraisal until we have an answer to this question?

Suppose, on the basis of no experience whatever with members of the type, we were to pronounce a characterization implausible, i.e., *false to* the type in question. The author might rebut us by saying that the fault is ours, not his, and that were our experience wider, our judgment would be different. And he now produces case after case from real life of persons behaving just as he has his characters act in such situations! He shows us passages in obscure volumes of abnormal psychopathology, latinized references from erotic orientalia, transcripts from police blotters in Balkan capitals in the nineteenth century. Somehow recourse to such documentation is a *reductio ad absurdum* of Hospers' criterion. Somehow the fault remains with the author. Consider, for the sake of analogy, a man presenting an elaborate argument to the effect that certain objects behave in unusual ways under rare circumstances, and we, never having had experiences of bodies so behaving, and finding his argument defective, announce that we are unpersuaded. He then produces example after example to show that he was right. Well, he was right in his conclusion, but the existence of bodies so behaving does not vindicate his *argument*. Had he convinced us, he would not have had to produce examples, and indeed we might remain persuaded by the argument (as in a *Gedanken* experiment) even though no instances were to be found. Similarly, a narrative must persuade us, and, if it fails in this, the fact that there are characters who so behave in no sense vindicates the narrative aesthetically.[2] No one, for example, needs to be instructed in perversity to appreciate the utter degradation of the Baron de Charlus: and one is persuaded, one's feelings are engaged by his actions, *whatever* one's firsthand or secondhand experiences might have been. Proust has *given reality* to this character and this episode, and this does not, I think, consist in these *resembling* real characters and real episodes, nor characters and episodes whose counterparts we have *experienced.*

III

Hospers has been accused of leaving no room in his aesthetics for the concept of *imagination.* This is unjustified, I think. His criterion for fictional plausibility bears a singular resemblance to what one might term the "Empiricist Theory of Imagination," and seems, indeed, to presuppose it. Basically, this is the theory, familiar to us from Hume, that an image is a copy of an impression, or else is compounded out of images which are copies of impressions though *it* is not itself a copy of an impression. According to the old formulation, there are no images in the mind (or no ideas if we identify, as Berkeley did, images with ideas) which are not either copies of sense-impressions, or compounds of such copies. An unresoluble image was declared *simple,* in contrast with *compound.* The imagination itself was impotent to produce any image not caused by an impression (one could not imagine red, according to this theory, without having *experienced* red), but it could call up a copy of an impression once had and, more importantly, it could *compound* new arrangements and combinations of simple images. Whether there were any limits upon the compounding imagination other than those imposed by criteria of analyticity is not, I think, much discussed. But presumably whatever is logically possible is imaginable if it does not presuppose an experience (as simple images do) which one has not had or cannot have.

Now Hospers has produced what I might term an "Empiricist Theory of Fiction" which shares a structural parity with this theory of imagination. We unfortunately lack a word which will do service for the literary counterpart to the psychological term "image." I shall therefore introduce the term "narreme." [3] A narreme is a literary unit which stands to experience in something like the relationship in which an image does, according to the Empiricist Theory of Imagination. Let us proceed to distinguish simple from compound narremes,

experience to *nonliterary* experience, when in fact it is through reading books that we amplify an experience which would be parochial without it. In fact it is through reading that I learn, for example, about characters and lives utterly out of consonance with any I have experienced. By reading history books I learn of lives as divergent as those of Henry the Eighth, St. Francis of Assisi, Petrarch, Commodus, Einstein, Mme de Maintenon, and Walt Disney. Perhaps *any* account must resemble the accounts of these lives as much as they resemble one another, and in this regard I have virtually no criterion for ruling out narratives as implausible. On the other hand, if consonance with my *own* nonliterary experience were a criterion for plausibility, I should have to reject *all* of these accounts as implausible. My own personal experience is, in most cases, too straitened a base for discerning between real and imaginary accounts, much less between plausible and implausible imaginary accounts. I *accept* some accounts as true of human beings and hence true to human nature, but this gives me too *wide* a basis to be of much service.

But secondly, it is a fact that people read *for* experience. The appetite for fiction falls off with age (and hence with increasing amounts of firsthand or secondhand experience). To the extent that it were false that we could acquire experience from books, it would be a fortiori false that we could acquire it from history books, and we should revert to the narrow base of personal experience. It sometimes happens that novels treat of experiences which, whether real or imaginary, are such that readers' own experiences serve hardly at all to differentiate plausible from implausible accounts. This happens when a heretofore censored subject is opened up for fictional treatment. Consider the erotic scenes in *Lady Chatterley's Lover*. These may have been wildly disconsonant with the sexual experiences of most readers, but not with the sexual fantasies of most readers. The disparity between art and life would here be blamed upon life. Reformers would tend to feel that life was implausibly puritanical rather than fiction implausibly salacious. The currently high value attached to sexual experience, together with the fact, as David Riesman somewhere points out, that sexual experience is a kind of permanent last frontier, explains the phenomenon of mature persons reading erotic descriptions with much of the same motives that young people read novels as such: not for entertainment, but for experience.

Thirdly, fictional description and characterizations may be disconsonant at a given time with the experience of readers, but, because they make appeal to fantasies and appetites, or awaken readers to undreamt of possibilities, they serve as causal forces in the modification of human behavior. And hence they become plausible through their own instrumentation: this is the famous phenomenon of nature imitating art. In this regard, Lady Chatterley has contributed to a sexual revolution widely commented upon today. The reverse, of course, can happen. A novel may be all too plausible, may hold the mirror up to nature, and readers, seeing themselves reflected in it and revolted by what they see, may rearrange their institutions and practices in such a way as to make the novel a self-defeating description. In after years readers may find implausible what once was shockingly true.

Fourthly, there are episodes, characters, and plot structures which we find recurring time and again in fictional writings, and which are accepted by readers not so much because they at all answer to situations experienced in real life, but because they satisfy conventions so deeply entrenched in literary tradition that writers hardly can rise above them: e.g., the personae in the *commedia dell'arte,* the triangles in the stock melodrama, the climax in the well-made play or the conventional romance. Later audiences giggle at conventions which moved earlier ones to fear and pity. Indeed, the conventions are often revealed as such only *after* a change in style. Once again, while in the grip of such conventions, it is often life itself which is condemned for any discrepancy between art and it.

Finally, the structure of the conventional novel demands conflicts and resolutions, oppositions and transformations of character, the tying up of loose ends, the elimination of episodes which do not further the action, as well as revelations and suspenses of a sort infrequently encountered in life save to the extent that life itself is structured novelistically. The extent to which we try to live our lives as fictional characters is not to be underestimated, which is perhaps one good reason why there is so considerable a congruity between life and fiction. Discrepancies, on the other hand, may simply be due to formal features of plotting. There may be plotless novels, but I am suggesting that what is required to effect congruity between life and fiction is a change in fictional *form*. And changes in form are, I think, difficult to achieve. It is not unfair to say that the novel has been the most conservative of art forms in recent decades, the breakthroughs here having been chiefly in the treatment of new (and erstwhile taboo) subjects.

V

The limits of the imagination, in actual practice, fall a good distance this side of logical impossibility. Who could produce, out of his own imagination, the immense variety of things we encounter in the universe? Who, asked to *imagine* a world, supposing he had never had experience with one, could have thought up such things as flowers (or birds)? The human imagination, unaided by experience, is hardly as creative as one might suppose: The best we might come up with, I should think, would be rocks. Left to imagine the world of the future, men have more or less transferred the present ahead, with only certain ills eliminated or intensified. Asked to populate a world, we would dot it with persons much like us, behaving much as we do. The characters of science fiction are the characters of fiction plus some apparatus, cowboys and Indians in different costumes, Romeos and Juliets in plastic bubbles. The newspapers outrace the most exotic imagination, as Professor Barrett's examples suggest. If you think that anything is impossible, the Duke of Wellington once said, read the newspapers. But with this I should like to return to the reductio ad absurdum which I mentioned in connection with Hospers' theory.

When we condemn a fictional account for implausibility, we are not likely to withdraw the criticism upon being told that in fact the things recounted are exactly like things which happen over and over. The fault remains with the author for having failed to convince us. All fiction is artifice, but artifice stands revealed when a spell is either broken or never achieved. In terms of counterparts, Lady Macbeth, or Oedipus, or Phaedra, or the Baron de Charlus are perhaps unduplicated. Who knows such people in real life? Next to them, people are pale and adimensional. They have a life of their own, and it is this to which we refer, I believe, when we speak of the reality of a character, or the reality of the world created by the fiction master: the world of Combray, or of Chandrapore, or of even Alexandria or Dublin. These are worlds alongside the real world, not worlds which have the world itself as model. The gift consists in making it appear as though one were adding to the world, rather than reflecting it. Questions of plausibility or implausibility arise only when this gift fails. Then we find what ought to have been horrifying merely preposterous, or what ought to have been moving only silly.

Now, there are certain splendid paintings of Gainsborough which *have* a light of their own in addition to whatever light they may show: they are, as it were, contributions to the world's stock of illuminations. A painting which only shows light is dead: an illustration rather than an image. Rubens' paintings have a vitality of their own in addition to whatever life they may show: a painting which merely shows life is dead, like an illustration from the biology text. A painting may be alive in the same sense in which a character in fiction may be, and artworks which do not attain to this have no claim upon our critical admiration. If they exhibit merely craft, merely virtuosity, they elicit pity or contempt: think of the wood carvings of the German craftsmen, or of Dürer at his technical best and artistic worst.

I should like to suggest that it is for the achievement of

reality that we prize works of art. And perhaps it has been in part through the growing recognition of this that in the past fifty years there has been a steady subversion of technical prowess, as though by destroying the very possibility of virtuosity one might capture the reality that art in its highest attainments possesses. Perhaps, again, it was through an awareness of this that the Imitation Theory of art so long held sway, for it must have seemed as though the only way that one might attain to reality would be through imitating objects which were real. Perhaps, finally, it might have dimly seemed that the best, and possibly the only adequate way to attain reality in this sense is simply to make real objects: Brillo boxes, for example. *Theories* of art are so many endeavors to trap the goose that lays the golden eggs, and to find some formula, some recipe, for producing what is at once art and has reality. But some crude drawings have life, and some do not; some imitations possess a reality of their own and some, though mimetically superlative, are inert, with only the life they show; some Pop objects are merely the objects they are, while others create a space of their own.

Pygmalion is the artistic hero par excellence, for his statue breathed: that tale is a parable for the aesthetic I am advancing. His success required the cooperation of a goddess. I do not know whether the concept of recipes is logically compatible with our concept of art or not: artistic theorists behave as though it is. Whatever the case, the connection between art and reality is to be found here, where our analysis ought to have begun.

NOTES

1. Our two senses of "real" might appear to converge: to say of a portrait that it is real might mean either that it is authentic or that it has a counterpart. But in fact this convergence won't work. A fake Rembrandt can still be a real portrait, and a real Rembrandt an imaginary portrait, e.g., like (presumably) "The Polish Rider."

2. The critical irrelevance of the riposte "But it actually happened!" is very nicely exemplified in connection with a recent play of Arthur Miller's, *Incident at Vichy*. In an article "Our Guilt for the World's Evil," *New York Times Magazine* (Jan. 3, 1965), pp. 10–11, Miller relates an incident which moved him deeply, in which a Jew was given papers which saved his life by a man he had never seen, with the implication that this immense gesture cost the latter his own life. Such an episode appears in the play. Despite the historicity of this episode, it apparently does not work well in the play itself, being, as Philip Rahv writes in a review "Arthur Miller and the Fallacy of Profundity," *The New York Review of Books* (Jan. 14, 1965), p. 3: "It is an ending dramatically unearned . . . a melodramatic contrivance pure and simple, a sheer *coup de théâtre*. . . . Everything indeed is possible in life, but in dramatic art what is required is the seeming inevitability of an end, however tragic, which is truly a conclusion vindicating the organizing principle of the work as a whole."

3. This term was once used by a former colleague at Columbia, Dr. Eugene Dorfman, a linguist. He has left Columbia long since, and I do not know his whereabouts. Neither do I know what he really meant by this term, nor whether my use in any sense whatever corresponds to what he intended. Nevertheless, it is an exceedingly useful word, and I borrow it for my own purposes, with apologies if I have distorted its meaning. So far as I know, it has not passed into the technical vocabulary of linguistics.

6

Symbols in Art

JACK KAMINSKY
Harpur College

WEBSTER'S THIRD INTERNATIONAL DICTIONARY distinguishes four basic ways in which "meaning," in its semantic sense, is employed: [1]

(1) The intension or extension of a term.
(2) The thing one intends to convey by an act.
(3) The sense in which something is understood.
(4) The thing that is meant or intended.

There are, of course, other contexts in which "meaning" is used. Thus the senses given in (1) through (4) are probably not applicable to "I'll be very annoyed with you if you don't eat your food. I mean it!" and "What is the meaning of this?" (said in anger). But even if these sentences do not fit any of the four categories, it is quite clear that "meaning" is here being used in a philosophically innocuous sense. The sentences are easily transformed into others which are, for all practical purposes, synonymous and yet lack the philosophically dangerous word "meaning." Thus they could become "I'll be very annoyed with you if you don't drink it. I'm serious!" and "Why did you do this?" (said in anger). There are still important difficulties in these latter sentences. For example, the conditional, interrogative, and imperative structures as well as the expressions "angry" and "serious" are indeed philosophically troublesome. But these are issues which at least do not directly involve the problem of explicating "meaning." We can, therefore, assume that even though categories (1) through (4) do not exhaust all the varieties of "meaning" they do include all the major semantic uses of this term.[2]

In art we are constantly referring to the meaning of the artwork. We can, therefore, ask whether categories (1) through (4) are applicable or at least of some use in explicating "meaning" as it occurs in artistic contexts.

Category (1) is familiar in logic and semantic analysis, but is it at all important in art? As Beardsley points out, we can regard pictures and perhaps sculptures as analogous to words or sentences and then instigate an entire analysis concerning extensions and intensions. But, first of all, in logic we apply intensions and extensions to linguistic elements and not to the entities themselves. We ask for the extension of "dog" but not for the extension of a dog. The object or designatum itself and everything similar to it is the extension of some linguistic designator. We do not ask for the extension of an extension.[3] Similarly, to present the picture of a chair and then to ask for its extension is at least a very odd question. We are apparently not asking what object the chair in the picture is a picture of. The very fact that we give a name to the chair is sufficient to show that we regard the chair as a designatum for a name and not as itself requiring a designatum. It might be argued that pictures are no more than intermediaries between the word and the extralinguistic referent which is really the extension. But even if this were a satisfactory analysis, we would not normally regard the picture as a signifier of an extension. Except in those cases where we might suspect that we are not dealing with what exists or where we might feel we are being deluded into acknowledging the existence of some object, the picture itself serves the function of extension. Unlike Swift's famous professors of language we do not carry with us every item which can serve to give the meaning of our designative expressions.[4] A picture is normally the best way of indicating extensions. Thus it would be quite strange for someone who has seen the picture of an object and recognized it to ask for its extension. Similar criticisms can be made concerning the use of intensions with art objects.

Furthermore, even if it could be shown that the semantic expressions of the logician were utilizable, can we truly be said to be dealing with the artwork? I could very well regard Matisse's "Anemones" as a painting of a vase of flowers, apples, and several other fruits. I might then go on to inquire about the kind of vase that appears and whether the apples do have the characteristics we attribute to apples. In fact, we could launch an entire investigation into whether what does seem to have the characteristics of an apples does not, on further consideration and observation, have the characteristics of an orange. These might be useful inquiries and might very well lead to all the intricate questions about intensions and extensions that have plagued logicians from Frege to Carnap. But it seems to me that what we are doing in such instances is precisely what we might be doing exclusive of the artwork. We are merely using the artwork to initiate some scientific or logical inquiry that could probably be better initiated by inspection of the physical world itself. But surely when we look for the meaning of a painting we are not playing the role of logician or scientific investigator. It would be irrelevant if not presumptuous of someone to tell us that the vase apparently stands for a vase and the apples for apples. These are matters whose determination we take for granted prior to a consideration of the meaning of the work. There may, indeed, be a question about what a picture pictures, but interest of this sort, with its need for precision and formality, is incidental to that interest which regards the object as a work of art. Dali's clock may be a fairly poor specimen of a clock. But in terms of aesthetic appreciation and evaluation who really cares?

Category (1), therefore, does not adequately explicate "meaning" when this expression is used in art. What of category (2), namely, meaning in the sense of that which one is trying to convey by an act? (2) has sometimes been taken to be the sense that is being employed when we speak of artistic meaning. But for the most part this view has been discredited. Artists are often dead before their work is acclaimed and their intentions and their aims simply cannot be considered. Furthermore, the artist himself, especially if he is not involved in the writing arts, may not have the linguistic ability to express his aims, or he may have forgotten his original intentions. Artists often refuse to state their aims and simply direct attention to the work itself where the intent can supposedly be plainly seen. Finally, the artist may indeed be able to state his intention, but it may have little to do with the really important meaning attributed to the work. Thus Shakespeare labeled the *Merchant of Venice* a comedy. But obviously the many critics who have been fascinated by Shylock have been interested in more than its comic significance.

We may, therefore, think of artistic meaning in the sense of (2), but then we are more concerned with the psychology of the artist than with the meaning of the work of art.

Category (3), namely, meaning as referring to the sense in which something is understood, can also be taken to be a disguised version of (2) in that it might allude to the intentions and motives of the artist. And then all the objections raised to (2) can be raised again. But we might think of (3) as referring not to the artist's motives but to the spectator's feelings or ideas. Then we might want to say that the meaning of the work of art is the composite of feelings or ideas that it can arouse in a spectator. But this is surely much too broad. The feelings or ideas we can have in relation to an artwork are often alien to the work. The observation of a painting may produce memories of some frightening incident, but these ought not to be taken as the kind of ideas or feelings that are in any way related to the meaning of the painting. Thus, if we are to consider sense (3) with some seriousness then some criterion must be formulated by which to distinguish relevant from irrelevant ideas and feelings. I am not sure that such a criterion can be found. As Kant long ago pointed out, it is exceedingly difficult to decide whether the feeling resulting from observing an artwork is due to the artwork itself or to the desire to own or to have created it. Nor is it any easy matter to decide what ideas about art are and how, if we finally do decide what they are, we can determine when one is relevant and another is not. But the important point is that any extraction of a possible subclass of feelings and ideas must depend upon the art object which, in the final analysis, is the determining factor. We would be required to look to the art object to affirm whether this idea or that feeling is appropriate while some other is not. Thus we sometimes hear a laugh from the audience at a certain place in a play and we criticize such behavior on the grounds that the words were misunderstood or that some subtlety had been overlooked. In fact we sometimes acknowledge our own deficiency in understanding a play or a novel by being given more information concerning meanings of the words used. A reader with a mastery of many languages would certainly better understand Joyce's *Finnegans Wake* than one who could only understand English.

We are led, therefore, on the basis of sense (3) to sense (4), namely, meaning as it applies to objects or events. But now it becomes rather important to disentangle the different ways in which meaning is used with objects and events. We have already shown that meaning in the strict sense required in logic is not applicable to extralinguistic entities. But we can distinguish three sorts of meaning that can or have been employed with such entities.

(a) First there is meaning in the traditional metaphysical sense. Thus the question "What does this event mean?" might elicit a metaphysical type of answer, e.g., "The gods are angry." But presumably meaning in this sense is no longer philosophically respectable, for the replies are such that there is no way of deciding, without circularity, their truth or falsity. Is there some way of showing that the gods are angry and have caused this event? Or, on the other hand, can we show the gods are not angry and have not caused this event? No answers to these questions can be given. Thus if one speaks of an art object, in Hegelian fashion, as being a manifestation of divinity or an exemplification of some creative process in the universe, he is using a meaning that may be impressive and have the ring of profundity, but it is irrelevant to the particular meaning of the artwork.

(b) A second meaning attributed to objects and events concerns their relationship to a rule or a law, either scientific or conventional. Thus we can ask "What does this event mean?" where the answer expected will be a reference to a scientific law, either its confirmation or disconfirmation. If I released a penny and it suddenly unexpectedly moved towards the ceiling, assuming that I am not completely struck dumb, I might ask "What does this mean?" where I am asking whether or not this incident is to be taken as disconfirming evidence for a familiar scientific law. This is a genuine use of meaning in which the answer given is both relevant and significant. But is it the sort that is applicable to artistic meaning? I think not. To ask for the meaning of a painting or a book is not to look for some scientific law of which the artistic subject matter is an instance. Insofar as we are involved in perceiving and appreciating a work of art we are not engaged in scientific scrutiny. As Beardsley points out in his discussion of the Immanence-Theorist, "the ideas that turn up in poems . . . do not purport to be predictions of future events, or laws of nature or of man. The poet uses them in a different fashion." Nor are we concerned with finding a moral law that may permeate or be exemplified in the work. The traditional Kantian argument still holds, namely, that a genuine involvement in a work of art means that we admire it for its own sake and not because it leads to some extrinsic supposedly more important end.

(c) A third sense of meaning as applied to objects is what I shall call symbolic, or humanly created, meaning. This covers all the various ways, both explicitly and implicitly, by which human beings, for a multitude of reasons, make objects stand for some set of directions, or for some theory, or for some other objects, or for some feeling, or for an indefinite number of other things. Such activities are not to be regarded as mystical or as endowing the universe with strange new entities. We use linguistic signs as our most priceless means for referring to objects without having the objects before us. It is surely not surprising that we use objects as abbreviations for other objects and as abbreviations for long discourses. We need shorthand techniques just as we need the formula $2 + 2 = 4$ instead of the lengthy formula that results when we employ strict logical terminology. Thus anything can become a symbol: colors, squares, circles, dashes, lines, dots, and even old tomato cans. They can be adopted either explicitly, as round pieces of copper called "pennies" have become indicators of a certain form of currency, or implicitly, as the color blue has in most contexts become a symbol for sad or melancholy situations, and, in its most obvious sense, as pictures of objects have become symbols for the objects themselves. The reasons why things are transformed into symbols are many and varied. For all we know, in many cases the elusive quality of primeval influence that Hospers mentions may very well be one of the important reasons, especially in those cases where the meanings are implicit. But asking for reasons here is like asking for the reason the word "dog" has become the linguistic component for signifying dog. Who knows why, out of all the possible sounds and spellings that can be created in the English language, "d-o-g" and not some other arrangement of letters became the way to indicate a given entity! Where it is useful for some reason or another, where we can make things easier in order to anticipate possible dangers or realize expectations, we will use anything as a symbol, both words and objects. And once we have made an object function in this way it tends to retain that function even when the original reason for making it a symbol has disappeared. A swastika can still cause a reaction and be taken to have some explicit connotations even though the context in which it was given a function has, at least for the most part, disappeared.

Meaning in sense (c) is not open to rigorous logical analysis. It can occur anywhere, anytime, and under the oddest conditions. One has only to think about the number of different kinds of traffic signs to become aware of how objects of the most diverse sort can attain symbolic status. Is this the kind of meaning that can be attributed to art?

Meaning in the sense of (c) does seem to have the most ready application to art. A very usual and important question in the perception of an artwork is: "What does that line mean?" or "What does that musical chord signify?" or "What does the Green Knight symbolize in *Sir Gawain and the Green Knight*?" And very often we will say that a given sound is joyous or, more specifically, symbolizes joyous situations. In the same artwork we can find an indefinite number of symbols. *That* line conveys serenity or situations in which living has been pleasant and serene. *That* color is warlike or signifies situations in which living has been hard and fearful. *That* person with *that* kind of expression on his face would be taken to be an angry or a frightened person. It doesn't matter how we came to symbolize these lines, colors, or facial expressions in the ways that we do. Perhaps the colors signifying serene or warlike situations have actually been very subdued and hardly noticeable in these situations. Perhaps some writer simply used these colors in giving a vivid description of periods of war or of peace and, as a result, they became symbols for his readers who, in turn, made others take them as symbols. But regardless of whatever makes something become a symbol, artworks are filled with marks that we ourselves have accepted as symbols. Some of these marks are easily understood because they are so familiar or we have made general stipulations about their use. But other marks require further investigation. Who but a professional philosopher or mathematician would know what is signified by "$\supset$" or "(Ex)"? But probably most people would know what an arrow signifies. Similarly, an artwork is laden with marks to which meanings have been given—some of which are so familiar that we immediately grasp them and others which we have to be introduced to or which we have to study. For this reason there is nothing contradictory about saying that the meaning of an artwork is both present and not present. Nor does this at all involve any form of transcendentalism or Hegelian mysticism.

The meaning is present in the sense that some symbols are present, even if they are merely pictures signifying what they picture, which would probably be recognized by everyone. But meaning is also absent in that usually some marks still have to be explicated.

An artwork, therefore, ought better to be understood as something which has many meanings and not simply one. And if there is any real mystery in art it is that most of us are not aware of marks that have become symbols for various groups. As Dewey once put it, energy must be expended on the artwork if we are to appreciate it fully.[5] The symbol may not be clear; there may be some confusion as to how it is to be taken. This does not mean that we must look for *the* meaning. There may be many meanings. We may have stipulated a mark to signify X in one context and Y in another and thus have produced confusion and ambiguity when the mark appears in some third context. But the fact that a mark may conventionally be used to convey many meanings should not be an argument against the need to understand how symbols are being used in art. For, as we shall argue shortly, an artwork does require an emotional response from a spectator, no matter how subtle that response may be, if he is indeed regarding the work as an object of art; and this response is a result of the kind and number of marks that have been taken as symbols.

Experiencing an artwork, therefore, can be, as Beardsley indicates, a kind of game in which a search is made for the meaning of symbols. But Beardsley is mistaken when he downgrades this sort of game, for meanings condition our response and our evaluation of a work. To become aware of something new or misunderstood is to enhance or detract from the value we attribute to the artwork. Furthermore, as Beardsley himself recognizes, there are rules of rejectibility—no matter how vague and ill-defined—by which one meaning is rejected and another accepted. Tomato cans can symbolize many things, but perhaps they should not be used to signify the pioneer spirit.

The emphasis on the symbolic status of art is perhaps quite commonplace. But what very often is not emphasized is the relation of symbols to emotional response. We do react to symbols. I do not mean that we scream or laugh with joy. There is a tendency to oversimplify human response as if the only emotions that we can feel are the few basic ones of hate, fear, love, and desire. And even of these we are sometimes told that all are basically forms of fear or of desire. But even if it were sensible to speak of these emotions as the basic ones—and I am not at all convinced that it is very sensible—their combinations and their different degrees lead almost to an infinite number of different sorts of emotions. Rather than hate we can envy and mistrust and dislike; rather than dislike someone we can feel annoyed or irritated by him. We can desire, but we can also crave rather than merely desire; and we can be somewhat attracted to someone rather than to crave for him or even to desire him. I can fear someone but I can also be cautious of him or be awed by him. When I envy someone, I desire and hate and also perhaps love, although in what amounts and in what degrees would be difficult if not impossible to tell. Some of these emotional responses we call moods, or simply feelings, or inclinations. I am not here trying to classify the various psychological components that make up human beings. Even if I wished to do this it would require a much more detailed psychological study than I could offer here. The important point to be stressed is that symbolic objects are emotion producers and that these emotions need not be of the sort that we experience in the clear-cut cases of love or hate or desire. There are also feelings that are so subtle that we have difficulty finding the appropriate word to describe them. We have feelings, for example, about what is remembered or what is anticipated and for many of these we have no explicit name except perhaps the feeling of nostalgia or of anticipation. But what of the feeling we receive when we think of some bad event that shocked us? This feeling is not like the original one that occurred during the event itself. The original one might be called fear, but how shall we name the feelings that arise in relation to some past feeling? For example, when Salinger in *The Catcher in the Rye* has Holden remember his dead brother, the feeling is not described simply as involving love or nostalgia. The description must include reference to loneliness and to the fear and inexplicable horror of death. Holden's feeling cannot be described by the usual predicates of fear, love, hate, and so forth. Perhaps these expressions partly describe Holden's feeling. But more is involved. When Proust writes of his grandmother, do we have some one word that could best be used to refer to the emotion he wishes to express in his remembering? Is it properly described as love or sympathy or nostalgia, or is it something different that takes a great deal of describing? In brief, the ways in which we emotionally react to objects or occurrences to which we have assigned meanings are many and diverse.

Emotional reactions are perhaps most frequently associated with those objects that attain symbolic status. The very fact that something is symbolic means that it has now or has had in the past a meaning of special importance to some group of society. For this reason we are much more apt to react with some emotion regardless of whether the symbol still retains its importance as a symbol. We react in a multitude of different ways. The color blue, if it retains its usual symbolic status, may affect us with the complex emotion of melancholy and/or sadness. A line that may signify may affect us with that special feeling that comes from remembered experiences of lightning and thunder. Certain proportions in a man's body may characterize strength and all lines suggesting these proportions may become a symbol of strength with the consequent emotional response. This does not mean that there is a one-to-one correspondence of emotional output between objects and events in the world and objects and events in art. The fear we might feel about an object in real life differs from the emotion we feel when we see the object in a painting. Some symbols remain the same in terms of their capacity to produce emotions. But others, because of their greater significance for human existence, when they are placed in different contexts cause an increase or decrease in emotional intensity. A blood-soaked handkerchief found on a kitchen floor would produce a far greater reaction than the same object portrayed in a picture. But an emotional response would still persist.

Thus the argument is that there is no aesthetic response *per se* to a work of art. We respond to the work in a variety of ways in terms of the symbols that are experienced. The response can be subtle, as when we are affected by a certain kind of line signifying the peacefulness of peaceful situations with its attendant feeling of peacefulness. Or the response can be to a color or to a facial expression, as in the "Mona Lisa," or to a shadow or a series of squares filled with certain colors which stimulate a still further response. In any work of art the responses are many and varied, just as visitors to a large city are overwhelmed by the sights, smells, and noises all of which combine to produce various impressions. But as in the experience of the city so also in art impressions change. As we learn more about the symbols of a work we obtain different kinds of emotions. This painting has lines that create feelings of anticipation as well as serenity. But the red color, as a symbol of rejoicing and hope, does not have the vividness of the same symbol that appears elsewhere. Or else the red is very similar to that in other paintings and, therefore, little if anything new has been added. But note the facial expression of the main character, the bare glimmering of a smile with the quizzical look of the eyes. Hasn't the artist here captured and placed before us the symbol of the vain man or the proud aristocrat? In this way we uncover and examine the marks of a work of art and then evaluate it in terms of affirmative responses rather than negative ones. In this way also we understand why appreciating a truly great work of art takes time and study. It takes time to encounter the various situations that call forth or make us witnesses of at least some percentage of the kinds of emotions that human beings often undergo. And it takes the hard work of study and reflection to determine what is being symbolized by the symbols of art and what responses are appropriate.

Finally, I should like to comment on conflict in symbolic

interpretations. It has often been taken to be an irresolvable problem in art that symbols can be given the most diverse kinds of meaning. The problem is especially pressing in abstract art. But it would seem to me that we ought to treat different sets of meanings in the same way we treat different possible languages. We use words to state what a symbol symbolizes, and it is at this point that all our notions of logic and semantic analysis begin to play a role, for languages can be adequate or inadequate. Some are more ambiguous than others. Some are not properly formed and involve contradictions that are eliminated in other kinds of language. Some are rich, others poor. Here, then, is how we check interpretations. Human beings talk or they write about what the symbols in an artwork symbolize. And the languages they use are open to examination. Some sets of statements about the same set of symbols are compatible, while others are not. We may never obtain the final interpretation of any set of symbols. But at least on the basis of our knowledge of linguistic and logical systems we can distinguish the adequate from the inadequate interpretations.

NOTES

1. This is not a complete list of all the definitions given in the dictionary. There is one other, namely, "The pattern of engrams aroused by a given stimulus." But I did not understand this to be significantly different from (2). It ought also to be noted that the order of definitions is not the same as the order in the dictionary. (1) is given last.

2. For an explication of other non-semantic ways in which "mean" is employed, see W. P. Alston, *Philosophy of Language* (Englewood Cliffs, N.J.: Prentice-Hall, 1964), Ch. I.

3. However, it ought to be pointed out that in oblique contexts where the extension of a term is its intension in other contexts, it does make sense to ask for the extension of the extension.

4. *Gulliver's Travels,* "A Voyage to Laputa," Ch. V.

5. "There is work done on the part of the percipient as there

is on the part of the artist. The one who is too lazy, idle, or indurated in convention to perform this work will not see or hear—his 'appreciation' will be a mixture of scraps of learning with conformity to norms of conventional admiration and with a confused, even if genuine, emotional excitation." *Art As Experience* (New York: Minton, Balch & Co., 1934), p. 54.

7

Literature and Reality

WALTER KAUFMANN
Princeton University

THIS TOPIC is too big for adequate treatment in a few pages, but Beardsley and Hospers discuss it as one topic among many. Both of them also deal with music, painting, and other arts, and not only fail to do justice to literature but seem to me to be wrong about it in important respects. Their mistakes are similar and by no means incidental to their central contentions. I shall consider Beardsley first and then Hospers, venturing some constructive suggestions along the way.

I

In his paper, Beardsley distinguishes two theories about art and suggests that they are "at bottom . . . recommendations about how works of art are best approached." Orally, he adds that the alternative is meant to be exhaustive and that he does not think that when it comes to literature there are any really good grounds for the Immanence Theory; literature, he says, calls for the Significance Theory.

Indeed, Beardsley says in his paper that he considers "literature—surely the most favorable case" for the Significance Theory; "plainly and thoroughly representational" painting or sculpture "the next easiest"; "nonrepresentational paintings and sculpture" more difficult but still manageable; and music scarcely more difficult. The Immanence Theory, conversely, seems to be based on music and nonrepresentational art, faces trouble with representational art, and breaks down confronted with literature—all according to Beardsley.

In fact, however, the Significance Theory does not offer fruitful recommendations for approaching literature: the "two rules which in effect define the Significance Theory" hardly make sense when applied to literary works.

"Rule 1: Works of art, as nonutilitarian human artifacts, are to be taken as indicating what they most resemble in form or regional quality." What does Milton's sonnet on his blindness ("When I consider. . . .") resemble in the form of regional quality? And what does it indicate?

Yet according to Beardsley himself Rule 1 marks the only hard-core difference between his two theories; for "a modified Immanence-Theorist, of course, might accept . . . Rule 2 as far as symbolism in literature is concerned. . . ." It is clearly implied that even the "modified Immanence-Theorist," and a fortiori the authentic one, would balk at Rule 1 when it comes to the interpretation of literature, while the Significance-Theorist, whose approach to literature seems the only feasible one to Beardsley, would insist on Rule 1.

Actually, the second rule does not make a great deal more sense when applied to most literary works. "Rule 2: Utilitarian objects prominently depicted or described in works of art are to be taken as symbolizing the dominant qualities of the activities in which they usually function." In Milton's sonnet on his blindness, for example, no utilitarian objects at all are prominently depicted or described. If these two rules really "define the Significance Theory" we have to conclude that this theory breaks down before Milton's sonnet, not to speak of other poems.

In fairness, we should recall that the Significance Theory is initially introduced as a comprehensive term for the claim that a work of art "copies, or imitates, or represents, or expresses," and what these admittedly different claims are said to have in common is the view that "it is the very nature of a work of art to point beyond itself to something else." At this point one may recall Plato's and Aristotle's influential term *mimesis,* which has been variously rendered as copy, imitation, or representation; and it seems that Beardsley lumps the expression theory, so different on the face of it, with the mimetic theory in order to form an inclusive and exhaustive alternative to the Immanence Theory. One may even wonder whether "Reference Theory" would not be better than "Significance Theory": the term "significance" is patently ill chosen, for "significance" and "immanence" form no exhaustive contrast any more than "significant" and "immanent."

The inadequacy of this scheme, however, is not reducible to a poor choice of words. When the Immanence Theory is introduced at the beginning of section II it is said to include statements not only about what the work of art *is* but also about what it "resembles," while statements about what it refers to are said to belong to the Significance Theory. After this, "resemble" drops out of Beardsley's paper—even in his discussion of examples from the visual arts where "resembles" would often be far more idiomatic and natural than "represents," which is often unclear—but the term "resemble" reappears again near the end of Beardsley's paper in the formulation, already quoted, of the first of the two rules "which in effect define the Significance Theory."

Let us return to Milton's sonnet on his blindness. We have seen how both rules are inapplicable to it. Neither does it seem to copy, imitate, or represent anything. It *says* a number of things, and the first task of interpretation is surely to lead readers to see *what* the work says. It is not clear that what it says lies outside it instead of being immanent in it. The biographical fact that the poet really was blind might be said to lie outside the poem, and so does the Calvinistic tradition which emphasizes action so much more than Luther did. Both the biographical fact and the tradition enhance our understanding of the poem: A Lutheran of the same period would not have found any such problem in being blind as Milton did. But what the poem itself says is in the usual sense of both words immanent in it as well as significant.

The same considerations apply to Milton's sonnet, "Methought I saw my late espoused Saint. . . ." Again the two rules break down and Beardsley's scheme does not help us.

The question "how people should be induced to approach works of art" of this kind remains wide open.

Let us try then to offer some suggestions of our own: In the case of such short and relatively straightforward poems the task of stating what they say may seem so simple that some critics are led to assume that a theory of interpretation should concentrate on what remains to be done after such an initial interpretation. But any interpreter must surely explain Milton's allusions to Alcestis in the second sonnet and to the parable of the talents in the first. Neither poem can be understood adequately without such explanations. It is not clear whether we depart from the Immanence Theory when we insist on this.

The reader who does not understand "Alcestis" and "Jove's great son" because he has not read Euripides and does not know the ancient Greek traditions is not in an altogether different situation from one who does not understand "God," "Saint," and "the Old Law" because he has not read the New Testament and does not know Christian traditions. Nor is the perplexity of such readers altogether different in kind from that of foreigners or "children from culturally deprived homes" who do not know the meaning of "chide" or "vested." It would hardly be difficult to describe analogous problems in painting and music where understanding also depends on some knowledge of the idiom, of conventions, and of earlier works, and those lacking such knowledge understand much less than those who do.

The *Iliad* plainly does not say something simple in the same relatively straightforward way in which Milton's two sonnets do. It offers us a more nearly self-contained world, and if there are allusions to earlier works or traditions we are less likely to notice them. What concerns the interpreter is plainly what is to be found *in* the poem. The following questions do not take us outside the work: whether the characters develop; what ethic, if any, is implicit in the poem; what conception of the human condition we find in it.

Most works of literature lie between the *Iliad* and a sonnet, at least in length; tragedies, for example. Here, too, the same questions are fruitful: what moral ideas are implicit in the *Oresteia*? do the characters develop? how is the Apollo of Cassandra's story in the *Agamemnon* related to the Apollo of the *Eumenides*? Even when we say that the *Oresteia* evinces a belief in the possibility of moral progress through the use of reason, we are not claiming that the work "copies, or imitates, or represents," or even "expresses" a belief which had existed outside the work before it was written. It is not as if Aeschylus here expressed his well-known belief in progress; rather the trilogy says or implies that such progress is possible. Whether the poet consistently maintained this belief in his private life is quite a different question.

We might go on to ask whether this belief is characteristic of his work generally or only of this particular trilogy. Even as the *Eumenides* must be interpreted in the context of the trilogy of which it forms, as it were, the last act, one may interpret an author's single works in the context of his whole *oeuvre*.

We can go a step further and ask whether the world view of the *Iliad* is also that of the *Odyssey*, or whether in the latter poem we find a concern with property and wealth that is largely alien to the *Iliad* which is much more concerned with honor and status. If we answered the last question in the affirmative we should have some grounds for doubting the common authorship of the two epics and some evidence, albeit not conclusive, for assigning a later date to the *Odyssey*. Comparisons of style and vocabulary might help to establish a higher probability.

Some critics may find some of the questions raised here philosophical and irrelevant to works of art as works of art. But when we deal with some of the greatest writers, including Homer, Aeschylus, Sophocles, Euripides, Dante, Shakespeare, Milton, Goethe, Dostoevski, Tolstoy, and many of the most interesting writers of the twentieth century, such questions as these are central to any understanding of their major works.

To return to Beardsley, we have seen that our questions form no part of his Significance Theory. Neither do they fit into his Immanence Theory which "considers no work of art, taken by itself, as being interpretable (unless the explication of metaphor—and, it might be added, the elucidation or analysis of implied character and motive in novels—be considered interpretation)."

Beardsley's dichotomy was evidently suggested to him by his assumption that meaning depends on reference, and interpretation on meaning. But his paper leaves the notion of reference, though it seems all-important for his scheme, utterly in the dark. On behalf of the Immanence Theory, he quotes two lines from Housman to point out a difficulty in the Significance Theory:

> The night my father got me,
> His mind was not on me. . . .

"Who is the 'me' in this poem?" asks Beardsley. And who, one might add, is Cordelia, or Oedipus, or Macbeth?

We are merely told that according to "some critics," evidently Immanence-Theorists of whom Beardsley disapproves, we are here offered "pseudo-references," and "the literary work uses only . . . the surface and contour and texture and emotional impact of ideas, but not their living substance. . . . How else could we enjoy the horrors of tragedy?"

If what we want are "pedagogical proposals about how people should be induced to approach works of art," we need not enter into the intricacies of recent philosophical discussions about "referring"; and short of that the alternative of references and pseudo-references is as unhelpful as that of surface and living substance. But it may be of some slight help to distinguish the following cases:

(a) Some literary figures closely resemble historical figures whose names they bear.

(b) Some bear the names of historical persons but differ from them in important respects.

(c) Others closely resemble historical persons whose names they do not bear.

(d) Yet others combine features of several recognizable historical figures.

(e) And others, finally, seem entirely "fictitious" or, to put it more positively, creations of the poet's imagination.

Whether historical names or resemblances to historical figures are crucial for an understanding of the significance of literary figures has to be decided in each case, not once and for all. To decide this, one has to see first how we can interpret a work without going outside it and then what, if anything, is added by bringing in additional information about the historical prototype. Sometimes what is added is a realization how the poet changed historical characters and events, and the changes he made are often invaluable clues to his intentions. But this is at least equally true in cases where previous authors have dealt with the same, or similar, material—in cases, in other words, which do not take us outside the world of literature into nonliterary "reality." The changes rung on the Orestes story by authors who came after Aeschylus furnish an outstanding example, as does the way in which Aeschylus himself departed from the Homeric tradition.[1]

II

John Hospers, in his paper on "Art and Reality," also overestimates the dependence of literature on nonliterary "reality"; and what he says about literature is in some instances simply wrong. Thus he says—and I interpolate numbers to facilitate discussion of his claims:

"Even if the character in question does a totally unexpected thing . . . [1] the novelist must have prepared the ground for us by characterizing him as the kind of person who is subject to such sudden characterological changes. . . . Otherwise [2] the event is left totally unexplained, [3] the reader is left baffled, and [4] the required tie between art and reality is broken."

All four of these claims are wrong, and so are the last two sentences of the preceding paragraph, which are in the same vein. To begin with the first claim, there is no good reason whatever why a writer cannot reveal character to us through unexpected actions, without first preparing the ground for us. If he wants to present one of "those wrecked by success," [2] he need not tip his hand before.

Nor does it follow that if the ground is not prepared for us, (2) "the event is left totally unexplained." Not only might the explanation come later but there is a wide area indeed between the *totally* unexplained and the completely explained.

Hospers' third claim, that if the ground has not been prepared for him "the reader is left baffled," is clearly meant to suggest that this would be bad and would invite just censure. In fact, precisely what is left unexplained invites attempts at explanations by readers and interpreters and is often found most fascinating. Thus Freud devoted the first half of his paper on "Those Wrecked by Success" to Shakespeare's characterization of Lady Macbeth and concluded, before considering Ibsen's *Rosmersholm* in the second half: "Confronted with the character of Lady Macbeth we have been unable to answer the question why she collapses, sick, after the success. . . ."

Kafka's two-page parable "Before the Law," in *The Trial*, furnishes a more extreme example. The behavior of the two characters in the parable is not illuminated "through prior characterization," yet this is not felt to be an artistic defect. It is from what they do and do not do that we learn to some extent what they are like, but Kafka deliberately leaves room for a wealth of conflicting explanations and actually goes on to produce such explanations, one after another. These pages, moreover, are probably intended to furnish a clue to his own conception of *The Trial*, and they also throw a great deal of light on *The Castle*—and on the problem raised by Hospers.

Hospers' fourth claim, that "the required tie between art and reality is broken," shows how his conception of reality differs from Homer's and Sophocles'. In the *Iliad* Hector says: "In a moment, Zeus can make a brave man run away and lose a battle; and the next day the same god will spur him on to fight." [3] Similarly, Menelaus says in Sophocles' *Ajax:*

> Nay, though a man should tower in thews and might,
> A giant o'er his fellows, let him think
> Some petty stroke of fate may work his ruin.[4]

While Menelaus generally does not speak Sophocles' mind in the *Ajax*, this sense of radical insecurity pervades not only this play as a whole but also Sophocles' other tragedies, as well as the *Iliad*. What matters in the present context is that this unreliability and unpredictability of the world do not even stop at the threshold of character: even such apparently strong and firm characters as Hector and Ajax may suddenly act, as we might put it, out of character. That is the sense of reality we encounter in some of the greatest works of Greek literature. And in this respect some existentialist literature is closer to the world of Homer and Greek tragedy than it is to the novels of which Hospers seems to be thinking.

It might be argued that Hospers is right about "reality" and that these writers are wrong and exaggerate the element of uncertainty and insecurity. This is not the place to try to establish a view of the human situation. But so far from being baffled and inclined to condemn the writer's characterization, as Hospers supposes, most readers simply fail to notice such difficulties—at least in some types of literature, such as Greek or Shakespearean tragedy and much twentieth-century fiction.

In a conversation with Eckermann, April 18, 1827, Goethe noted that Lady Macbeth says in one of her most striking speeches:

> I have given suck and know
> How tender 'tis to love the babe that milks me. . . .

But after the murder of his children, Macduff says of Macbeth: "He has no children." Most readers overlook this problem. And even Goethe ignored a really profound difficulty when he excused this apparent inconsistency by saying: "the poet always lets his characters say what in some particular place is fitting, effective, and good, without worrying a great deal, or anxiously calculating, whether these words might not perhaps offer an apparent contradiction to another passage." Of course, the Lady might have had a child from a previous husband; but why does Macbeth try to murder Banquo's sons to keep them from inheriting the throne if he has no children? The impression we receive from Shakespeare's play is that Macbeth has no children. Here is a matter of central importance, left in utter darkness by one of the world's supreme poets in what is generally considered one of his most successful plays. It would seem that the characterization of Macbeth violates that "fidelity to human nature" which Hospers considers crucial.

That *Hamlet* abounds in similar difficulties is well known among Shakespeare scholars, yet most of these problems escape the attention of all but a very few readers, not to speak of playgoers. In Greek tragedy absolutely central points are frequently left unexplained. Take three of the seven extant tragedies of Sophocles whose masterly plot construction has been admired by critics ever since Aristotle.

In *Oedipus Tyrannus* the hero is outstanding in his relentless attempts to discover the truth, and the plot depends on this characteristic. Oedipus also tells us that when a drunk told him long ago that he was not the son of the king and queen of Corinth, he first tried to pry the truth from them and, failing in that, went to Delphi to gain enlightenment, and there he was told that he was fated to lie with his mother. To avoid this fate he left Corinth. Jocasta, who had much earlier received a similar prophecy, had exposed her son to escape the calamity. Yet Oedipus married a woman old enough to be his mother, and it seems that neither of them asked any questions at the time or for years thereafter. It would be misleading to say that we are asked to believe this; for the atmosphere of Greek tragedy and the conventions governing it are so remote from naturalism that such points are almost bound to be overlooked—unless one makes a deliberate effort to imitate the Higher Critics of the Old Testament who on similar grounds would infer that there must have been two or three different authors.

In *Antigone* it is never explained just what the heroine

believes ought to be done to her brother's corpse, and why —to prevent what. She is caught when she returns to the corpse for a second ritual; but it is left unexplained why she came back—and whether, if not caught, she might have come back again.[5] Yet *Oedipus Tyrannus* and *Antigone* are generally admired as the two most perfect works of the most perfect tragedian of all time.

In Sophocles' *Philoctetes* the central purpose of Odysseus' and Neoptolemus' mission remains unclear: do they need Philoctetes with his bow to conquer Troy, or only the bow? Kitto has discussed this question very fully, and there is no need here to go into it. C. M. Bowra has said in his book on *Sophoclean Tragedy*,[6] and Kitto agrees: [7] "There is uncertainty about almost every play of Sophocles . . . about the whole meaning of an episode or even of a play."

These considerations are anything but tangential to Professor Hospers' arguments about "Art and Reality." He tells us at the outset: "We shall begin with the art-medium in which it is most obvious that there is a relation of art to reality . . . namely literature, and then see whether any conclusions that emerge therefrom can also apply to visual art." Two paragraphs later Hospers speaks of "the closest relation that exists between art and reality: the relation between characters in literature and people in life." I have tried to show that he misunderstands this relation, presumably because he takes his cue exclusively from one kind of novel while ignoring other types of literature.

Thus Hospers' naturalistic standard of "fidelity to human nature" does not stand up any more than Beardsley's assumption that literature "copies, or imitates, or represents, or expresses" some independent reality. Great works of literature often say something or crystallize an experience of life; but it is not necessarily an experience that existed—even in the artist's mind—before the work was created: it may be an experience that is crystallized for the first time in the work and of which the writer himself never had any clear and articulate consciousness.

I agree with Beardsley that recommendations "about how works of art are best approached" could be helpful, but neither he nor Hospers seem to me to furnish fruitful recommendations, at least as far as literature is concerned. I have tried to be constructive by suggesting some questions that it *would* be fruitful to ask.

NOTES

1. See my article on "Nietzsche Between Homer and Sartre: Five Treatments of the Orestes Story" in *Revue Internationale de Philosophie,* 67 (1964.1), 50–73.

2. Sigmund Freud, "Die am Erfolge scheitern" in *Einige Charaktertypen aus der psychoanalytischen Arbeit, Imago,* 1915, often reprinted; e.g., in *Gesammelte Werke,* X, 370–89.

3. 17.176 ff. Rieu translation, Penguin Books, p. 320. Cf. also pp. 377; 20, 433 ff.

4. 1077 ff., Storr translation in the bilingual Loeb edition.

5. H. D. F. Kitto discusses this and the following points more fully in his *Form and Meaning in Drama* (1956).

6. 1944, p. 2.

7. *Op. cit.,* pp. 90 f. Many of the questions touched here I hope to treat more fully in a book on tragedy.

8

Three Problems in Aesthetics

JOSEPH MARGOLIS
University of Cincinnati

THE ISSUES of the three opening papers are rather unrelated to one another. My comments are addressed to each serially.

I. PERFECTION, COHERENCE, AND UNITY

Schapiro's discussion centers on the "ascription of certain qualities to the work of art as a whole, the qualities of perfection, coherence, and unity of form and content, which are regarded as conditions of beauty." I think it is unfortunate that the concept of perfection remains relatively unclear in the account. It is difficult to see what the sense is in which these three "qualities" are of a sort that would support a common finding. The epithet "perfect" seems to invite the question "in what respect?" which the other attributes do not. Also, Schapiro does not use the term consistently, as designating a coordinate attribute. So for instance, in speaking of Rembrandt's "Night Watch," he employs the phrase "perfectly proportioned." I am inclined to think, from a scanning of his discussion, that Schapiro (contrary to his own insistence) never uses "perfection" to designate a distinct attribute.

But if we allow the attributes Schapiro is interested in to pass muster as being of comparable sorts, we find ourselves confronted by a more serious and fundamental difficulty. For Schapiro wishes to hold that "the judgment of perfection in art, as in nature [and the judgments of coherence and unity of form and content], is a hypothesis, not a certitude established by an immediate intuition." The reason, he insists, is that these judgments "are never fully confirmed, but are sometimes invalidated by a single new observation."

It may be seen at once that Schapiro is not concerned with all aesthetic "qualities" that may be attributed to a work of art "as a whole." For example, one may say that a particular work is *dainty;* here is an attribute that belongs to the work as a whole, but it is surely a quality that a more and more detailed study of the work to which it is ascribed is not at all likely to invalidate. Daintiness is, so to say, a quality of the work as a whole, rather like an air or manner, a quality which, in Schapiro's phrase, may be "established by an immediate intuition."

I agree with Schapiro that there are great works of art that, in certain respects, may be said to lack coherence and unity and even to be imperfect in all sorts of ways; as he says, "as criteria of value they are not . . . indispensable." But there is, nevertheless, a curious ring to his narrower and more interesting thesis, namely, that these judgments are of the nature of *hypotheses.* There is no clarification of this notion beyond the insistence that "they are never fully confirmed" but are rather "sometimes invalidated by a single new observation." The difficulty I see is this: if I could anticipate the "single new observation" that would invalidate the "hypothesis" of coherence or unity, presumably I could examine a given work of art with respect to that observation; in that case, against what Schapiro says, I could validate my claim conclusively. What I am suggesting is that it is logically improper to hold both that the claims of coherence and unity are hypotheses and that they cannot be conclusively confirmed. I do not think one can make clear sense of the view that a hypothesis (concerning nondispositional properties) can be invalidated unless one can make sense of the view that it can be validated; the seeming caution that it is "always possible" that one has made a mistake *does not bear at all* on the actual procedures of validating and invalidating hypotheses. It should also be noticed that, with respect to works of art, our primary concern is perceptual (with due adjustments for the literary arts). It is, therefore, additionally unlikely that, *if* the judgments of coherence and unity were hypotheses, they would not be capable of being conclusively confirmed; for such "hypotheses" would simply involve a scanning of all the discriminable or perceivable properties of the work and never causal relationships (with respect to which, classically, one speaks of the possibility of new disconfirming evidence). In short, if the judgment of coherence depends on complex perceptual discriminations alone, it is difficult to see in what sense it could not be "fully confirmed." Again, it does not seem to fit our way of proceeding to construe these judgments as hypotheses; for no one supposes that he can state, *in advance,* anything like a reasonably complete set of criteria on the strength of which he would ascribe the qualities of coherence or unity to any particular work of art or even "a single new observation" that would invalidate a judgment of the relevant sort. But the entire enterprise of validating and invalidating hypotheses supposes that we can formulate necessary conditions and sufficient conditions in terms of which to try our claims.

In a word, hypothesis does not provide a suitable model for characterizing the logical properties of judgments of coherence and unity. It is much closer to the truth to suppose that the discovery of features of a work of art hitherto unnoticed may incline us to *alter* our judgment that the work is coherent or unified. That is to say, it is not that a hypothesis of coherence may be invalidated by "a single new observation" but rather that "a single new observation" may affect our judgment of a work so that we now judge it to be coherent (or incoherent) where previously we thought it incoherent (or coherent). We may *assess* the work differently now that we have additional information. It is a question of whether, knowing what we now know, we would say that the work was coherent or not. The issue concerns taste and appreciation rather than hypothesis. Put perhaps most tellingly, it is a question of whether we would or would not take the ascribed qualities of the work to justify a judgment of coherence; it is not a question of whether, having claimed that a work is coherent, the evidence will support the claim. *It is a question of putting a value on the actual qualities we know a certain work possesses; it is not a question of searching for evidence which we know in advance will tend to confirm or disconfirm a certain claim.* On the first alternative (and relevantly here), the facts are given and the work is assessed in the light of these; on the second (and not relevantly here), the facts are what we are to search for.

II. INTERPRETATION

Beardsley is concerned, as he says, primarily with "the nature and validity of critical interpretation-statements." There are at least two preliminary difficulties confronting his enterprise that are based on his own formulations. For one thing, he defines interpretation in such a way that one of the most central issues regarding the matter is thereby prejudged; "to interpret," he says, "is verbally to unfold or disclose meaning (either sense or reference)." One may of course insist that there are forms of interpretation, by no means irrelevant to Beardsley's concern, that are not verbal at all—for instance, the sorts of interpretations provided by performing artists. One may also insist that interpretation does not always disclose meanings, in a sense bearing on language and symbol—for instance, the effort of a music critic who seeks to provide an interpretation of a piece of electronic music so as to ascribe to it a certain musical coherence otherwise difficult to appreciate. But far more important than these adjustments is the objection that Beardsley holds interpretations to *unfold* or *disclose* meanings. The implication is that an acceptable critical interpretation makes *explicit* what is, in some sense, present or implicit or hidden in the work itself. Hence it is that Beardsley speaks of "correct" and "incorrect" interpretations: "One who advances an interpretation," he says, "tacitly claims correctness for it, and thus allows the logical possibility that it may be incorrect." It is important to see that, if criticism *discloses* meanings and if the statement of such disclosures may be *correct, it is not possible to provide for the defense of plural and incompatible interpretations of a given work of art.* Actually, Beardsley already had, in his *Aesthetics,* argued that all admissible interpretations of a work of art converge ideally toward some comprehensive account (which it might not be possible to formulate). That is to say, Beardsley's theory construes interpretation as an analogue of factual truth. But if critics characteristically (though not always) generate plural and incompatible interpretations of complex works of art—think of musical interpretations (which Beardsley wrongly rejects) or of such literary works as *Hamlet* or Kafka's *The Trial* or Yeats's "Among School Children"—Beardsley's thesis cannot be regarded as the result of an analysis of the nature of criticism, must rather be a stipulation laid down altogether without defense.

The argument may be put very simply. If critics, in their professional practice, provide *different* interpretations of a given work of art and if these different interpretations are such (as they often are) that one cannot *jointly ascribe* to a work of art the alternative meanings allegedly "disclosed," either critics are not justified in offering incompatible interpretations *or else criticism cannot be viewed as disclosing the true or correct interpretation of a work of art.* Now, if Beardsley is prepared to admit that such incompatible interpretations are indeed reasonably defended by practicing critics, he cannot hold to his "disclosure" theory of interpretation. It should also be noticed that it is a mistake to think that speaking of incompatible interpretations involves a transferred use of the logical notion of incompatibility. It does not, as one may readily see if he sees that the *statements* that a given work *has* meanings A and B (where A and B are incompatible) are themselves incompatible statements; contrariwise, if the statements are incompatible, the interpretations are incompatible.

On the other alternative available, I submit that Beardsley (not having addressed himself to the problem here formulated) never considers the grounds on which a critic's interpretation can be disqualified (apart from the question of its compatibility with other interpretations offered). But I think we may safely say that if he had considered the issue, he could only have argued for a *reform* of critical practice; his account could not possibly have been an analysis or description of the practice of critics.

The second difficulty facing his account concerns the specimens of interpretive statements given. Beardsley himself acknowledges that some of his instances of descriptive statements might be construed as interpretive statements and that some of his interpretive statements might be construed as descriptive statements. This is true and important. But it is more significant that Beardsley's instances all concern linguistic symbols or symbols of other sorts and, further, that in exploring his variety of interpretive statements, he is all but exclusively concerned with reference beyond the work of art to the actual world. That is to say, Beardsley considers problems of interpretation that bear on what a work "depicts," "portrays," "suggests," "connotes," "denotes," "symbolizes," "represents," "refers to" in the real world. I would not deny that *some* works of art, in some sense, *refer* to the real world; I cannot see that every work—and every work that invites interpretation—makes such reference. And I would not deny that *our* consideration of the actual world may illuminate a work of art by way of interpretation; but I cannot see that this presupposes that the work actually refers to that sector of reality that illuminates it. Think of fiction—at once the most relevant and the most damaging instance. To interpret a work of fiction and, at the same time, *to preserve its character as fiction,* one clearly does *not* construe the language of the story as referring to the actual world, even if *our* reference to the world illuminates the story. Beardsley's central discussion, therefore, is taken up with a tangential issue: the quarrel between the Significance Theory and the Immanence Theory falls with the admission that critical interpretation concerns reference only in a minor and rather special setting. Interpretation is not restricted to meanings, in Beardsley's sense, nor even to representational art, certainly not to references to the actual world. But one can now more fully appreciate how —on this limited view of interpretation—Beardsley would plump for a "disclosure" theory. The oddity of the view proposed is focused tellingly in Beardsley's claim that "Since there are no rules for musical significance, there is no such thing as interpreting music." What we notice, finally, is that if the question of reference be set aside, Beardsley will be seen not to have provided any logical distinction between description and interpretation.

III. ART AND REALITY

Hospers says that his "main concern will be with the relation of art to *external* reality," which he characterizes carefully so as to avoid obvious paradoxes involving the work of art itself and the minds of artists. He is interested in finding a relationship between art and reality that holds for "*all* art." But if I find that he discusses three entirely discrete issues, that cannot possibly be brought together usefully under his rubric. For one thing, he concerns himself with the Aristotelian question of "fidelity to human nature" in literature; he finds that the thesis of fidelity, on any interpretation, is somewhat strained for the visual arts and altogether inappropriate for music. For a second, he concerns himself with the nature of "affective qualities" in works of art; he argues against holding that there are "intrinsically expressive" qualities, insists instead that qualities become expressive, universally recognizable expressive qualities, by "being rooted . . . in the most primordial reactions of human beings to conditions of nature which all human beings confront." And finally, he concerns himself with the power of particular works of art to move us affectively; he finds himself inclined to hold that this power depends, in some way, on touching certain "deeply-rooted life-experiences."

On the first issue, "fidelity to human nature," there are several small difficulties to be noticed. It is not always clear that Hospers is really concerned with matching art and reality (in literature), however that may be supposed to be accomplished. Often, it seems that he is rather more concerned with the coherence of the characters presented, with elements of behavior ascribed to them for which we may not have been prepared by the author. He finds such characters "implausible and unconvincing," though he casts his account in terms of correspondence with reality. It should be noted here that Hospers regularly insists that the author must give us *prior* notice of the developments that are to come. Again, with respect to literature, Hospers claims that "human beings in fiction . . . must behave, feel, and be motivated as actual human beings behave, feel, and are motivated." I see no argument given why this *must* be so. If it can be violated—and it is not entirely clear that, on Hospers' conception, it is actually possible to violate this rule—I cannot see why literary art may not have merit in departing from the relevant constraints.

Still, I am prepared to concede that some test of "fidelity to human nature" can be formulated, in principle, in a non-vacuous and non-circular way. My objection to such a test, as Hospers formulates it, would then be that he has surely reversed the practice involved in praising a character in terms of fidelity. For Hospers holds that we must be able to identify persons "of type T" (for instance) in the real world and match our fictional characters to these. I do not know that we ever catalogue human beings in the required way and then match characters with them. It seems to me that, in praising a character in the relevant way, what we do is assimilate human beings *to the type of the character*. I am not saying that this is, as such, a very important criterion of the merit of a work of art, but Hospers has created an extremely difficult, and altogether unnecessary, puzzle for himself by formulating his test of fidelity in the way in which he does. We do not praise Hamlet by searching for flesh-and-blood Hamlets; we praise him by noticing (now that the author has arranged a new perspective) that certain human beings strikingly approach in various ways and degrees the fictional character we know so well.

The shift to the second issue, that of expressive qualities, is a little baffling. The reason is that no question of matching the qualities of a work of art and the qualities of "real" things arises. The only connection with the topic lies in Hospers' effort to provide a general *explanation of the origin* of the expressiveness of certain qualities. He offers, broadly, a theory of association that insists on relations so pervasive that qualities do indeed appear phenomenally and universally as expressive. Now, I think that *any* theory of the sort Hospers seeks here must link art and reality, that is, *some* part of the external world; in this sense, his effort trivially concerns his original topic. On the other hand, his actual discussion of the expressive quality of colors, for instance, is extremely elementary. I doubt very much whether colors as such *have* affective qualities—as Hospers insists; it seems rather truer to the mark to suppose that colors and lines and the like have affective qualities in this particular setting and in that. But the point remains that the perception of these affective qualities requires absolutely no account of how they may have arisen. In short, Hospers' discussion of the alleged relation between art and reality bearing on expressive qualities is altogether irrelevant to aesthetic questions as such. There is, therefore, no way of linking significantly the first and second issues.

The third issue, that of the "moving power of some combinations of elements in artistic media," Hospers clearly takes to be an empirical matter. It is, in fact, a causal matter, as he sees it. Consequently, it too (though for reasons quite different from those that bear on the second issue) only trivially concerns the relationship between art and reality—at least as far as aesthetic considerations go. The affective power of particular works of art does not itself involve any attention to the *relation* between art and reality: at stake, rather, are the *real* properties of works of art. In this sense too, the question has nothing whatsoever to do with the evaluative considerations regarding fidelity in literature (or in the plastic arts).

In short, I cannot see that any of Hospers' three lines of inquiry promises to lead to a comprehensive account of the relation between art and reality that would hold significantly of "*all* art."

9

How Not to Talk about Art

KAI NIELSEN
New York University

IT IS TRUISTIC to remark that communication between disciplines is not easy. This was much in evidence in the reactions to Professor Schapiro's paper. Here a man of unquestioned distinction as an art historian only succeeded as an aesthetician to either confuse and frustrate or simply bore. For all his very evident knowledgeability about and sensitivity to art, his talk about perfection, coherence, and form was such that it will leave philosophers or at least many philosophers (as it did Ziff and Black) baffled and frustrated. Schapiro's "theses" remain so opaque, so fuzzy, that one is tempted at the very start to give up and once more to raise the lament about "the dreariness of aesthetics." (Schapiro was genuinely enlightening and entertaining when in the discussion he dropped aesthetic theorizing and talked to us about art. Again the moral is: one can talk about art without being able to talk about the talk about art.)

Professor Ziff has adequately exposed many of the confusions of Schapiro's paper. Here I want simply to examine one aspect of Schapiro's arguments about perfection. Schapiro tells us "that the judgment of perfection in art, as in nature, is a hypothesis, not an attitude established by immediate intuition." Upon reading such a remark, one is sorely tempted to read no further. What, if anything, could constitute 'an immediate intuition' is (to put it mildly) obscure and how a judgment of perfection could possibly literally be a hypothesis, e.g., something like Dollard's frustration-aggression hypothesis, is even more obscure. Yet to refuse to read on would be unfair to

Schapiro, for it becomes reasonably apparent from the context what Schapiro means. He means that in judging a certain work of art to be perfect, we are not simply talking about our immediate reactions to it, but about how we and others will react after repeated exposure, after study, after dwelling on it, and after seeing it against the background of the history of art and criticism. But to make this perfectly sane observation is to say little about the logical status of such statements as 'There is a perfection of form in *Madame Bovary* that Zola never attained,' or 'Rembrandt's "Portait of a Rabbi" is a perfect portrait.' Schapiro's remarks do not in the slightest show that such statements are hypotheses, or empirical statements, or that perfection is an empirical quality of a work of art. Schapiro does indeed give us to understand that such judgments of perfection are neither simply expressions of preference nor do they record what we are immediately aware of. As Thomas Mann's character Hans Castorp quite meaningfully remarked of his cigar, "it tastes vile, but I know it's good," so one can meaningfully say of Rembrandt's "The Polish Rider," 'I don't like "The Polish Rider" but all the same it exhibits perfection of form.' These are the evident linguistic facts, but accepting them does not commit one to the claim that judgments of perfection are hypotheses or that perfection is an empirical quality or characteristic.[1]

Much of the discussion of Schapiro's paper turns around what he was saying about perfection. What is it to say that a painting lacks perfection? In what way, if at all, could perfection be a quality or a characteristic of a painting? How could we teach a child what a perfect work of art is? How do we decide when a work of art is perfect? Schapiro insisted that whether a work of art was or was not perfect is an empirical question. But *if* it is an empirical question, it most certainly is a very odd empirical question indeed. Consider Goya's "The Third of May"—a work that many might say is a reasonable candidate for a perfect work of art. How could we go about establishing in an empirical way that it is a perfect work of art? Contrast:

(1) "The Third of May" is a perfect work of art.

(2) "The Third of May" is a picture of a firing squad.

(3) One of the figures in "The Third of May" is a man with a white shirt and yellow pants.

Without kudos or charisma, with normal eyesight and standard lighting conditions and a mastery of English, and without any "training in sensitivity," a man can confirm or disconfirm (2) or (3) without any difficulty at all. Whether (2) or (3) are true or false is a plain empirical question. But how would we establish the truth or falsity or probable truth or falsity of (1)?

No doubt one might say that whether (1) is true or false is an empirical question, but hardly a *plain* empirical question like (2) and (3). But if so, what then would constitute a confirmation or disconfirmation of (1)? In saying "The Third of May" is perfect, there is nothing we can point to comparable to the white shirt and yellow pants to establish the truth or falsity of one's claim. Nor is there anything we can point to, like the guns, soldiers, blood, dying men, dead men, and praying men that confirm (2), to show that (1) is true or probably true. To say that it is a perfect work because it is flawless, complete, consistent, or fulfills its form, is not to point to features of the artwork that are there to be observed in some empirical manner. It is not like saying he was rude because he deliberately stepped in front of her, or he is courageous because he risked his life to save the child. It is rather more like saying this ought to be done because it is right and fitting that it be done. On hearing this last remark, we are still not told what it is that we ought to do, or how it is that we can in some empirical manner determine what we ought to do. We no more have empirical criteria for identifying a flawless work of art or a complete work of art than we have for identifying a perfect work of art. If Schapiro is to do anything at all to establish that he or anyone else has empirical criteria to determine whether or not a work of art is perfect, he must do something comparable to what Phillipia Foot has been trying to do for such homely words as 'rude' and 'courageous.'[2]

He must give "perfect-making" criteria; that is to say, he must point to empirically detectable features of works of art, and he must do it in such a fashion that if a work has these features, it is true or probably true that the work in question is perfect and if it lacks these features it is false or probably false that it is perfect. If judgments of perfection are expressible as empirical statements, or if they are in any literal sense hypotheses, it must be that some conceivable experiences count for or against the truth or falsity of the statements in question. But Schapiro has not even given us the slightest hint concerning how that may be possible.

There is a further point that needs to be made. If they are hypotheses or empirical statements, they are true or false; and if they are true or false, they, unless they are autobiographical statements or statements about the tastes of some culture or subculture, must be statements whose truth or falsity is publicly determinable by informed, experienced, normal, and careful observers who are apprised of the relevant facts. If it is not possible to do this—if the acceptability of the judgment in question depends on some cultural or individual idiosyncrasy of the person(s) making the judgment in question—we cannot say that that judgment is objectively true or false. It is evident that Schapiro does not think that all statements to the effect that a work of art is perfect are autobiographical statements or statements about what some cultural elite would approve. But how is it possible for judgments of perfection or statements like (1) above to be true or false in the above objective manner? For questions of perfection to be empirical questions of the sort Schapiro intends, and for judgments of perfection to be hypotheses, we need some empirically identifiable criteria for determining whether a work of art, no matter of how limited a *genre,* is or is not perfect, and we need to show how it would be possible to confirm or disconfirm a statement like '"The Third of May" is a perfect work of art.' Schapiro, as far as I can determine, has not given us one iota of help in doing this. Yet if what he says about perfection in a work of art is so, this is just what he must do.

Some may think that I am behaving like a truculent and brash positivist when we all know, or at least should know, that positivism is dead. I am making demands concerning the validation of judgments of perfection that could not possibly be satisfied. I am inclined to think that this last claim is correct. But I am not saying anything that depends on the acceptance of positivism, or the verifiability theory of meaning, or anything of that sort. I am only taking Schapiro at his word. He is the one who claims such judgments are empirical, are hypotheses, are capable of empirical test. I have only shown how he has not made good his claims.

It might well be fair to say that Schapiro, not being a philosopher, had something less precise in mind. This no doubt may be so, but a philosopher has every right to show what Schapiro would be committed to if he were saying anything that was at all clear. Perhaps Schapiro could explain how we can in an objective and empirical manner determine whether a given work of art is or is not perfect, if we only try. But then I can only point out the obvious: that he has not done so and he has not even provided us with a blueprint of a program about how this might be done.

In reaction to difficulties of this sort there is a tendency in some quarters to take an obscurantist turn. This was much in evidence in response to the penetrating criticisms of Schapiro's arguments given by Black. Professor Hofstadter in arguing about how one would handle questions about perfection in a work of art made a remarkable flight to a metaphysical enchanter, for he argued that there can be an "inexpressible norm fulfillment" and that if one has somehow had such a fulfillment one would know if a work was perfect; if not, not.

He talked as if what would constitute 'an inexpressible norm fulfillment' was something that would be evident to anyone who took art seriously. By all means let us take art seriously, but this neither licenses us nor in any way calls for speaking in such obfuscatory terms. How would Hofstadter meet the stock questions concerning the unintelligibility of that which cannot—cannot even in principle—be expressed? Or was he simply engaging in hyperbole: saying in effect, what is surely true, namely, that there are many things in life which are very, very difficult to express—things that take a Marcel Proust or a Thomas Mann to express? If this is so, then it is the philosophers' job, difficult as it may be, to give, or at least to try to give, a perspicuous representation of these areas and not to hide behind expressions that have no use and have been given no use.[3]

Professor Barrett, as a true shepherd of Being, engages in a somewhat different kind of obscurantist talk in the final sections of his reply to Professor Hospers. In the middle sections of his "Art and Being," he made the by now familiar point that 'art' is open-textured and argued convincingly for the importance of historical considerations in understanding and assessing a work of art. But when he traded in Wittgenstein and Collingwood for Heidegger, he too made his flight to the enchanter. To really understand art it isn't enough to understand the relation of art to reality or to human nature, but we must understand how art reveals Being. We must see through the work of art how Being projects itself. To really understand art and presumably to really understand life we must somehow be grasped by Being. Through art we encounter Being. In a footnote Barrett quotes with approval Heidegger's claim that in a painting of a pair of peasant shoes "Being, as presence, emerges through the painting of the shoes." If we but dwell on those shoes, imaginatively and sympathetically reflect on the kind of life a man would have who wore a pair of shoes like that, Being will become present to us.

It is the manner here and not the matter that stultifies. There are enough genuine perplexities in life without multiplying perplexities without need. Described asceptically one can say of such a painting that if we give ourselves to it, dwell on it, reflect on it, allow ourselves to face honestly our own feelings about it, we can—if we really do these things—imaginatively re-create what the life of such a man would be like. But there is no mystery here and no need to beat the drums of ontology or the tom-toms of phenomenology. There is no need to do this here any more than there is a need to use such a vague conceptual structure to characterize or explain what is at the forefront of our attention when we dwell on Picasso's "La Vie." The feeling we have when we look at those figures is one of a controlled yearning, yet a yearning that carries with it an understanding and acceptance of such yearning together with a sense that there is "nothing new under the sun." But to articulate this, to find our way through the great paintings of the world, we do not need such an inarticulate ontological Virgil. What we are talking about is complex enough, we do not in our talk of art need to mystify the mind with such gobbledygook as Herr Professor Heidegger ladles out.[4]

It is indeed true that in looking at a painting we will often feel that no description will ever really convey what we feel as we stand before it. But there is no great mystery here—no need to talk of an "inexpressible norm fulfillment" or of "being grasped by Being." It is simply that no description of an experience, however accurate, however faithful could—logically could—ever be identical with the experience itself. Of course it couldn't, for then it would be the experience itself and not a description of the experience. To feel something is one thing, to express it is another. However, we can, and on occasion do, talk about an artwork and what we feel when we dwell on it. But in doing so we add nothing but a delusive sense of mystery of Being. Such talk sounds profound—sounds as if through it one had at last an entry into the irrational core of human destiny—but in reality it is only obscurantist: its sense of revelation being entirely dependent on the work of art itself, the significance of which can be described, as well as it can be described in plain terms, without metaphysical jargon whose very intelligibility is open to the most serious doubt.[5]

My remarks may seem captious and tendentious. It may seem that I am saying that all is dross that is aesthetics. But that is not my aim at all, though it was my aim to object to certain styles of philosophizing that unfortunately have been and no doubt will continue to be all too prevalent in aesthetics. But one need only remind oneself of some of the things that Hungerland, Sibley, Hepburn, and Weitz, among others, have written to recognize that aesthetics is not *intrinsically* dreary.[6]

NOTES

1. These are linguistic facts. I speak, of course, of the translation of *Der Zauberberg*. But here the translation is faithful: "Sie schmeckt miserabel, aber ich weiss, dass sie gut ist." Thomas Mann, *Der Zauberberg* (Frankfurt am Main, 1960), p. 82.

2. Phillipia Foot, "Moral Arguments," *Mind* (1958), "Moral Beliefs," *Proceedings of the Aristotelian Society* (1958), "Goodness and Choice," *Proceedings of the Aristotelian Society,* supplementary volume XXV (1961).

3. See in this context William Kennick, "Art and the Ineffable," *Journal of Philosophy,* 58 (1961), 309–20, and Alice Ambrose, "The Problem of Linguistic Inadequacy," in Max Black (ed.), *Philosophical Analysis* (Ithaca: Cornell University Press, 1950), pp. 15–37.

4. After all, it was Professor Heidegger who had the profound insight and historical sense to tell university students in Germany "Not theorems and ideas be the rules of your being. The Fuehrer himself and alone is the present and future German reality and its law. Learn ever deeper to know that from now on each and every thing demands decision and every action, responsibility. Heil Hitler!" (Reported in the *New York Times,* April 11, 1964.) A man with such an understanding of the human condition is either a fool or a knave or, what is more likely, a little of both.

5. Lest it be thought that I trade too much on the derogatory force of 'obscurantist,' 'gobbledygook,' 'mystery,' and the like, see my specific remarks about such philosophies of Being in my "Linguistic Philosophy and Beliefs," *Journal of Existentialism,* forthcoming.

6. Paradigm cases are: Isabel C. Hungerland, "The Logic of Aesthetic Concepts," *Proceedings and Addresses of The American Philosophical Association* (1962–1963), pp. 43–66; Frank Sibley,

"Aesthetic Concepts," *The Philosophical Review,* LXVIII (October, 1959), 421–50; Ronald Hepburn, "Literary and Logical Analysis," *The Philosophical Quarterly,* 8 (October, 1958), 342–56; Morris Weitz, "Truth in Literature," *Revue Internationale de Philosophie,* 31 (1955), 116–29.

10

Reality and Art

BRUCE WILSHIRE
New York University

PROFESSOR HOSPERS admits that he probably should have begun his paper which deals with the relationship between art and reality with proper definitions of "art" and "reality." But to do so, he says, "would undoubtedly mean getting involved in the definitions of these terms for the entire allotted length of the paper, without ever coming to grips with the substantive issues into which they are supposed to lead." I appreciate the difficulty Professor Hospers faces, but I wonder if it would be better never to get to these substantive issues at all than to get to them by way of the working definitions which he stipulates. "Reality" he simply takes to mean "external reality," that which is "apart from" the artist's "states of mind" and his works of art. It seems to me that these initial formulations predispose his analysis toward dualism, and that dualism creates artificial and misleading problems for aesthetics. The presence of dualism is further suggested by Professor Hospers' contention that "representation" is the relationship that obtains between art and reality. If this term were used merely to mean that one cannot have a concept of an individual, but only a representation *qua* intuition, then dualism would not necessarily be involved. But it is taken to mean, I think, that there are two sectors of reality: one composed of states of mind (or art) which represent, and another composed of things which are represented. Professor Hospers is led to say that music, for example, cannot represent, and thus the problem is created of how music can be related to reality. I think this may be an artificial problem, given the manner in which it is raised. Though I owe an apology for the brevity of my own remarks, and though I admit that the great importance of the subject matter may be a reason for saying nothing rather than a little, I do wish to offer a few comments.

We might remind ourselves that dualism has been under attack from nearly all of Western philosophy since Kant. This is not to say that dualism is wrong, of course, but it is to say that we might reasonably expect from Professor Hospers some passing thrust at the Kantian notion that any discussion of reality is possible only because it is already at the outset a discussion of reality in relation to mind (or experience). And we might reasonably expect some defense of Professor Hospers' own implicit notion that we can discover the relationship of mind to reality by some method other than the transcendental one—other than through the exposure of a priori assumptions about the very relationship in question.

It is not just absolute idealists who would object to Professor Hospers' analysis. Take William James for example. After nearly two thousand pages of psychological writings in which he attempted to carry through a dualistic program he was forced to admit that he did not know what a "state of mind" was. The upshot was his "pure experience": the common ground for both the physical and the mental; that without which neither could be specified. What is a mental "state" but experience taken as experienc*ing*? What is a physical thing but experience taken as experienc*ed*? Early he criticized the notion that mind was a representation or mirror of reality. Something must be *taken* to be something; it must be intended. The a priori is the interest we bring with us and which governs the intending. We select out those characteristics which are most important to us relative to our interests; they become the standard, typical or ideal views of things, and they comprise what we call the essence or specific nature of the thing. It is *what* the thing is.

Following James's lead, I want to try the hypothesis that all perception is selective and involves an ideal, in a word, that all perception is art-like. If we can specify reality only in terms of characteristics common to thought, art and reality, then a revision of Professor Hospers' position would be called for, I think. Art would not *represent* reality but would simply *express* characteristics through a specially created instantiation of them—characteristics which existing things other than the artwork *might* share. There would be no immaculate perception in which reality itself is presented in itself and then compared to an artwork to see how the artwork represents it. The position would be that we perceive the existing, physical world only through our expressions, some of which are our artworks.

We cannot avoid the conception of intentionality of mind, and using James as a touchstone we see why. If thought is specifiable only as thought *of* things (or instantiated characteristics) and things are specifiable only as things thinkable *of*, then the of-ness, the intrinsic referentialness of mind, must be considered. Professor Hospers wishes to dispose of any egocentric predicament in his dualism by asserting that "experiences are experiences *of* something, and of what are they if not of reality?" But to invoke intentionality as a bridge in a foreordained dualism is to obscure intentionality in two ways. First, the conception of intentionality involves one in nonsense, it seems to me, if one uses it to link two sectors of reality (mind and reality, or art and reality) specifiable antecedently of the intentional relationship between them; for if intentionality is used, it is logically prior to the specification of the sectors. However gropingly James deals with intentionality he sees this much: we must begin metaphysical analysis by positing an all-encompassing pure experience. Second, the conception of intentionality involves one in nonsense if one simply says that what thought is *of* is reality, and then does not distinguish between existence and essence, actuality and possibility, the individual and the universal—handle the distinction as you will. Certainly, if what one thinks of exists, then *what* it is (its essence) is just what *it* is. But it need not exist.

The element of ideality or essence common to all thought

and all expression (and to all the things expressed by the expression) must be present in an artwork as well. Except that the ideality seems pushed to a higher level, and this, paradoxically, because the expression that is the artwork is itself a concrete existent and is intended as such. It is unlike the expression of ordinary speech, say, in which we just look *through* the expression at a possible state of affairs in the existing world expressed by the speech. In art the expression and the expressed are one. Hence, the question of whether there exists another existent which the art in turn may be *of* involves the matter of a *further* expression: e.g., the caption on the bottom of a painting.

Professor Hospers' analysis of the relation of art to reality encounters peculiar difficulties in the case of music, and I think these difficulties arise because of his dualistic approach. On the one hand, he says, is reality—such things as movements of bodies, psychic processes, and *sounds.* On the other hand is art—such things as musical *tones.* Music relates to reality, he says, when its tones remind us of reality, e.g., our sounds. It can be shown, I believe, that characteristics common to both art and reality must be used to describe both, and that the expression of characteristics (often *via* artworks) is logically prior to our apprehension of reality. Professor Hospers himself writes that when people are sad they talk in "hushed tones." Now "tones" is a word that was to be used to describe music only. We might add other examples: Jane has a melodious voice; Joan speaks in flutelike tones; Jim has a commanding bass voice; Jill is trumpet-tongued and speaks in a staccato rhythm. What is more, Professor Hospers speaks of psychic processes as "surging." The word expresses what surge does, and "surge" is a synonym for "waves" or "surf." Could we ever have dreamed of describing our psychic processes as "surging" unless the characteristics of surf had already been recognized? And might it not be the case that recognition overlaps with expression? Perhaps the surf was first recognized through the expression of poetry, song—or *music!*

Referring to the tone poem *Don Quixote* by Strauss, Professor Hospers writes, "Music cannot possibly be about a Spanish knight in the way that Cervantes' novel is." Of course we could grant this if all he meant were that music depicts things in a different way from literature; because it does. But he goes on to say, "Music cannot depict the Don and his adventures with fidelity to reality or without it, for the simple reason that it cannot depict them at all." Really? We are brought back to fundamentals: What is reality? How do we get to know it? I believe we can say that Beethoven's Third Symphony (*Eroica*) lacks fidelity to Don Quixote and his adventures, and I believe *part* of our reason for saying this is that this music differs in a definite way from Strauss's tone poem. Professor, Hospers maintains that music cannot be *about* human nature because it does not *represent* anything at all; but if there are ways of being about reality other than representation, then his criticism loses its force.

We are stuck with fundamental philosophical questions, and I can see no value in postponing them. What is reality? How do we know it? Cervantes' novel is not about "reality" either, if we mean by that "existence." The knight never existed. It might be said, though, that the knight represents a *type* of man who did or does exist. Benedetto Croce, however, has already pointed out that Don Quixote is a type only of all Don Quixotes. That is, what do we perceive some existing men to be? Quixotic. They are like him, more than he like them. "Quixotic" is explained by reading *Don Quixote*. Cervantes' novel is an expression of an archetypical character from which we derive an archetypical characteristic. It is in terms of this characteristic that we *may* cognize existence. It does not seem, then, that we can say that Cervantes' novel is about reality because it resembles or represents reality. The point is that we do not know what reality is until we characterize it. But if we characterize it in terms of an artistic expression, it is gratuitous to say that art depicts reality because it *represents* reality. Reality in this case would be *presented* in artistic terms. If we begin with the assumption that art is one thing and reality another, we are almost sure to miss the common ground on which the expression and the thing expressed meet. Of course it is true that the book or the music is one existing thing and the quixotic man that may exist is another existing thing. But surely this is a secondary consideration, and one which can be entertained only because we already grasp the characteristic as already expressed.

It seems to me that music can express the same characteristics as are expressed in a painting, a statue or a sentence. As Croce points out, it is a mistake to think that a particular art-medium yields only one kind of impressions which then do or do not represent reality. It is a mistake to think that a painting, say, yields only visual impressions.

> The bloom on a cheek, the warmth of a youthful body, the sweetness and freshness of a fruit, the edge of a sharp knife, are not these, too, impressions obtainable from a picture? Are they visual? What would a picture mean to an imaginary man, lacking all or many of his senses, who should in an instant acquire the organ of sight alone? The picture we are looking at and believe we see only with our eyes would seem to his eyes to be little more than an artist's paint-smeared palette.

The sensory "conduit" involved (a misleading word used by British empiricists) is quite incidental. We see Don Quixote, we hear him, we read about him—the same man in all cases. It need not be that the tones of the music remind us of sounds made by quixotic men. If we think of anything like sounds at all when we hear the music, it may be more like the sounds *we* might make if we listened a bit more intently, a bit more sympathetically, a bit more understandingly.

Though the expression which is art does not *qua* art contain any reference to existing things *qua* existents, it is nevertheless true to say that in art we express ourselves less abstractly than we do in the language of science or in the worn counters of everyday speech. In art we preserve the original given-to-us aspect of all phenomena—the subjective pole of the subject-object whole of cognition—our care for things, our interest, our joy with them. Where is our joy, where is our pleasure? As James noted, it is indifferent whether we speak of a feeling of joy or a joyous event. Joy cannot be bottled up in a dualistically conceived mental container. It is intentional in the sense that it characterizes a whole lived-situation, and it is logically prior to any abstraction of a part of the situation for the purposes of controlling the situation or predicting future events. As Collingwood put it, art is the imagined experience of total activity which achieves the expression of emotion. I do not think we can control our subjectivity, not directly at any rate, but only through expressing ourselves, which includes the expression called art. I do not agree with Professor Hospers that Collingwood's formula is incompatible with the fact that the process of creation is cool and emotionally detached in the case of many artists. On the contrary, Collingwood's whole point is that art involves an expressing of emotion through a fixing of it within an imagined whole of experience, and that this is to attain a perspective upon it in which we learn about it and in which we are *relieved* of its perturbation; we master it, rather than it us, and in this sense we are detached from it. Expressing an emotion is not just having the emotion. There is a difference between the gesture of the actor and the grimace of the sufferer. I think that Collingwood has been misinterpreted at this point, and I wonder whether this has occurred because Professor Hospers takes the *process* of creation and the expression of emotion to be analogous to letting liquid out of a container: perturbation would last until all the contents had been let "out"—out in "external reality" amidst pigment and canvas, say, which is the finished *product*. Neither Collingwood nor Croce, however, would conceive of expression in such a dualistic manner. Neither of them would accept the distinction between expression *qua* process and expression *qua* product, because for them, so far as I can discover, process and product are identical. That is, an expression can occur as process only after it is already "out" as product: but "out" would not mean mere spatiotemporal location in the "external world"; it would mean the realm of intelligibility or communicability (even if no one else actually gets the communication)—what Croce calls Spirit or objective mind.

I agree with Professor Hofstadter that art expresses the original given-to-us aspect of all phenomena, the subject-objective whole of experience. To think that relativity to a subject is adequately suggested by an example of mirrors reflecting different aspects of a single situation is to forget that mirrors do not cognize or intend anything at all. (The mirror analogy is not Professor Hospers'.) Needless to say, they do not cognize their own cognition; nor their own expression; nor their own submission to that which is other than the self but which can be grasped together with the self in a nonthematic or prereflective cognition.

Music is not so different from the other arts when it is considered in a philosophical framework different from Professor Hospers'. To be sure, in cases like Handel, Bach, or Palestrina it is hard to *say* what the music does express. I suppose that is why we have music to express it. To assert, as has been done in the past, that music expresses ideal (or desirable) states of mind is to slip back into dualism. Better to leave it rather general and to say that what music expresses through the medium of sound is just this: ideal relationships as intended or intendable by a subject. For then we would preserve the subjective-objective whole of experience. The question of the point at which sound ceases to be music and becomes mere sound borders on the broader problem of intentionality and intersubjectivity which I do not step into. It may be that a necessary condition for applying the predicate "art" to a thing or process is that it be takable (or intendable) as that which was intended by *another* (the artist) as a work of art. I do not know. It does seem, though, that a minimal understanding of the artist's intentions is essential, and that it is wise to adopt the same caution as that adopted by the music reviewer for the *New York Times* who admitted that he might be incompetent to judge the artistic quality of Anton Bruckner's symphonies because he "could not enter into Bruckner's world." He did not mean, presumably, that he could not inspect Bruckner's sense-data, or that he could not hear Bruckner's sounds, but that Bruckner's music expresses ways of being-in-the-world which he, the reviewer, has not yet learned to experience. Perhaps we could say that Bruckner's music expresses ways of being-in-the-world which the reviewer has not yet even dreamed of, but which are dreamable.

11

But What about the Reality and Meaning of Music?

PATRICIA CARPENTER
Barnard College

I

AS A MUSICIAN, I have been struck throughout these meetings by the persistent clustering of difficulties about the question of musical meaning. Indeed, to raise that question seems to force to light a fragmentation in the meaning of 'meaning,' which must then, as it was remarked, be either broadened until it is useless or narrowed to the point of meaninglessness. This seems to me curious, for surely music is the most meaningful of the arts.

Theories of meaning—developed with an eye to other art forms—ultimately founder against music. Perhaps then it would be wise to look to music first in an effort to discover the meaning of 'meaning': to think of musical meaning not as exceptional, but as paradigmatic.

Sound, even before we move to the level of musical tone, is eminently a sign, an omen. Its function is to announce happenings, in the external or internal world; and the function of hearing is to attend to those happenings. One might say that "gesture"—the gesture of pointing, for instance—is dumb, unheard, and visible sound. Like pointing, sounding is an act both of directing attention to something and of bringing something into attention. And music, like drama, is made up of such acts of calling-to-attention. How then does sound become so severed from its connection in the world that it is possible to say, "Music has no meaning"?

In one sense, I stand—as do most musicians, Professor

Beardsley observes—on the side of the Immanence-Theorists. Certainly a musical work of art is a being that rests in itself. But it is, as well, a being that speaks. Just as surely, I must agree with the Significance-Theorists: if it speaks, it is art; if not, it is matter. I find myself in this quandary because of the claim the Significance Theory makes on a verbal model of meaning: that meaning is to depend upon translation into, or interpretation by, words. Then, in relation to musical meaning, I distinguish sharply between music as a language and the musical work of art. The meaning of music is immanent in that music as a language is sufficient in itself adequately and eloquently to express musical thought. Untranslatability is one of the essential qualities of the musical, as it is of any artistic medium. But the musical work of art is significant: certainly it says something. What is said, in the musical work as in any other, does not need interpretation, is often not comfortably interpreted; indeed, verbal translation of the musical work especially slips easily into heresy.

The problem seems clearer if the question is put more concretely: what can I say—or what can I make—with sounds? And then it seems to me to arise whenever we hear and speak, in any "language." We can say—or make—a poem, for instance, or a fugue. I think that to ask about the meaning of music compels one to ask whether meaning in general does not ultimately lie in the doing, in both saying and making, "expressing" and "forming." What can I *do* with sounds?

Sense and sound become separated in two directions—toward words, as well as tone. But on the other hand, both in the language of words and in the language of tones, the original unity of sound and sense is heightened—in poetry, and in that fusion of words and music which since antiquity has been understood as "melos." In our tradition, this ancient unity has only recently been broken; and the controversy between referentialist and nonreferentialist begins here: when it can be asked, as by the Encyclopedists, for example, "Sonata, what are you trying to say to me?" Only in the nineteenth century did the separation become so self-conscious that music was asked to do what it had never been called upon to do before, i.e., to "represent" without benefit, and more fully than, words. An antithesis such as Beardsley sets up, between music that is "austerely formal" and "the twittering of birds," is in the context of a recent and local style. The cadenza of Beethoven's *Pastoral Symphony,* for example, stems from a venerable tradition of "bird music," from the great polyphonic programmatic chansons of the French Renaissance, through the myriad eighteenth-century "hen" and "cuckoo" fugues—music no less "formal" because it utilizes the familiar rhythm of hen-clucking or expands upon the cuckoo's interval of a third. Indeed the fugue itself is a formal principle abstracted from what was originally a vivid depiction of the hunt, a poetic genre, the *caccia.*

In music the attitudes represented by these two theories are not a mutually exclusive opposition, but rather two extremes of a continuum—both equally important in the fluctuating history of musical style, both equally valid aspects of music.[1] It is interesting to see where a particular work falls within this range. A piece of music fashioned after a rhetorical model of expression, for instance, is not comfortably dealt with as a closed system. However, any particular process resembles process in general; and any closed structure has features in common with others, and can resemble the structure of the real. *How* music relates to reality—whether it refers, resembles, exemplifies, or, as tradition has it, reflects—varies in relation to other varying factors: the manner of speaking, the idea expressed, the genre, the model of the world it bespeaks. To the question, then, of whether music is *essentially* either referential or nonreferential, I would answer, "Neither." But it is nonetheless meaningful.

The problem of musical meaning lies, not with puzzles involved in musical reference, but rather with an "immanently" significant form and with the various senses in which 'autonomous' applies to music. It is these which I want briefly to explore. Contemporary issues in aesthetics stress the differences, not similarities, between musical and verbal language, and turn on the fixed, specific, and separable meaning of the word: music is autonomous in that its meaning is embodied and nonspecific. This comparison rests, first, on a conception of music as rhetorical expression; and, secondly, on a model of rhetorical order as the stringing together of a train of static, discrete entities. In late nineteenth-century aesthetics, music was a paradigm of autonomous form in virtue of the "purity" of its language: it was not *able* to represent. However, today in the light of other contemporary art forms, the issue is seen to be the potency of a self-subsistent form, an issue applying as well to the literary as to the musical art form.[2] Following a line of thought suggested by Professor Hofstadter,[3] I want to look at some of the analogies between music and verbal language, using as a guideline a question raised by Professor Nagel: "What is the content, for example, of a fugue, if we take content to be distinct from applications of form?"

To this end I propose, for a few minutes, to turn the notion of 'meaning' around: music, I maintain, not only has meaning, but typifies the meaning "situation." Meaning emerges in verbal language as it does in music, as a mode of experience is crystallized, called to awareness, and translated into sound.[4]

II

Difficulties concerning the meaning of music do not arise because the matter of music is not found in the external world. True, tones, like words, are made, not found. True also, music does not belong to the visible and tangible world. But we nonetheless encounter a piece of music as outside us, as we do a painting. And it is deeply connected with reality, standing as a powerful demonstration that the visible world is not all there is of the "real" world.

Musical hearing, it has been said, "really deceives us in a most peculiar manner about external happenings, so that they penetrate our inner being in complete disguise." [5] Uneasiness with the "signification" of music has more to do with those peculiarities which arise as experience is translated into tone than with the nonspecific way in which the tonal medium "refers" to reality. Music is first of all sound. And sound lessens the distance between sign and signatum, and between hearer and heard. It raises in a vexing way questions about intuitive knowledge, about the intimacy of the relation between the knower and the known.

First, sound connects subject and object in a unique way, which tends to isolate the transaction between them, i.e., by interpenetration. Auditory perception strikingly exemplifies the wholly interdependent situation that holds between the self and its world; hearing appears to be "the most central and important sense in the general synaesthetic complex which shapes perception." [6] Sound mobilizes the hearer and engages him immediately in a situation of tension, of attention, of taking notice. The auditory situation is one of expectation, concentration, quickened alertness, heightened presentness. Hearing is a bent of the entire organism toward action, fundamentally involving motor response, a response which the growing child learns to inhibit and transform into kinetic imagery. Sound, more than most sensations, seems fragile and evanescent, partly because its very perception requires our active participation and intent. Ordinarily we must attend to a sound or it is not heard. A primal fear of the new-born infant is a noise that penetrates unexpectedly.

To sound is to make known by announcement. Like gesture, sounding intensifies and emphasizes what is singled out merely by calling attention to it. The mark, the omen, is first that which is noted, then that which is named. Like gesture, sounding is motion, a stretching forth and toward. And the gesture, seen or heard, is intention as well as extension; it springs from a purpose: the aim of reaching out, the effort of voicing a sound. Hearing, too, is a tension toward the happening to which one is attuned. Sounding or hearing is an intentional act, of mind as well as body—an act of meaning. Further, like gesture, sounding is not only an act of meaning, but also the meaningful act. What is meant is what is designated, but the meaning is in the pointing, in the emphasis. What is meant is what is happening.

But the audible gesture is peculiar in a way visible gesture is not. As vibration, it is a motion into as well as toward, a connection between. A sound not only carries its message outward, but also brings it in through the ear; it is not something "here" nor "there," but rather something that sensuously moves out into the world and sensuously penetrates in; the thresholds of hearing are felt as pain. We hear sounds as "things," i.e., at a distance, but it is not easy to keep them there. We ask of a sound, not "Where?" but "Whence?" And to hear requires not only our engagement and participation, but also our assent. To listen is to accept what is heard, to take heed, to hearken. It is not possible to hear, or to speak, except in a context of understanding.

Secondly, it is very hard to disengage a sound from the source to which it "refers." The audible gesture does not point to things; nor is it about things; what sound makes known are events, what is happening. It announces a connection, like smoke to burning; but, unlike the smoke, it is the burning. Even a single sound is its own "personality"—a sinister noise, the hot note of a trumpet, a quiet murmur. And although we can speak of an empty noise ("mere sound," like an empty gesture), emptiness itself is a quality—empty courtesy, mere form. It requires a sophisticated act of abstraction to hear bare sound, apart from the sounding world. Sound embodies a portion of concrete life.

III

Now the problems of Significance already are apparent here, in the primitive auditory situation. Meaning is (at least) a three-term relation. And although it may lie, not in the stimulus nor its referent, but rather in the relation that holds between them, "in the pointing," [7] the Significance Theory depends on a distance maintained between sign and signified. But how does sound "refer" to its source? Is not hearing at once an "interpretation" of the sensation? And is not meaning, rather, a situation in which something happens between subject, object, and the concrete bit of world their encounter calls to attention—a feeling that something has been said. Something is immediately translated into sound and immediately grasped by the listening imagination. The difficulty becomes crucial when the medium of translation is tone, a medium itself, so to speak, "syntactically absolute." Weight is thrown to the side of Immanence by the peculiar nature of the tonal "thing." What kind of meaning is immanent in tone? In the object made up of tones?

A tone, first of all, transcends its source. Whereas sound traces back to the sounding object in a striking way, the tone becomes disembodied; it is solely the happening.[8] It is not the property of a body, like other sensations. "We touch a cold wall, see a blue flower, hear a tone." [9] It is a peculiar kind of thing, an incorporeal sensation. Like thought it transcends the space in which bodies are located; unlike thought it is external, both disembodied process and object encountered.[10]

Sounds are perhaps nonspecific words; they are surely uncrystallized tones. Whereas words connect in virtue of their relation to the external world, the tone takes up its meaning into itself. What it loses in specific external reference it gains in a precise "logos" of its own.[11] It is not only sensed quality, but also sensed form, in itself organized, "sensible number." The sonal object is difficult to keep distanced and in self-repose, but an object made of tone is "solidified" by its own intermeshing relations: tones point to each other.

It is not, then, that tones have no connections in the external world—number, for instance, is one such connection; but ordinarily we are not interested in looking so far. We are interested rather in the connections of tones with one another. And "autonomous" music is music put together only in terms of its own connections, made up "only" of tone.

On this view, the formal aspect of music is its physical, material shape; whereas its "meaning" consists in those qualities which reveal no correspondence with the physical properties of the stimulus.[12] Ordinarily this view of a work of art supports no distinction between form and content. And music is, again, a paradigm case for it: because tone embodies both qualities and relations, the problem of an "empty" form does not arise. But what is sometimes lost from view is the *total* concrete form. If, for instance, a text is part of the music, then the words—bringing with them their meaning—are part of the acoustic stimulus, as is a title given by the composer.[13]

In point of fact, what is not "in" the stimulus is the whole of the work. (And for those who follow—along this line of thought—the nineteenth-century tradition, the overall shape of a musical work lies in its movement: meaning hence is related to musical "motion.") Musical hearing strikingly forges its own *Gestalt*. The acoustic mode of perception is successiveness, and the auditory object is in fact never given as a whole. The tonal "thing" is *only* form, in this sense, persisting through time, not space, and maintaining its identity only in the realm of the mind. It exemplifies the "intentional object."[14] Musical hearing deals with a "pure" sensation that nevertheless functions much as thought does, and has been called "antilogical perception," for it depends upon the ability to perceive the non-simultaneous as simultaneous.[15] Although a piece of music is presented discursively, like an idea, yet it can be heard as a whole, in a meaningful way. Fundamentally, its "relevance" lies in this: that it fits the imagination that made it and the imagination that will grasp it, the musical mind that speaks and the musical mind that hears.

The problems of musical form stem from this: that the whole is in fact never "there." During the Baroque era, for instance, when fugue was a "live" form, it was also a "habit of form"—a repository of techniques, accumulated over centuries, for fashioning a temporal *Gestalt*. As a form, it is a specific procedure for presenting a musical theme, the conventional pattern of the so-called fugual "exposition," which utilizes specific kinds of repetition, relation, and emphasis—a procedure that lay in the fingers of every musician of the time, a cliché for getting things going. As such, it was a serviceable "tool" for the manipulation of musical material, applicable to any particular theme, i.e., its *soggetto*. This was taken as "the given" by the composer, whether he had in truth "found" it or, perhaps, invented it himself. For generations of composers, the fugue served as training ground for the articulation of musical matter, for making a suitable musical "thing."

IV

Sound, then, can carry its own meaning or, in its free-floating way, is readily at hand as sensuous matter—for play, for improvisation, for making, as well as for "fixing" into words. And tone, especially, is disengaged from its anchor in the real world, available for sheer perception, for sound-play. This is the primary sense of "autonomous" music: music that serves no practical end.

But the distinction should be made, in respect of both musical and verbal language, between sound used as sheer matter, as an element in babbling, and sound used for symbolization. The child, it is said, learns to speak by catching simultaneously both meaning, and the mutual differentiation of sounds that is the basis for language, because there is no connection between communication and babbling.[16] Tonal sound is also used for many purposes. But the music we know as an art, in our contemporary world, is not mere play with sound, but language. A piece of music, like a piece of verbal language, is meaningful discourse—a continuous, connected act of meaning that takes time—time for give and take between speaker and hearer, hearer and heard, time for meaning to emerge. One makes music in order to say something in tone. There is no verb in modern English that can accommodate the "autonomous" music of the modern Western world, i.e., nonvocal, nonfunctional music; 'to sing,' 'to incant,' 'to intone,' or 'to speak in tone' reflect the ancient function of music as melody. Perhaps we may use the word "musicalize." To discourse in tone is to "musicalize."

And then, on the other hand, tones "musicalize" the work. Because music is so strikingly a system of tones, not an assemblage of sounds, it is tempting to ontologize the musical language itself. And indeed, certain shaping forces do seem more definitely preestablished, more generally valid, in the musical medium than in most others. A single tone is not concrete in "music," nor even in a particular musical work; it has meaning only within the musical language as a whole. Like the phoneme, a tone is only a function; its meaning is "syncategoremic," i.e., only its power to differentiate and distinguish itself in relation to other tones and to the total system. Like a single sound, a single tone can be expressive; on the side toward unorganized noise, each tone has its individual color, or timbre. But in virtue of its pitch-organization, it takes on a precise kind of "character." As soon as it is fixed in relation to other tones, it is available in the construction of a system, and can thereafter be placed with more or less accuracy. We can observe the musical language in the same attitude that a linguist takes toward an "ideal" verbal language, concerned with its material basis rather than with "content" or "meaning." And thereby the language itself becomes a model which serves as starting point as well as end. There are certain laws inherent in the medium; and meaning is the uncovering of these laws. To speak musically presupposes this language: if I choose to speak logically in tone, then I must obey the tonal laws.

Autonomous then means "syntactically absolute": autonomous musical discourse looks only to its own internal laws. The language informs of nothing but itself; music "means itself." This immanent musical sense is seen to hold not only from tone to tone, but on different levels, among any elements grasped as unitary—from what has traditionally been considered as the fundamental musical-acoustic phenomenon, consonance/dissonance, to Meyer's "sound-term" or musical gesture. In contemporary music, the basic element has become the "sound-configuration." But whether on a "phonemical" or "grammatical" level, the connection of part to whole is seen as syntactically correct and intrinsically interesting.

Tonal "meaning," in this sense of "structural meaning," i.e., consisting in the changing relation of one element to another and to the whole, seems to me more concrete and precise than verbal meaning, perhaps because the system itself, the context, is more formally rigid. In this regard, music is more like a mathematical than a linguistic system—an aspect of music that has fascinated man throughout the ages.

Seen in this light, the fugue is not a generalization that musicians habitually make from particular fugues. Rather, it is a formalization of a basic musical datum, the proportion 2:3:4, the so-called "division of the octave." Each fugue is a demonstration of this musical fact in terms of a concrete subject matter. A particular fugue is "about" a specific octave and its fifth. One proceeds, in an attitude of strict analysis toward the given, to explicate the "meanings" inherent in the *soggetto* —much the same attitude, for example, that the contemporary composer takes toward his basic "set."

If meaning is to be understood as opposed to "sense-content," then it is just these inherent relations that are specifically musical: yet they hold aside from any concrete tone, in the abstract. It is these, especially, that can be interpreted only imprecisely in another language. And autonomous, i.e., "abstract," music is that which is preoccupied with these meanings. Not all music is. Some, for example, is absorbed with the sensuous element of sound, the surface of the "Klang," which is taken from the world most immediately in perception. Further, the kind of "system" changes. In sixteenth-century Venice, the musical "organism" corresponded to a model of corporeal, harmonious proportion. Contemporary permutational order, by contrast, resembles a self-referring mathematical structure. But in any case, such a view emphasizes the nontemporal, the "omnitemporal," character of music.

In a musical context that exploits this aspect of language, what is intended is usually quite definite. For example, in the music of the so-called "common practice" era (the eighteenth and early nineteenth centuries), a handful of structural schemes governs the legitimate procedures for reasonable musical thinking—these are the "rules" learned by the beginning harmony student. And the student learns to read and hear as he learns to differentiate tones as functions of these procedures. In this style, the linguistic structure is so rationally transparent that ambiguity is endlessly interesting, a musical "idea" that cannot adequately be explained in terms of its verbal analogue. I think, for example, of the last movement of Beethoven's Piano Sonata, Op. 101, a most peculiar fugue that is "about" a musical ambiguity: the double meaning of the interval of the third, which is either the proportion 4:5 or 5:6 and which functions as both the lower component of one triad and the upper component of another. On the primary level of text analysis, Beethoven's fugue can be read in terms of musical dynamics; i.e., tones acquire their meaning according to their function in the overall process: they are structural or prolonging, goals or means of motion, empty of meaning except as they point to, support, contain, continue, delay, or obstruct, the motion. But, at one point in the fugue, the musical passage must be read two ways, not because it is vague or imprecise, but because the ambiguous relation has forced the issue of an ambiguous motion. Then this detail clarifies the peculiar application, in this fugue, of the formal pattern of exposition: that the voices answer each other at the third, not the fifth. Beethoven's commentary is one more in the long history of musical dialogue about the idea, "fugue." The relation he explicates, 4:5:6, is a "division" not of the traditional octave but of the fifth, that interval which serves as pillar to the system of classic triadic tonality. His fugue not only makes a statement about tonality which will be explicated by Schubert and Brahms. It is as well a comment that prepares for the dissolution of that system (which by its very clarity allows for ambiguity) and foreshadows a world in which there is no preestablished harmony. Bartók, a century later, will "divide" the third, but by that time the system, in the face of an extraordinary internal integration, will have shattered itself.[17]

Now in this case, it seems to me, ambiguity has more than a sheerly "syntactical" meaning; its meaning is nevertheless purely musical. The musical syntax, like any other, tends to function as an organism, according to its own laws. And preoccupation with the marvellously rational system of classic tonality has led to preoccupation with the particular kind of dynamic, "goal-directed" form which is its issue. But we can distinguish between a psychological feeling of motion, of tension and release, and the self-propelling forces inherent in the medium itself, the purely tonal "logos."

Ultimately, in this line of thought, the temptation arises to consider musical "time" separately from musical "substance" —i.e., the temporal perspective of music becomes "form." And as the system tends toward stability of function, form also becomes a kind of "frozen time" (an observation leveled at some contemporary music, but applicable as well, for example, to the great *organa* of the late Gothic era). Thus the musical work, as well as the language, moves toward an internal equilibrium at this formal level, is "stylized toward the pole of Being." [18] Again I cite the fugue, a great pun, throughout its long history, on *fuga*, "to follow"—to follow after, to follow from. Although it began as a very concrete kind of chase, the "fleeing of voices" was soon abstracted from the hound-cries and horn-calls, to be utilized as the pursuit of one voice after itself, the deduction of "many out of one." To musicians in fifteenth-century Italy, this principle exemplified form in an ideal sense, the relation of particular to model, "Imitation." Technically, it was a manner of dealing with a prior given subject as strictly as possible, "modus optimum organisandi." And ultimately it epitomizes musical "research," the pursuit of all possibilities inherent in a given theme. In the great *summae* of Bach, the connections laid bare are no longer temporal, but musicological. The *Art of the Fugue* was not conceived for any real instrument, but for the musical mind, in a "sound" removed from the concrete sounds of time and space.

Many of the problems about musical meaning arise from the confusion of system and rhetoric, the manner of speaking. Like so many issues, this has been brought into focus by contemporary art. When Schoenberg described his new method as being "for composition with twelve tones related *only* to one another"—i.e., with single tones, not triads—he might well have said he was writing now with musical "phonemes," for he was taking apart the entire fabric of the musical language in order to reconstruct it as another system. But he still spoke in the classic rhetoric. However, a change in the language ultimately entails a change in what can be said. Today's composers (like those at the turn of the seventeenth century) are attempting to speak in a new rhetoric, to say something only this new language can say. They work, in fact, with a new matter-sound, not tone; and it generates its own new system.

V

Finally, I want briefly to return to my original distinction between the musical language and something "said" in that language, the piece of music. The language is not only sufficient in itself to embody musical thought, but also its immanent "syntactical" meanings are intrinsically interesting. Nevertheless, although the language itself tends toward equilibrium, toward "perfect" form, its end is in the speaking, in the work. Man speaks in music because he has something musical to say. And the meaning lies not in the linguistic structure, but in the speaking.

The question of immanent meaning, then, must be asked not of the medium, but of the work: is it "semantically absolute"? The tonal object, like any other, can be perceived for its own sake, if the whole it forms—that which is "musicalized"—is sufficiently absorbing. To some extent, any perception is for its own sake, for the sake of whole-making; material is coherent only if it is part of our universe, graspable as a whole or part of a whole. And a piece of music is not in some way removed from the real world of time and space. Like any object, it is never adequate, never wholly there, always a synthesis of appearances; its meaning is never finished, but always seen against the continuing background of the world —"musical" world and "real" world.

Like verbal language, musical language can be used in many ways, to say many things. And the language is subject to the idea made manifest. It is uncomfortable to attempt to distinguish the extent to which a musical thought is "about" the real world or "about" the tonal world—at least, to do so is to construct different layers of meaning in both the work and the "world." Once we leave the syntactical level, the "rules" for interpretation do not apply with any assurance to wholes. Bach, for example, says something about "real" space, but inseparably from the tonal space he shapes: by the new way in which he "completes" the octave; by his extension of this principle of closure to the entire space the octave includes, the "circle of fifths"; by "letting be" the new possibilities for combination which this frees. Bach establishes a spatial conception that musicians two centuries before had begun to probe; his own implicit notions were not finally worked through until the "extended tonality" of the late nineteenth century.

The composer shapes his thought in tone; but there is constant interplay between the composer who thinks and the tones that "think." Discourse might be more broadly conceived—in musical, as it has been in verbal language—as time taken to shape, rather than recount, experience: self and world speak first to one another. In this sense, any language—verbal, musical, or whatever—is, as Professor Hofstadter put it in his commentary, the "articulation of being." It is possible to use the language at hand—verbal or musical—in a secondhand way, to reach for the counter that goes under each thought. But in music, at least, this is not creative thinking; the musical language shapes a musical idea as the experience itself takes shape, in the act of articulating. Musical meaning, I would say, lies in this fundamental act that at the same time both acquires knowledge about the world—i.e., "hears"—and voices that knowledge in sound—i.e., utters.

The musical work is not autonomous because it translates experience into a medium uniquely set off from the external world. Rather, like any work of art, it transforms and isolates experience, somehow making the transaction between subject and object in itself sufficient. The crux of the problem of musical meaning lies here, in the absolute nature of any work of art, rather than with particular musical matters of reference, interpretation, or immediacy.

NOTES

1. "Not only does music use no linguistic signs but, on one level at least, it operates as a closed system, that is, it employs no signs or symbols referring to the non-musical world of objects, concepts, and human desires. . . . [But] unlike a closed, non-referential mathematical system, music is said to communicate emotional and aesthetic meanings as well as purely intellectual ones. This puzzling combination of abstractness with concrete emotional and aesthetic experience can, if understood correctly, perhaps yield useful insights into more general problems of meaning and communication. . . ." L. Meyer: *Emotion and Meaning in Music* (Chicago, 1956), p. vii.

2. Hofstadter, for instance, distinguishes between the scientific and literary uses of language, the former as tool, the latter as an element in the expressed content; further, he distinguishes two kinds of linguistic form: separation and distinction are vital to the logical form of scientific usage, but death to aesthetic "rhetorical" form, an intrinsically interesting whole, a "whole-for-effect." "The Scientific and Literary Uses of Language," in *Symbols and Society*, L. Bryson *et al.*, eds. (New York, 1955).

3. "These remarks hold not only of the language of literature, but of that of science and of every other field of human experience, and, more generally, of the whole attempt to deal with expressive human experience, i.e., experience in which human beings make a content in and for experience by the use of materials as a medium." *Ibid.*, p. 310.

4. ". . . the man who speaks never says exactly what he meant to say; and further, he never knows exactly what he meant to say before speaking. . . . The words that I bring forth do the thinking for me, just as the hands of the composer, moving over the keys, do the composing." M. Dufrenne, *Language and Philosophy*, tr. H. Veatch (Bloomington, Ind., 1963), p. 17.

5. E. Kurth, *Musikpsychologie* (Bern, 1947), p. 1.

6. The thesis of H. Reinold in, "On the problem of musical hearing," in: *Reflections on Art*, ed. S. K. Langer (New York, 1961), pp. 262–97.

7. Meyer applies this definition to musical meaning, *op. cit.*, p. 34.

8. "If now we place the acoustic mode in the 'hierarchy of the senses,' which . . . reaches from the more object-related to the more subject-related sensory perceptions, the quite special and significant position of auditory perception in this scale becomes evident. For at one end of the scale are the existence and condition of material objects, at the other, the fact that we feel this way or that. . . . Beyond their capacity of not being experienced as affects of a bodily part, auditory perceptions can become separated from their object, move to the forefront of experience . . . stand and hold attention by themselves, as for instance in music. . . . Sensory impressions of both the object-related and the ego-related poles of the hierarchy may appear in hearing." Reinold, *op. cit.*, pp. 268 f.

9. V. Zuckerkandl, *Sound and Symbol: Music and the External World*, tr. W. Trask (New York, 1956), p. 272.

10. J. Handschin, in distinguishing between central and peripheral tonal properties, considers whether it be legitimate to differentiate the tone from its properties, since it does not have the same relationship to them that an object customarily has to its properties; the paired concepts, object—properties, should not be applied to tone, since a tone is not just another object. "A tone is neither tangible nor visible but fundamentally a process." *Der Toncharakter* (Zurich, 1948), p. 1. H. H. Dräger, commenting on this passage, adds: "A tone is both an object and a process, not only because the perceived process traces back to an object (which is also the case in sight), but also because in hearing it is the process transmitted (not the case in sight) that we perceive as an object. . . . Accordingly, a tone is a hypostatically perceived process." "The Concept of 'Tonal Body'" in: Langer, *op. cit.*, p. 175.

11. Handschin, *op. cit.* and W. Wiora, "Der tonale Logos," *Die Musikforschung*, 4 (1951).

12. C. Pratt, for instance, maintains this position in *The Meaning of Music* (New York, 1931).

13. Wiora illustrates interesting ways in which Brahms, by

changing a word or two in a folk tune, changes the shape and character of the melody. *Die rheinisch-bergischen Melodien bei Zuccalmaglio und Brahms* (Godesberg, 1953), pp. 134 f.

14. A point of view developed by R. Ingarden in *Untersuchungen zur Ontologie der Kunst* (Tübingen, 1962).

15. Reinold, *op. cit.*, p. 268.

16. "The important point is that the phonemes are from the beginning variations of a unique speech apparatus, and that with them the child seems to have 'caught' the principle of a mutual differentiation of signs and at the same time to have acquired *the meaning of the sign.* For the phonemic oppositions . . . appear and are developed without any relation to the child's babbling. . . . It can be said that beginning with the first phonemic oppositions the child speaks, and that only afterwards will he learn to apply the principle of speech in diverse ways." M. Merleau-Ponty, *Signs,* tr. R. McCleary (Northwestern University Press, 1964), p. 40.

17. Interesting in this respect are Arnold Schoenberg's remarks on tonality in *Style and Idea* (New York: 1950), for instance, p. 106: "Formerly the use of the fundamental harmony had been theoretically regulated through recognition of the effects of root progressions. This practise had grown into a subconsciously functioning sense of form which gave a real composer an almost somnambulistic sense of security in creating, with utmost precision, the most delicate distinctions of formal elements."

18. A criterion for analysis developed by G. Brelet in *Le Temps Musical* (Paris, 1949), and discussed by Wiora in "Musik als Zeitkunst," *Musikforschung,* 10 (1957).

12

The Problem of Musical Hermeneutics: A Protest and Analysis

EDWARD A. LIPPMAN
Columbia University

THE PRESENT PAPER was provoked by the almost total absence of historical considerations on meaning and truth in art. Even the discussion of aesthetic values, which suggested that there was an intrinsic limitation in an "instantaneous" apprehension of visual art and that the verdict of one generation is in general corrected or supplemented by another, failed to develop a systematic historical theory of aesthetic judgment. A point of utter childishness was reached in the contention that the understanding of a musical composition can be achieved solely through repeated exposure to a given recorded performance. That a nonhistorical approach to art could produce or endorse insensitivity of this kind has led me to assemble by way of protest the humanistic factors of interpretation, which I have surveyed here as part of a general view of musical meaning.

Since a musical work is written in a social and cultural setting and is intended for an audience and for some particular occasion, it is generally able to fill its role in the world without explication or aid. Yet the necessity for interpretation or explanation repeatedly arises, either because the composer is following a train of thought that is not completely understandable to his contemporaries or because the lapse of time has transformed obvious meanings into obscure ones.

What interpretation seeks to make clear is the complex of feelings, associations, and ideas that were initially formulated in tone by the composer and produced by an adequate performance at the time the work was composed. The conceptions and feelings that are embodied in a composition are in large measure specific to music itself; they are essentially unknown in any other way. Meaning of this type nevertheless resides in a community of understanding and ways of feeling and in subtle departures from tradition; it is by no means inevitably attached to given acoustic patterns. A melodic phrase of a particular work, for example, may reappear literally in a composition written decades or centuries later, but the new stylistic context will give it a meaning that is often almost completely unrelated to its earlier one. Chordal progressions undergo the same transformation. The quality of an elementary pattern is of course determined by the whole configuration of which it is a part, but when there has been a general change in style, the new significance of the pattern will not be due entirely to the influence of a different musical Gestalt. The more fundamental alteration of meaning can be seen readily when not only a component pattern but a whole melody or an entire composition is reused in a work of a later stylistic period; each element of the borrowed whole remains within the same musical context in an objective sense, but we respond to it in accordance with another sphere of musical experience. The tradition of student life and university songs gives something of a hearty atmosphere to the Columbia "Alma Mater," a quality that is completely alien to the melody as Haydn conceived it in one of his last string quartets.

Yet the social and cultural foundation of musical significance often escapes our notice, for we become familiar with style by an intuitive rather than a conscious process; we understand a particular repertory of tonal phrases and forms in an immediate way from the hearing of only a few representative works of the same idiom, provided these are not too distant from us in time. Indeed the spontaneous appreciation of musical expressiveness is a remarkable example of historical insight, and it argues the presence of an elemental basis for music in the constant or slowly changing properties of human physiology, whether of sense perception or vocal expression. In spite of this, our understanding of music is quite susceptible of error, and it is not difficult to discover instances of the flagrant misconception of older music. We may even be able to define the more popular responses to music in terms of historical naiveté, for what is most symptomatic in the recent recording "Bach's Greatest Hits," for example, which boasts of not tampering with the musical text in any objective sense, is precisely the curious effect of listening to the tonal patterns of the early eighteenth century by bringing into play the auditory responses associated with present-day jazz. Or to turn from an attractive trick to an unconscious process, we find the same kind of transformation automatically accomplished by a concertgoer when in listening to a Beethoven symphony he recognizes a melody that he came to know originally in a commercial jukebox version. In cases such as these, a text that belongs to a given sphere of thought and musical feeling is flooded with the reactions and ideas and emotions of the listener's own time and culture, typically in the happy belief that the composition in question has been correctly understood and appreciated. Interpretation will obviously prevent or correct basic errors of this kind in musical apprehension, for it undertakes to make the various symbols of past music, and the peculiar responses provoked by motifs and progressions again familiar.

In this process of reconstruction, performance and verbal explication are equally indispensable. Language can point to meanings that cannot be revealed at all in performance: it can explain the significance of individual symbols, and elucidate the import of the composition as a whole, defining whether it is subjective, spontaneous, liturgical, or pedagogical. But a third problem, putting us in intimate touch with the precise quality and the temporal course of musical experience, remains relatively intractable to verbal description and is perhaps best approached through performance. Yet even this problem has seen solutions in language, first in the poetic criticism of the Romantic era, which sought to create linguistic parallels of musical compositions; then in the hermeneutics of Kretzschmar, which was inspired by Dilthey; and again in the writings of Ernst Kurth, who employed a systematic and sensitive terminology derived in part from psychology and in part from physics. What words and images can claim in respect of capturing the actual flow of musical experience, however, is doubtless little more than a limited pedagogical value which will be more instructive than a fine performance only for those who are musically insensitive.

A great many kinds of meaning in music are clearly symbolic in nature; but unlike religious, verbal, and logical symbolism, musical symbolism has never received the attention it deserves. The epistemological investigations of Peirce have no counterpart in musicology, while the historical studies of Arnold Schering have never been expanded into a general treatment. These are deficiencies that must eventually be eliminated, and as an initial approach to the problem of interpretation, I have tried to develop an outline both for the analysis and for the history of musical symbolism. The typical effect of a musical symbol will not unequivocally determine an object, for music lacks representational power and is accordingly restricted to the presentation of elemental qualities. These necessarily have an ambiguous reference and require further specification if their meaning is to be made precise. In general, however, they will retain more than one significance, so that audible symbols may point simultaneously to physical objects, images, emotions, and concepts. A further peculiarity that distinguishes musical from logical symbolism can be seen in the effect of length: as we proceed from a single tone to a phrase and then to a whole composition, music does not show the abrupt changes in character that we designate by "term," "proposition," and "argument," but rather a more gradual accumulation of symbolic types. Still another distinctive feature of symbolism in music is its complex and diversified nature, which must be held responsible for its resistance to analytic and historical investigation. The triadic relationship between symbol, effect, and object is obviously a complicated one; its nature is simultaneously physical and psychological. In general, the effect that is produced or intended will point towards the object through the mediation of the symbol, but the variety manifested in situations of this type is nothing short of remarkable. Social symbols depend upon range and richness of meaning, scientific ones on restriction and precision. It is understandable that a whole series of terms has arisen to designate the different expressions of symbolism, for the variety and scope of symbolic activity are as wide as the nature of mentality. Each field of human expression has its array of designations, from the signs of unreflective behavior, through the maps and graphs of mathematical thought, the icons and emblems of visual art, and the terms and propositions of logic, to the figures, tropes, and metaphors of rhetoric. But traditional descriptive terms such as "emblem" or "metaphor," which are taken from visual and verbal expression, cannot be applied to music without qualification.

The peculiar complexity of musical symbolism is perhaps due largely to the fact that music involves more than one sensory mode and more than one kind of activity. Also musical symbols demands considerable attention in their own right, and thus superimpose other kinds of meaning on their symbolic function. The problem of separating nature from convention in the genesis and operation of musical symbols seems again to be unusually complicated. A major source of difficulty exists in the intimate connection of music with language, for linguistic symbolism possesses its own complexity and its own elaborate terminology. Indeed the concepts of musical symbolism have often been borrowed from those of rhetoric, and it is obvious that vocal music always contains verbal symbols as well as tonal ones. Musical symbols vary in size from the constituent elements of form such as rhythmical patterns, chords, melodic intervals, tone-color, dynamic configurations, and verbal components to whole compositions and groups of compositions. Each kind of symbol will exist in various modes, from actual sonorities, notational signs, instruments, and performers, through images of such concrete entities, to the general concept or type of which they are exemplifications. The objects of these symbols will comprise material and perceptible things and events, a category that includes music itself; individual emotions; and images of these physical objects and feelings. The effects of the symbols will be concepts and images of such objects. Both the effect and the object of any symbol are dependent upon the producer and the observer. The realized effect may not correspond to the intention of the composer or performer; indeed there may be no audience at all. On the other hand, if the music is spontaneous no symbolism will be intended; vocal music can be an unreflective expression of feelings, and instrumental music a muscular play with kinetic and tonal possibilities; yet in both instances various kinds of symbolism may exist for a listener.

Although the typology and historical nature of musical symbolism must ultimately be related to those of symbolism in general, they are best examined initially in their own right. Types may be distinguished on the basis of the connection between symbol, effect, and object; this would appear to provide the most significant determination, and thus the one within which subtler distinctions may most logically be elaborated.

Among the visual symbols of music, notation is probably the most varied and interesting. It may be either arbitrary, as in the case of a system using the letters of the alphabet, or natural, as in the high-and-low representation of pitch. Medieval note-shapes, such as the brevis and longa, and left-to-right distance in general, also contain an inherent conformity to duration. In many instrumental notations, numbers, letters, or other marks designate the position of the fingers on the instrument, but the more usual objects of notation are the tones of voices and instruments, and the effects of the symbols are the concepts of these sounds and the intention and effort involved in producing them. Ideas and physical objects may also be represented, however; black notes can symbolize mourning, or sharps the Crucifixion. In one of the madrigals of Marenzio, the text "of five pearls," "di cinque perle," is set to five successive whole notes at the same pitch, so that the notation presents a picture of five strung pearls, the line of the staff doing duty as a string. Somewhat similarly, one of the chansons of Baude Cordier, around 1400, is written in the form of a heart; while a motet of Heinrich Schütz traces out the outline of a baptismal basin in illustration of the text by a slow descent and rise of the voice parts. The notational symbols of Cordier and Schütz are purely visual, but this is generally not the case, for a sharp that represents Christ's cross, for example, is not only seen as a cross, but also heard as one. If a musical score is examined silently, of course, without dramatic or auditory realization, the notational symbols will point only to visual and auditory images as their objects. In the imagination of a composer, on the other hand, the symbols themselves will not have a physical existence, but will exist only as concepts or images of notational signs.

Apart from notation, visual symbolism is found in music whenever it comprises drama, pantomime, or representational dance, for actors and dancers, and also their individual physical motions and gestures, will have their own series of symbolic objects, even though these are often intimately related to those of the tonal component of the music.

As far as the auditory symbolism in music is concerned, an initial type can be defined by the basic perceptual role of tones, which can be regarded as signs of the instruments and singers that produce them. This is a natural symbolism in which part stands for whole; it is largely but not altogether transcended in the realm of musical art. But the recognition of instruments and voices as well as their localization can become important constituents of musical experience. This is especially the case in program music or in opera, where the represented instrument or singer becomes a further symbol in its own right, but it is true to some extent also in every variety of antiphony and polyphony and in every manifestation of virtuosity. The fanfare that announces the critical arrival of the minister in Beethoven's *Fidelio,* for example, is significant as the sound of a *trumpet* in particular. And the piano music that is played in Carnegie Hall by Artur Rubenstein, to take another instance, has a special importance as the sound of a *piano* that has a particular *location,* and indeed as the playing of *Artur Rubenstein* in a particular location. Perceptual symbolism is obviously reinforced by visual symbolism—we even summon up some vague image of the invisible herald in *Fidelio*—but it is capable of acting unaided, and in principle is purely auditory.

Related to perceptual symbolism is a type based on the imitation of sound, for we may suspend the normal presentational function of tones and use them to duplicate the sounds of the outside world of those of other instruments or voices. In addition to the naturalistic imitation of birdcalls or thunder, the violin may imitate a guitar or the voice a trumpet; instrumental music may imitate recitative; and in many genres of vocal music a singer must assume another personality than his own, or having adopted one character, must disguise himself vocally in order to be taken for another. Symbolism of this kind, based on resemblance of tone-color or melodic style, is of great musical importance; the fundamental impulse of instrumental lyricism is an outstanding example, for in rising above their nature as mechanical contrivances, instruments always have at hand as their most obvious model the expressive values of the voice. But the imitation of extra-musical sounds can claim at least one highly significant example in the vocal representation of speech that motivates recitative and realistic dramatic styles.

Another type of symbolism in music resides in the texts of song, opera, melodrama, and religious music, for the voice will obviously command the whole symbolic range of language, from denotative and connotative meaning to the emotional and volitional qualities associated with conceptual and logical functions. Although the verbal symbolism in music rests on sound, it is obviously neither simply perceptual nor specifically tonal; nor, like the visual symbolism of drama and dance, does it only accompany and interact with the symbolism that is peculiar to tone. It can be regarded instead as a distinct but proper part of our auditory experience, and it provides in addition the most important framework for supporting and defining the meaning of tonal symbols. The interpretation of the verbal symbolism of musical texts is at times a matter of considerable complexity; obscurities or reference and simultaneous levels of meaning arise in places as different as the medieval motet and the librettos of Wagner.

Returning to tone itself, we find that it is not restricted to the representation of its source or to acoustic imitation, but becomes the basis in addition of an allegorical type of symbolism by means of analogy, which permits musical patterns to symbolize a wide range of non-sonorous objects, both visual and conceptual. This type of symbolism depends upon a formal resemblance that is consciously apprehended, and it requires the aid of visual expression or of language to make its meaning evident. An important formal equivalence is that of number: a repeated tone or pattern, the number of voices for which music is set, or the number of tones in a motif can symbolize the corresponding number of persons or events, and become an allegory of the Trinity or the Ten Commandments. Motion provides other formal relationships between music and external events; a prolonged tone will symbolize sleep or enchantment, an undulating figure will represent the rocking of a cradle. Similarly, imitative figures may depict the rotation of a wheel, or canonic structures the act of pursuit or adherence to law.

The interconnection of the senses is the basis of another type of symbolism in which visual and tactile objects are represented by the direct route of a felt resemblance between different modes of sensory experience. Bright tone-colors will suggest bright or flashing visual objects; patterns of motion are also intersensory, with tempo as the counterpart of speed in the physical realm and the dimension of pitch serving as the natural depiction of up and down. High pitch serves not only for physical ascent and celestial phenomena, but also figuratively for God or the Resurrection, just as low pitch depicts not only descent and the submarine world, but hell and death and the fall of man. But when pitch is used to depict right and left rather than high and low, the symbolism interestingly becomes one of formal resemblance instead of heterosensory effect. Physical size, weight, and distance also have their psychological duplication in musical terms, even without the reinforcement of the visual symbolism that can be provided by the properties of instruments and the placement of performers. It is often difficult to distinguish formal correspondence from synaesthetic immediacy, for a given musical configuration may readily have the capacity of acting in either way; in such cases only historical study can uncover the true nature of the symbolic effect.

Perhaps the most ramified and problematic type of musical symbolism is that based on the subjective sphere of emotions, feelings, and moods. Music has physiognomic and emotional qualities, whether these are experienced inwardly or only contemplated, and it is therefore comparable in some degree with external situations that give rise to emotion. In addition, there is an immediately recognized kinship between the feelings entering into our musical response and those known in other contexts, so that we readily accept music as a natural symbol of both heteronomous emotions and the concrete situations provoking them, as well as of the general classes of emotion known as sadness, joy, and so forth. Not only melodic patterns but chords, or instruments, or also whole passages or works, arouse feelings and moods adaptable to symbolic purposes. Every chord, even every interval, has its own physiognomic character, strongly dependent, of course, on its context; and each instrument can become symbolic of a characteristic realm of emotional experience: trombones awaken their own feelings and moods, and so do horns, a flute, or the organ. Chromaticism is an important example of symbolism that acts largely by means of emotive response. It has a formal basis also, for chromaticism bears the same relation to diatonic music that unusual events do to normal ones, and this is an additional factor that helps to make chromaticism the natural vehicle of the extraordinary and the strongly emotional; it is the inevitable symbol of pain, sorrow, and ecstasy, and especially of great suffering. Like chromaticism, any scale or melodic pattern whatever will excite specific feelings and moods, so that the modes and melody-types so widely found outside of recent Western music have easily been able to serve symbolic purposes in their application to particular functions and texts.

Associative symbolism is a final type, dependent upon a prior connection between the symbol and its object. The connection is an arbitrary one by definition, so that any likeness or natural relationship that may exist between symbol and object must have become ineffective and have been supplanted by association. Thus apart from any inherent suitability, the trumpet will bring a military atmosphere to mind, the organ will suggest a religious scene, and functional music in general will recall the whole occasion of which it is a component. Similarly a familiar vocal melody will point to the meanings of its text even when it is performed by instruments alone. Keys also appear to exemplify a symbolism due to prior association, for the differences between them that have been based on pitch, instrumental idiom, melody-types, and tuning ratios are either variable, elusive, or imperceptible; yet their use to represent spheres of conceptual-emotional experience such as pastoral atmosphere or heroism is often surprisingly consistent.

We can thus distinguish several large categories of symbolism in music, which may be designated as visual, perceptual, imitative, verbal, formal, intersensory, emotional, and associative. The actual occurrence of these types in music, however, represents a hermeneutic problem largely because of its variety and complexity. The most characteristic feature of musical symbolism is its composite nature. In any given instance, it may be difficult to specify which of the enumerated types is exemplified; the types must often be thought of as modes that are active simultaneously in the operation of a single symbol. When vocal music suggests speech, for example, the symbolism can be due both to formal resemblance and to sonorous imitation. Or if we consider the motif by which

Wagner represents Wotan's spear, the decisive and deliberate scalar descent in the low register which is sounded by the trombone uses physiogonomic qualities as the basis of emotional symbolism, conveying the feeling of authority that attaches to the spear, itself a symbol of law, through the tone quality of the instrument and the irrevocable step-by-step descent along the tones of the scale. But formal symbolization is active also, for the extended and unvarying progression in constant durations and without deviation from the scale contains a formal analogue of legality, rigorous consequence, and rule, and in addition a formal counterpart of the simple and severe shape of a spear. Intersensory effects are involved as well, since the auditory qualities we have mentioned spontaneously evoke the visual image of a straight shaft, and the penetrating and inflexible tone of the trombone something of the visual and tactile property of pointedness. Visual symbolism obviously plays a role also, for the stage spear represents the mythical one as well as its associated powers of authority; but in addition to this, the sound of the trombone is a perceptual symbol of the instrument itself, and the unusual length of this, together with the progressive extension of the slide that is called for precisely by the scale motif in question, become visual symbols in turn of the shape of the weapon. Wagner's orchestra is invisible, however, so that the performing motion and the instrument are perceptual objects and visual symbols only as images. This is also occasionally true of the spear itself, since the motif is sometimes heard when the weapon is not on the stage. Still another procedure of interest is that in the absence of the spear, Wagner will characteristically make use of imitative symbolism, and sound its motif on instruments other than the trombone.

What is true of the spear motif is true in general of musical symbols. The trumpet motif that represents Siegfried's sword has a sharp rhythmical outline, a high and therefore bright pitch, and a swiftly rising character that suggests the withdrawal of the weapon from a sheath and the raising of it in the air. The tone-color is the most cutting one available in music, and it belongs to a musical instrument that is metallic, silver-colored, and shining, and associated in addition with military signals and exploits. Or again, the motif symbolizing the gold under the Rhine is a simple triadic pattern sounded in the mellow tones of the French horn, an instrument round in shape and gold in color. The triad, as the perfect harmony and—for the nineteenth century—the physical as well as the mathematical source of music, represents something of the primeval power and beauty of the metal, especially in its pristine form and in the natural setting of the river. It is significant also that the triad is sounded on an instrument that makes direct use of the harmonic series for its tones, and that the triad is taken, in fact, just as it occurs in this series. The shimmer of the metal is incidentally increased by a kind of restrained trembling of the strings that surrounds the motif as a kind of halo.

The complexity of musical symbolism is certainly connected with the fact that tonal experience in itself is essentially incapable of representing a specific external object other than its acoustic source. It must therefore be complemented by an independent symbol in the form of verbal or visual indication. As soon as we specify the intended object, however, the music reveals unsuspected richness of significance; each of its aspects develops a concrete and appropriate reference, and every side of our experience appears to bear on the one representation. At the same time, the immediate object of the musical symbol is in general not coincident with the reference of a text or the visual event of a dramatic representation. Thus the object symbolized by music becomes in turn a symbol that points to these more definite and final objects. Melodic motion may symbolize waves, for example, when the text refers to the sea. Clearly the triangle relating symbol, effect, and object is not an adequate representation of such a situation, and must give way to a more complex depiction. But this characteristic instance is only an example of the bewildering simultaneity that confronts us when we turn from an isolated tonal symbol to a complete musical work. For music is composed of melodies, rhythms, and harmonies, of tone-colors, dynamics, form and spatial arrangement, even of two or three melodies at once. And this still omits its development in time, which can increase the number of its elements almost without limit. There may be a series of physical objects or happenings depicted variously by formal analogy or intersensory resemblance, melodic quotation may simultaneously invoke prior associations of meaning, harmonic expressiveness may produce a peculiarity of mood, key and mode may have their own emotional significance, and style may point to a particular historical, social, and physical environment. To these we must still add verbal and visual symbolism. Each constituent symbol will have its own group of observers and its own mode of origination. Furthermore the possible objects of musical symbolization are not sharply separated from one another: emotions and moods are generally the concomitants of physical situations, and are often attached to abstract notions as well, while abstractions have their eventual basis in concrete experience, both factual and emotional. Finally we do not respond to music in a compartmentalized way, nor is it written or performed according to any single mode of conception or comprehension. The constitution of musical experience will differ at different times and places, but it will never be precisely restricted to any given symbolic type.

This complexity will obviously have its reflection in the history of symbolism. No symbolic type can be assumed to apply to all music; even visual and perceptual symbolism may be absent, for music may be conceived as a purely auditory world of experience unrelated to material conditions; and even when a type persists the symbols exemplifying it can change completely. Symbolic types and particular symbols both have their own historical course, some maintaining themselves and others disappearing in the progress of time, some marking the style of an individual composer, others that of a whole epoch or country. Symbolism may originate in a special context and subsequently spread to other genres and to a wide geographical area. Intended meanings are occasionally directed to a restricted audience, and even when they are generally comprehended they can be quickly forgotten; the symbols of an older style easily become unintelligible as cultural attitudes and interests change. On the other hand, symbols can be carried over from one stylistic period to another, and when tradition is strong, as in the case of church music or of chromaticism, symbolism will display surprising longevity. But besides the varying selective action of history, tradition exerts a constant transforming influence upon all symbolic types, deadening their initial mode of activity so that they all run down to the level of convention and arbitrary association. In any event, loss of familiarity with symbols and their meaning creates insurmountable barriers to the historical understanding of music, and the penetration of an older symbolic system can be a matter of considerable difficulty. Precisely because symbolic conventions are always presupposed, it may be impossible to find any explicit statement of their existence and character, so that a knowledge of other arts, of other contemporary fields of expression, and of the dominant interests and ways of thought of the time will provide the only reliable means of uncovering the unknown symbolic aspects of the musical language of a distant period or culture. What is more, the symbolic configuration of music is a complicated texture that is constantly changing, different meanings being transformed at different rates. Thus we cannot characterize the symbolism of a composer or a historical era in terms of a single symbolic type, but must encompass in our description whatever trends are ascendant, whatever other types of symbolism accompany these, whether more durable or more superficial, and the way in which all the symbols are interrelated, the pattern of the whole. Because of the complexity of a complete account, the general historical course of symbolic attitudes and interests will provide an indispensable orientation for a more detailed picture.

In ancient Greek music, symbolism was controlled by the notion of mimesis, which was logically complemented by the concreteness of an art that comprised dance, melody, and language. The representation of man was complete; gesture and melody expressed the outer and inner aspects of his nature, while language presented the rational power of conceptual thought. The appropriate criteria of an imitation that was capable of precision and force were its fidelity and its ethical character. The symbolism was given additional meaning by social and religious function; style and genre reflected the specific virtues that were embodied in ceremony and ritual, and unmistakably designated in the content of poetic texts. Each component of music pointed to a corresponding aspect of what was represented; meter and mode possessed whole systems of ethical meanings that were the ancestors of the symbolism of keys and rhythmical patterns found in recent Western music. The aulos and kithara, which were distinct even in their modes of symbolic action, represented two separate spheres of meaning that were contrasted in feeling, ethical properties, and Weltanschauung. In creating the symbolic properties of medieval plainsong, Christian liturgy takes the place of the praise of gods and heroes, and the concrete physical object is removed. There is a corresponding dissolution of the unity of verbal and melodic rhythm, and the symbolism is directed solely to idealized religious attitudes. The intended effect of music is to impose an attitude appropriate to the religious purpose. Stylistic variety, from the *accentus* of the celebrant to the melismatic Responds of the Mass, reflects the significance of each occasion and each section of the service. Text and music cooperate in this purpose, and the individual features of melody naturally tend to represent verbal structure, particularly in the parallel verses of psalmody with their medial and final points of articulation. But the symbolic use of modes and of the expressive values of melodic intervals has been established with certainty in only a few instances, and the same is true of the symbolic application of melisma and the introduction of numerical symbolism into the structure and repetitive features of melody. It is logical to assume, however, that conscious symbolism of these kinds played a considerable part in the composition of liturgical music, even if not in its realized effect. The same considerations apply to organum, for the symbolic implications of liturgical polyphony are in general controlled by the significance of the chant underlying it. But the rise of measured music added a new group of symbolic possibilities, the most important of which were the juxtaposition and interplay of sacred and secular significance and the structural and numerical complexities developed in the fourteenth and fifteenth centuries, although the extent to which these were symbolic is difficult to determine. It is compatible with the outlook of the time, however, for mathematical form to appear as a sensible manifestation of cosmic structure, and for music to take on the values of the quadrivial sciences in providing philosophic and theologic insight.

In the period 1500 to 1750, elaborate techniques of rhetorical symbolism became important, as manifested most conspicuously in the concept of an *ars poetica.* Every aspect of linguistic meaning and expression was adopted by music, from a projection of the rich content of the individual word through an imitation of the external form and sound of impassioned speech, to the detailed explication of the complex connotations of an extended text. This linguistic interest made its appearance when speculative structural techniques were still a dominant feature of music, and its initial manifestation was a conscious depiction of verbal meaning by formal analogy, but the principle that succeeded this was a more properly humanistic one that encompassed both expressive elements and poetic meter. The insertion of homophonic sections into a predominantly contrapuntal texture served not only the aesthetic end of balance and variety, but also the symbolic intent evoked by the text in settings of such passages as "ex Maria Virgine" or "alleluia." Indeed the musical incarnation of the words became the chief manifestation in music of the ideal of the imitation of nature. Expressive symbolism developed an esoteric trend with *musica reservata,* but became a commonplace in madrigalistic word-painting. A basically rational mechanism persisted, however, and was especially evident in the visual symbolism of *Augenmusik* and in the imitative symbolism of the programmatic chanson. The concept of *maniera* introduced the purely musical but equally conscious symbolism of a representation of older styles. Even the more powerful expressive intent of the *seconda prattica* and the *stile rappresentativo,* which brought speech patterns directly into melody, did not displace the conscious construction of symbols, which is conspicuous in the work of Monteverdi and leads gradually to a musical formalization of verbal and emotional expression. In the sphere of *musica poetica,* first in Italy and then in Germany, all the procedures and devices of rhetoric were reflected in musical terms. Vocal music duplicated the patterns of effectiveness that had been codified in the rhetorical figures, and either reinforced the content of tropes or added new ones that were purely tonal, such as ornamentation and metaphor. The whole compositional process and even the structure of instrumental compositions both as wholes and in detail came to exemplify oratorical modes of thought. Music was planned and perceived within the framework of *dispositio, elaboratio,* and *decoratio* and performance became *elocutio.* In the late German Baroque, however, the union of religious spirit and rationalism endows the order of music with a metaphysical significance that transcends human expressiveness and the empirical world of speech. Coincident with the highest development of verbal symbolism in the works of Bach, tonal and rhythmic organization take on an inexorable quality that reflects the divine regulation of the cosmos; and the symbolic richness of the music derives from the combination of rhetorical and mathematical symbolism.

The succeeding "Platonic" world of Classic-Romantic symbolism is centered in the flow of emotive and volitional experience, first in its own right and then as the subjective manifestation of cosmic will. The social representation of Mozart is transformed into the universality of the Beethovenian "idea," which projects, instead of eighteenth-century society, the ideals of freedom, humanity, love, and heroism, and the powerful emotions associated with them. Symbols no longer arise from either language or mathematics, but from the properties of tone itself, which is identified with the ontological nature of man and the world. Symbolism takes on an immediacy that contrasts with the conscious equations of the Baroque, and the description of nature depends not on the imitation of sound and on analogy, but first on indirect depiction by means of feeling, as in Beethoven's *Pastoral Symphony*, then on the poetic "character" of music, the distinctive tonal quality into which Schumann transmutes external conditions; and finally on synesthesia and the fundamental identity of the tonal symbol and its object. But if this tendency rests on the metaphysical suggestiveness of inner experience, it nevertheless becomes increasingly realistic in an external sense, and achieves a vividness that goes far beyond the formal imitation of the eighteenth century; synaesthetic response and new resources of color form an alliance of seemingly limitless power. Cosmic symbolism is found in its purest form in Bruckner; it is fused with realism in Wagner, and combined with personal elements in Mahler. The symbolism of Brahms, on the other hand, is essentially historical, and has older music itself as its object. Post-romantic trends exaggerate either realism or subjectivity, while the two are intensified in combination by Expressionism, which places them in the service of the subconscious.

In more recent times, classicistic tendencies lead to a musical objectivity that discourages both realism and expression, although it is not unfavorable to a historical symbolism that parodies older composers and styles. It also revives both the auditory and visual interest in instruments and performers, in contrast to the Romantic era, which often eliminated perceptual elements entirely from music. That there are any cyclic or continuous trends in the history of symbolism is doubtful. We can discern at most a general tendency towards the alternation of formal and expressive periods, but hardly any progressive course of development. The symbolic constitution of primitive music seems relatively simple; yet the music of higher cultures reveals no graded increase in complexity. Nor does musical symbolism progress from any one type to any other, even though it appears to contain limited but suggestive parallels to the development of other varieties of symbolic expression. The increasing abstraction of scientific symbolism, for example, and the discovery that the reality it depicts is essentially constituted by the symbolic system itself, seems to have a counterpart in the fate of music as a language of the emotions, with its sudden autonomy and objectivity in the instrumental works of Webern.

If the complexity of musical symbolization is due to the composite nature of music, its variability is certaintly due in part to the dependence of music upon other modes of expression. In any cultural setting, tonal patterns themselves produce a precise response in the domain of specifically musical experience, but this response is related only imprecisely to other varieties of experience. By analogy, by association, and by inherent resemblance, musical symbols may then become established in the most varied fashion. In the concrete world of Greek music, where melody, poetry, and dance are combined in fulfillment of particular functions, the significance of specifically tonal forms in the whole economy of human and social experience is well defined. Western music loses much of this specificity of meaning, although it achieves similar definition time and again in the realm of vocal music and in dance music. If tonal experience seems almost inevitably to suggest verbal structures and gestures, this symbolic fertility may be due in part to frequent intimate association and conformity with both language and bodily motion. Behind this association however, there is also a dependence, for tonal experience lacks the independence, strength, and utility of conceptual thought and of visual and haptic perception. Still more fundamentally, the persuasive connection of tone with kinesthesis would appear to have a physiological basis, while the equally intrinsic relation to language seems to be grounded in properties of temporal experience common to both. The similarities of melody and speech are remarkably close and persistent. Since the advent of Renaissance humanism, it is only with Webern in the twentieth century that music achieves formulations and patterns which are independent of verbal structures and of verbal expressiveness.

But if the dependence of music seems to account for its symbolic suggestiveness and its adumbrations of referential meaning, the new prominence of instrumental music in the eighteenth century inevitably focused attention on the existence of any peculiarly tonal meaning that melody might contain apart from symbolization, and eventually on the possibility that such meaning may possess features that do not vary with time and place. Does music in any degree derive from the natural world or from inherent factors of human anatomy and intelligence? It is perhaps a prejudice of the nineteenth century to believe that it does, to make music a transaction of nature and man, with society excluded. Principles of physics and mathematics are regarded as its significant determinants, along with the anatomical structure and the primitive emotional constitution of human beings. Greek music is seen as molded by the forms of Pythagorean harmonics and the structure of the soul, and Western music as formed first by the specific proportional theory of consonance and rhythm, subsequently by the mathematical and physical nature of tonality, and finally by the properties of sets, while the complementary picture of psychic constitution is constructed first in terms of an objective and essentially physical theory of temperaments and affections and subsequently in terms of the oneness of creative imagination and divine power. Great music is conceived as gradually uncovering natural and organic laws, and as revealing mathematical principles. In accordance with such an outlook music would contain inherent factors of consonance and dissonance, rhythmical components of inherent expressive value determined by norms of pulse and locomotion, and a repertory of elemental motifs based on the intrinsic attributes of high and low tones and the changeless physiognomic qualities of intervals. Even tone-color would be inherently bright or grave; the trombone would inevitably produce some specific variety of sublime or religious feeling, and the trumpet some sense of prophetic announcement or command. Emotional expressiveness would consist in an inevitable formulation of excitement, sadness, or joy in the tone-color, loudness, and pitch of the voice and in their rapidity of variation, or in the duplication of these qualities by instruments. Musical hermeneutics would simply await the compilation of its dictionary of basic musical patterns, discovered, perhaps, by laboratory investigation.

But for one thing, this view entails a certain atomism that overlooks the strength of context in determining the values of any part of a musical work. Nonreferential meaning in music seems to me to exist outside the area of fixed physical and physiological determination, in the realm of culture. For the composer is always confronted by an objective but socially determined inventory of melodic phrases and rhythmic patterns, and on these he imposes the peculiarities of his own personality by means of modifications of current practice and novel conjunctions of material, the whole being dictated by the unique conception of an individual composition as well as by the general constitution of his personal style. The laws of physics, the structure of mathematics, and the elemental physiological properties of his nervous system would seem to have very little to do with the wealth of significance contained in the musical work.

But if we replace the notion of fixity with that of slow change, we may salvage something of the conception of natural expressiveness, and perhaps succeed in establishing it as one of the two major types of nonreferential meaning that music seems to possess: the first a more immediate and intrinsic property of tonal experience, and the second best described as stylistic. Neither of these has any precisely defined symbolic reference. Defining either of them closely—whether from an analytic or a historical point of view—would be a lengthy and difficult enterprise, so that again I have undertaken no more than a brief characterization.

The more immediate nonreferential quality of musical

experience can be described as an almost inescapable involvement in a flow of tonal events that seem to be the product of careful and precise planning. There is an insistent demand made upon our consciousness and attention; other conceptual, emotional, and conative contents are suppressed; other awareness of the passage of time subordinated; and our feelings are caught hold of with a force that extends to compulsive effects upon musculature and respiration. Our participation is so direct and so pervasive that the auditory character of the experience loses the definition of a particular sensory mode, and the inner constituent becomes at least as prominent as the externality of the stimulus in both its acoustic and phenomenological aspects. At every instant, this immediacy exists in a context of past and future that extends roughly to the limits of the musical phrase being presented, or, at any point of formal articulation, to the image of the phrase just completed and of the one about to start. There is a larger context also, of the whole section or movement of the given composition—a synthetic configuration with a specific emotional character, which has been built up by memory or previous knowledge; and every moment of our progressing experience is realized as a part of this essentially static totality of tonal form.

The musical experience we are attempting to characterize involves meaning because it contains a duality of outer and inner, or stimulus and response. If it does not entail the triadic relationship of symbolic meaning, neither does it have the monistic character of an event. It can be inspected if we separate the perceived tonal forms from the experience that can be considered as their content or effect. The inner experience formulated by the composer will be reproduced by our response, and both will constitute equally a specific variety of intrinsically musical feeling. The existence of this kind of meaning is indicated by the fact that music "makes sense," that it is not a chance combination of tones but is faithful to native or acquired ways of feeling, that it gives rise to an experience consistent with stylistic tradition rather than completely determined by each individual composition. Also, it is only on the basis of meaning that we can account for the developmental course of musical history: there is no reason for any one trend or occurrence instead of another if the sounds of music have no significance. In music that is removed from our cultural tradition, meaning of this kind tends to disappear, for the experience it creates has no independence, no past connections; the same is true of extremely novel works, while on the other hand, nonreferential meaning becomes conspicuous whenever music draws heavily upon existing material.

The visual aspect of music contains its own nonreferential meaning, although there seems less likelihood here of isolating an elemental variety that is not the product of social and cultural conditions. In notation; in the gestures of singers and performers; in nonrepresentational dance; and in the physical motions, tableaux, and pattern of the action in drama apart from their obvious representational meaning, there appears to be less possibility of isolating immediate components determined by gravity, for example, or physiology, than there is in the case of tonal expression. Even high and low can be ignored by notation; even gravity disregarded in gestural dance, for example; even entrances and exits eliminated from drama; while we know that the motions of instrumental performance are dependent upon the instrument, itself a cultural product, and that gesture and physical behavior in general, like the meanings of colors and shapes, are products of society and culture quite liable to be misunderstood by outsiders. In physical and visual matters, much more than in tonal, we seem to deal solely with stylistic significance rather than with a composite of style and nature.

Unlike many types of symbolic meaning, which have an occasional character, nonreferential meaning is apparently an inevitable feature of music; we are powerless to escape from it; but unfortunately, we are also powerless to escape from the specific character that such experience possesses in our own time, and the question whether we can correctly recreate such meaning for the music of other cultures and eras is one we cannot easily answer. As we have indicated, the assumption that even the most immediate and elemental layers of our response to nonrepresentational dance motion and performing gestures and to tonal succession are unchanging is attractive in its simplicity, but probably incorrect, in spite of the inescapable presence of gravity, human anatomy, and high and low pitch. This is not to maintain that such primitive facets of response do not exist in any body of music; but like every other variety of musical significance, although perhaps more stubbornly, these must also undergo transformation in accordance with historical and cultural forces.

But style, which commends itself to us not as rooted in physiology but as more artificially produced by culture and taste, very nearly exhausts the nature of the intrinsic visual meaning of music, and it is doubtless the dominant kind of implicit meaning in tonal experience also. Here analysis will reveal a whole family of meanings, still without precisely defined symbolic reference, but now always accompanied by a curious suggestion of external entities, and indeed dependent for their value and interest upon just this suggestiveness. The feeling that is conveyed by music is also and primarily a way of feeling, and it is therefore adequately conceived as style, a distinctive aesthetic quality that mirrors the peculiarities of the forces that have formed the music. Not all types of style belong to the sphere of nonreferential meaning, for some designate aspects of form or kinds of workmanship, and thus simply classify a work as homophonic or fugal, its rhythm as free or metrical, its melody as stepwise or additive. This is no more than a description of what is given and not the distinction of some entailed reaction or some separable facet of music that exists alongside its acoustic nature. But personal, local, and period styles, and also styles of function and medium and physiognomic quality are types of meaning, for they are ways of expression with characteristic qualities of feeling that can be recognized as such and identified, even though they are not known in isolation from music. They are, however, known apart from any given composition or particular passage, and in that respect they have a certain measure of separateness and independence. Also musical style often bears a resemblance to the style of other arts and other products and conceptions of the same place or time or person, and in this it assumes a still greater independence of its acoustic embodiment and a similarly increased tendency towards objective reference. But style is essentially a self-contained meaning: it is Mozartean or Wagnerian, French or Viennese, Rococo or Romantic, religious or convivial, symphonic or chamber, grandiose or delicate, pianistic or choral, but it does not point to or represent Mozart or Paris or the piano or even the conception of grandeur or delicacy as a further object. It may suggest these, but the Mozartean quality or the grandeur is a specifically musical property and a specifically musical kind of significance which needs no complement and for which we simply try to find an appropriate verbal characterization based on cause or effect. Interpretation here makes the greatest possible demand on the musical knowledge of the exegete, for stylistic purity in music is as rare as racial purity in anthropology, and the controlling interest in the study of style is not so much the investigation of the scope and attributes of the various styles as it is the understanding of their mixture and transfer. The style of a composition is a Gestalt that reflects the environmental pattern of stylistic forces, and each force defines a stylistic type. Thus the style of the work contains the styles of the period, locality, composer, genre, and medium. But it includes mixtures of another kind also, for each one of these larger styles is itself a composition. The period style is a combination of past and present, the regional style a composition of different nations and localities, the personal style a compound enriched by the influence of other composers living and dead, the genre style a mixture containing features of other genres, the medium style often in part a parody of a style proper to a different medium, and the stylistic novelty of the work itself a conception not uninfluenced by other individual compositions. In the eighteenth century in particular, we find not only the finest stylistic sensitivity, but for that very reason also the most complex stylistic mixtures and fusions and transfers. In the *St. Matthew Passion* of Bach or in Mozart's *Zauberflöte,* the interwoven strands of past and present, of sacred and secular, of different nations, genres, forms, techniques, and melodic and polyphonic idioms present the greatest challenge to stylistic analysis.

If we were now to consider the combination of intrinsic with symbolic meaning in the actual course of musical history, I believe we would obtain a more or less adequate notion of the scope and nature of musical hermeneutics. As I have suggested, words are probably incapable of fully describing intrinsic meaning, although they may separate out the strands of style and thus define the locus of this meaning if not the particularities of its course. A full account of interpretation must deal also with functional meaning, for a knowledge of the purpose and use of a composition is a decisive factor in understanding it, but this is a matter quite amenable to historical investigation and description.

Simultaneous meanings, whether symbolic, intrinsic or a combination of the two, are very probably not merely a troublesome complication for the interpreter, but a significant or even a central property of music that can be identified with its essential nature. Even a single melody may contain a multiplicity of meanings, but in a polyphonic composition, different intrinsic meanings can simultaneously secure a remarkable distinctness. This peculiarity becomes most conspicuous in an operatic ensemble, such as we find in opera buffa, for example; for here symbolic meaning clearly defines a number of different personalities and emotions. There is in this property of music a strange analogue of the physical world, where similarly objects coexist and events simultaneously transpire within an encompassing spatial universe. It is not so much the simultaneity that is striking in music, but the coherence of the whole, the separateness of the parts within a single realm of existence and a unified temporal flow of experience. The spatial individuality of the participant instruments and singers and their defined positions in the tonal system, which has its own laws governing the relationship and motion of the constituent voices, provide a striking counterpart of the material world which is at least in part a literal microcosm, for the separate auditory entities are also separate physical objects. But even as a whole, music—like material reality—provides the frame and the conditions of existence and change for the auditory events that interact complexly and harmoniously within it.

The conception of interpretation that I have outlined identifies it quite closely with history, but I would like finally to introduce a distinction that I think may usefully be made between musical hermeneutics and musical history. Interpretation is certainly involved in both fields, but in somewhat different senses. For one thing, hermeneutics applies more to the individual work, and historical interpretation to the conjunction of works and the larger patterns they form. The work in isolation, however, as I conceive the nature of its meaning, can hardly be subjected to interpretation at all, since every symbol it contains, every emotional implication, every intended response and qualitative expression is essentially formed by historical currents of musical meaning. Hermeneutics must be thought of as revealing the whole significance of a composition as this significance existed when the composition was produced. It will uncover the thought and the experience that were incorporated in the work, whether by intention or unconsciously, since even the meaning unconsciously introduced might have been available to a discerning reader of the time. But this is by no means a task unconcerned with historical factors, for the meaning as it existed when the work was created would in general have comprised some awareness of tradition, of the prior development of musical language, even if this awareness was limited or inaccurate, and these historical components would necessarily be part of the reproduction of the original experience.

In a historical interpretation, on the other hand, the significance of the work will contain the future course of the style and forms it displays, values and meanings that could not be known at the time of composition. In addition, the history of these symbolic and stylistic features before this time will be extended and corrected in accordance with the new interests and the better (or at least different) knowledge of the historian, as well as in the light cast on them by an awareness of their continuing career beyond the work in question. Thus the chromaticism of *Tristan and Isolde,* for example, will be seen not simply as an idiom of personal and infinite longing that embodies simultaneously the essence of love and the desire for death, and that grows out of, say, the increasing flexibility of music in developing media for subtleties of feeling. This would include the harmonic and chromatic innovations of Schubert and the operatic predecessors of Wagner. To the modern historian rather than the hermeneut this chromaticism would become deepened in its meaning as an epochal step in a course that reaches from the religious symbolism of the Crucifixion in Bach to the suffering and longing for death of Amfortas in *Parsifal* and to the expressionist atonality of Schoenberg. However prophetic Wagner felt his achievement to be in creating *Tristan,* he could not possibly have foreseen these larger dimensions of the meaning of his opera, and they can be separated from the hermeneutics of the work as belonging to its historical interpretation viewed from the station point of the mid-twentieth century.

Index